DISCARD

Structure and Process

in Modern Societies

TALCOTT PARSONS

Structure and Process
in
Modern Societies

THE FREE PRESS, *NEW YORK*
COLLIER-MACMILLAN LIMITED, *LONDON*

Collier-Macmillan Canada, Ltd., Toronto, Ontario

Library of Congress Catalog Card Number: 59–6821

Fifth Printing April 1967

Contents

PART IV

The Structural Setting
of Some Social Functions

INTRODUCTION

The present volume consists of ten essays written by the author for various occasions during the past five years. Though very much concerned with theory in sociology they are for the most part oriented more directly to problems of empirical generalization with reference to large-scale society of the modern Western type. The one partial exception in this respect is Chapter III which deals with the problem of economic development in societies oriented to achieving a closer approach to that type. Within modern Western society the primary focus of interest is on the United States.

Though the occasions for undertaking these essays have been diverse there is a double basis of unity which binds them together. The first lies in the fact that they reflect a relatively definite and I hope coherent theoretical orientation. In this respect they belong to the period following the working out of the scheme presented in my book *The Social System* (1951) and the important extension of that presented in *Working Papers in the Theory of Action* (with Bales and Shils, 1953). They have constituted in various ways attempts to use and further refine this general conceptual scheme by taking up a series of problems in the interpretation of structural phenomena and types of process in this area.

The second basis of unity lies in my long-continued interest in the treatment of the social system as a whole. The most salient single case is the total society. I have committed myself to a kind of full-length attempt of this kind, using contemporary American society as the test case, in a book which is currently in process of writing. Its keynote will be the attempt to go as far as present theoretical resources and available data in the critical fields permit in

1

treating the society as a whole as a social system in the technical theoretical sense.

It is because of this double basis of interest that I have welcomed the various opportunities which provided the occasions for writing most of these papers. They presented challenges to a theorist to see how well he could use his theoretical knowledge and skill to handle the problems in the light of their place in the larger system. Furthermore the very diversity of the subjects presented opportunities to fill in gaps in different aspects of the total field which any future attempt to deal with a complex society as a whole would eventually have to enter into. Obviously it is impossible to treat a society as a whole and still be a specialist in one of the commonest senses of that term.

The ten essays published here are organized in four groups. In each group at least one other paper might well have been included, but for reasons of space this has not been done. The main criterion of selection among my otherwise appropriate papers has been to include in the present collection papers which are not readily available to sociologists in books to which they are likely to have access in the ordinary course. I shall mention the other most closely related essays at the appropriate points in the course of outlining the contents of the volume.

As I have noted the central theme is the analysis of some of the characteristics of the modern Western type of large-scale, more or less urbanized and industralized society. One of the most salient structural characteristics of such a society is the prominence in it of relatively large-scale organizations with specialized functions, what rather loosely tend to be called "bureaucracies." At the role level these organizations are composed of relatively pure-type "occupational" roles where the status and responsibilities of the incumbents are relatively fully segregated from their "private" affairs in terms of premises, kinship relations, property, and the like.

In the sociological literature perhaps the most important

landmark in concern with this problem area has been the work of Max Weber. In American work, however, besides the important literature in the field of public administration, it has been particularly salient in the field of industrial sociology, taking off from the classic studies of Mayo and of Roethlisberger and Dickson, and in the widespread influence of the book of Chester I. Barnard, *The Functions of the Executive*. More recently there has been another important phase, much of it inspired by Robert Merton's teaching, in which the work of Selznick, Gouldner and Blau is particularly prominent.

Part I of this volume consists of two papers which were intended to make a contribution to this area of discussion and analysis. Broadly my aims have been, first to strike some kind of balance between the more "formal" emphases of Weber and Barnard on the one hand, and the emphasis on "informal organization" which has been more prominent in the tradition of industrial sociology and in the more recent "bureaucracy" literature on the other. Secondly, it has seemed important to attempt to analyze the range of different types of formal organization rather more fully than this has ordinarily been done. Third, finally, I have wanted to work out the relevance of this field and some of the principal generalizations with which students in it were working, to the more general scheme for the analysis of social systems with which I have been working in a variety of other connections.

The writing of the first of these papers, Chapter I, was occasioned by an invitation to give a lecture in this field at the Cornell University School of Public and Business Administration. The manuscript of the lecture was subsequently revised and extended and published in two successive issues of the *Administrative Science Quarterly* (April-June, 1956). This work had awakened my interest sufficiently so that the following fall I decided to devote my seminar in *Topics in the Theory of Social Systems* to the field of the theory of organization. The second paper, Chapter II, is in part the fruit of that seminar and owes much to the graduate students who participated in it. It was written specifically for a conference on Administrative Theory in Education, held at the Midwest Administration Center of the University of Chicago in the fall of 1957, and was published by the Center in 1958 in the volume *Administrative Theory in Education* edited by Andrew W. Halpin. It shows both what I hope is a further level of analytical development beyond that of the first paper, and, because of the occasion, a special emphasis on educational organization.

In time of writing, a third related paper, not included in this volume, comes between these two. This is "The Mental Hospital as a Type of Organization" which was published in *The Patient and the Mental Hospital* edited by Greenblatt, Levinson and Williams (Free Press, 1958). This dealt with one particular type of formal organization and is a kind of "case study" within the more general framework with which I was concerned.

Chapter II and the paper on the Mental Hospital are "follow-up" papers from the starting points of Chapter I and emphasize one theme in particular. I have long felt that the most important single basis of criticism of Weber's discussion of bureaucracy, from the structural point of view, concerned his neglect of the significance of the professional type of role relative to the type of "administrative hierarchy" which was organized in terms of line authority. Since the rise of the professions to increasing prominence has been one of the principal characteristics of modern industrial society, this becomes a very salient problem in its interpretation. The ways in which such roles are structured and related to administration in the organizational context of the medical and the teaching functions, hence present problems of great interest. This theme will come up again in the essays treated in Part IV of this volume.

The two most salient functional areas of the incidence

of large-scale formal organization in modern society have been the economic and the political. Parts II and III may be regarded as, on the one hand, oriented to the problem of the larger structural setting in which these phenomena of organization appear, since they cannot be understood in terms of their internal features alone, but must also be seen in reference to the social "environment" in which they operate. On the other hand there has been a continuing concern in clarifying the nature of economic and political functions and the social structures crystallizing about them in modern societies from the point of view of their place in the social system as a whole.

Essential to the background of the two essays which comprise Part II are two considerations touching the development of my sociological interests. The first is the fact that the problems of the general relations of economics and sociology constituted the main point of departure for my own theoretical orientation in the field generally (cf. *The Structure of Social Action*, 1937). The second is the fact that, after a considerable interval, I had quite recently returned to these interests with the result of a substantial revision of perspective and further theoretical development. This broad theoretical shift was documented in *Economy and Society* (with Neil J. Smelser, 1956). The most essential points were perhaps two; first that the conception of an economy, as the main trend of economic theory treated it, should, from our point of view, i.e. that of the analysis of social systems, be treated as referring to a functional subsystem of a total society, namely that organized about adaptation. Once this reference was clearly worked out, a much more determinate set of relationships between the economy and other subsystems of the society, notably the "institutional" aspects which had been central to the sociological point of view, could be worked out. Secondly, we came to the conclusion that, on the theoretical level, economic theory could be treated as a special case of the more general theory of social systems. These two propositions gave a broad theoretical underpinning to our interpretations of the place of the economy in the social system generally.

Chapter III deals with the application of this type of analysis to the problem of economic development of the kind that leads into the industrial type of economy. It was written for the symposium on "The Challenge of Development" held at the Hebrew University, Jerusalem, in June 1957 and was published in the volume bearing that title by the Hebrew University in 1958. The version printed here, as in the case of Chapter IV also, represents a condensation of the original paper in order to meet the limitations of space to which the present volume is subject.[1]

The analysis presented in this paper revolves, in the first instance, about the problem of the role of political agency in the process of industrialization. It is argued that the original development of the industrial pattern had to occur, to a large extent, independently of political agency because the latter tended essentially to be bound to relatively short-run interests. Once, however, an industrial economy has come into being, it serves both as a model and as a focus of certain competitive pressures between politically organized societal units, and, in these circumstances, political agency is likely to play a very prominent part, precisely because it is in the interest, in the short run, of the politically leading elements to promote this development.

Chapter IV attempts to generalize the pattern of analysis outlined in Chapter III and to carry it somewhat farther in terms of technical analysis of institutional structure in the economic and political fields. The central theme is the problem of defining the conditions under which relative maximization of the mobility of resources can be carried out

1. The work of condensation has been skillfully carried out by Mrs. Carolyn Cooper. I do not think anything essential has been lost and in some respects both papers have been made more readable and better organized. Mrs. Cooper has also compiled the index to the book.

through the institutionalization of contract, property, and of occupational roles in the primarily economic field, and of leadership authority, and regulation in the political. The relevance of this pattern of analysis to the theme of Part I should be clear; it is only with a background of institutionalization of resource mobility of these types, and the attendant solution of problems of order in the social system, that large-scale effective formal organization comes to be possible, and its development is a central characteristic of the industrial type of economy.[2]

Chapter IV was written as a "background paper" for a conference on "The Transformation of Russian Society since 1861." It will be published in a volume of approximately that title, edited by C. E. Black, by the Harvard University Press in 1960.

Part III consists of three essays dealing with the political aspect of social systems. As background to their interpretation it may be noted that the theoretical work on the place of the economy in the society, carried out in collaboration with Smelser, naturally led to a consideration of the relations of the economy to other comparable "primary functional subsystems" of the society. In this connection I have undertaken, in ways still very incompletely worked out, a program of analysis of the "polity" as a concept parallel to that of the economy. This has involved a rather drastic revision of my previous conception of the relation between economic and political theory (for example as stated in *Social System*, Chap. IV). The focal conception which has emerged is that, just as the economy is organized about the functional imperatives of *adaptation*, seen in terms of the total society as a system, so the polity is organized about the

2. With respect to the themes dealt with in both of these papers I am particularly indebted to the insights developed in an informal discussion group conducted by Dr. Clifford Geertz (now of the Department of Anthropology, University of California, Berkeley) and myself during the academic year 1956-57. A further important stimulus came from association with Professor David S. Landes, also of the University of California.

conception of *goal-attainment* as another equally basic functional imperative. An important part of the rationale of this analysis is given in Chapter IV, in less technical terms in the body of the paper, in a more technical formulation in the "technical note" appended to it.

Chapter V is centered about a reconsideration of the concept of "authority" with special reference to its place in the complex of political institutionalization and consequently its relations to such concepts as legitimation, leadership, and the like. In my own intellectual background the problems posed by Max Weber's famous classification of three types of authority *(legitime Herrschaft)* have been particularly salient, and the essay comes around to suggesting an interpretation of these three types. It seems to me that the three do not lie on the same analytical level and that an attempt to squeeze them into comparability in such terms leads to a misleading distortion of their significance.

The paper was written for the volume entitled *Authority (Nomos,* I, a publication of the Society for Political and Legal Philosophy, Edited by C. J. Friedrich, Harvard University Press, 1958).

The other two papers in Part III are oriented to problems of the American political system. Chapter VI is a review article, dealing with C. Wright Mills' book *The Power Elite.* It was originally written (in the fall of 1956) for a proposed new "journal of opinion" which did not appear, but it was then published in *World Politics* (October, 1957). The essential theme of the paper is the analysis of the institutional setting within which the roles of the higher "managerial" elements of business and government in the United States should be placed. Its relevance to the problems of Part I should be clear. The general thesis is that Dr. Mills seriously exaggerates the degree to which the undoubted power of these elements is left uncontrolled, because he does not adequately analyze the institutional matrix within which the organizational structures with which he is concerned are placed. One of the most striking evidences of the bias associated with this neglect is his gross underestimation of the importance of the legal system in a society of the American type.

Chapter VII is the oldest of the ten papers included in this volume, and is the only one written without specific occasion. During the academic year 1953-54 I served as Visiting Professor of Social Theory at the University of Cambridge, England. It is perhaps understandable that an American social scientist living abroad should have been particularly concerned with the understanding of the dramatic events which were going on in his country during that period, not least from the point of view of trying to explain them to his English friends. The paper was written in the spring of 1954 essentially as an attempt to clarify these issues. It was published in the *Yale Review*, Winter 1955, as " 'McCarthyism' and American Social Tension: a Sociologist's View" and reprinted under the title "Social Strains in America" in *The New American Right* edited by Daniel Bell. Its theme is the sociological analysis of a problem in the "dynamics" of the American political system, with special reference to the reactions produced in the system by a situation of severe strain compounded in part of the situational immediacies of the loss of China to the Communist cause and of the Korean war, but underlying this, of the structural changes necessitated by the emergence of the United States as a major world power in a situation of very serious international political instability. It is gratifying that the broad prediction of a subsiding of the acute disturbance with an expected relative stabilization of the system, has been fufilled.

There is a fourth paper in this area which might have been included in Part III but which, for reasons of space, has been omitted. This is " 'Voting' and the Equilibrium of the American Political System." It was written for *American Voting Behavior*, edited by Eugene Burdick and Arthur J. Brodbeck. This deals with another "dynamic" aspect of the

American system, the way in which the two parties function to maintain an equilibrium in the regulation of the relation of the polity to the general process of social change going on in the society. In particular the findings of the study *Voting,* by Berelson, Lazarsfeld and McFee, throw a great deal of light on this process. My attempt was to interpret these findings in the light of a more general analysis of American society as a dynamically changing social system.

Part IV is somewhat more miscellaneous than the other parts. It consists of three papers which deal with aspects of the large-scale society not directly included in any of the three categories which define the contents of the other three. The first of them, Chapter VIII, deals with the relations between the social system and its physical environment, with special reference to the territorial location of action. This is the area dealt with in older sociological theory mainly under the heading of ecology. I have started out with the traditional ecological foci of residential location of populations, on the one hand, and of the places of work, on the other. I have then attempted to relate them as systematically as possible to jurisdiction as a category of the political and legal systems and to communication and physical mobility as principal modes of interrelation of territorially distinct units of a social system. This paper was written for a meeting of the Society for Political and Legal Philosophy in December, 1957, and will be published in *Nomos,* Vol. II, edited by C. J. Friedrich.

Chapter IX returns to a subject of long preoccupation, that of the professions and their place in the social structure. Within this field my greatest interest has been in the medical profession, and more particularly at the role and formal organization level. This paper however, is oriented to the more general place of medicine in American society, with special reference to its involvement in the processes of structural change which have been going on in the society. It was written as an address to the Conference on Medical Education and Licensure of the American Medical Association in February, 1958 and published in the *Journal of the American Medical Association,* May 8, 1958. Because of the occasion there is a special emphasis on the bearing of the analysis on the problems of medical education.

Two other recent papers might also have fitted into this general theme of the place of the professions and their functions in modern society. One of these is "The Definition of Health and Illness in the Light of American Values and Social Structure," published in *Patients, Physicians and Illness* edited by E. Gartly Jaco (Free Press, 1958). This paper is less concerned with the professional group as such and more with the situations within the society which define the functions of the medical profession. It attempts above all to relate these to American values and to reinforce the analysis by a brief comparison with the "meaning" of illness in the Soviet Union and in Great Britain. It was written almost immediately before Chapter IX and the two, in an important sense, belong together. The second omitted paper deals with the sister profession of law. Entitled "The Place of Law in Social Systems," it attempts a broad sociological analysis of the functions of the legal profession in the society. It was written for the Seminar in the Relations of Law and Sociology at Rutgers University in 1956, and will be published in 1959 in a volume of papers from that seminar, edited by Harry C. Bredemeier, by the Rutgers University Press.

Still a third paper not included in this volume has a certain relevance which deserves mention. This is "The Link Between Character and Society," written in collaboration with Winston White for the volume of the Free Press series of "Continuities in Social Research" on the work of David Riesman to be edited by Seymour Martin Lipset and Leo Lowenthal. This paper deals, in a broad way, with the problem of the relation of personality to American society, partly in terms of the relevance of American values, but more specifically of the part played by family, school and peer group respectively in the process of socialization. There is an important sense in which the problems dealt with in this paper lead into those of Chapter X.

Finally Chapter X deals with the pattern of religious organization in the United States. It was written for the new French journal of the sociology of religion, *Archives de sociologie des religions* (Janvier-Juin, 1958) and was published in French translation there. A slightly revised and extended version was published in *Daedalus* (Summer, 1958), which is the one reprinted here.

The religious background of a society has come to be understood to be of paramount significance to the values institutionalized in it. American society, however, has been very widely interpreted as having become secularized in a sense which would imply that the values originating in religious orientation had largely ceased to be operative and had been replaced by "secular" or even "materialistic" values.

This essay presents an analysis of the system of "denominational pluralism" in the United States which gives an alternative interpretation of the relation of current religious organization to the historical background, an interpretation which is consistent with the view that the most general value-orientation of the society has not changed, at least since the later 18th century. The essential keynote of the discussion is the importance of the processes of structural differentiation, which have quite fundamentally changed the status of "organized religion." Since this involves very substantial "loss of function" to the church or churches, it in one important sense clearly constitutes a process of "secularization." It does not, however, follow that secularization in *this* sense is synonymous with value-change.

Taken as a whole the ten essays brought together in this volume, along with the others which have been mentioned, should be interpreted as a variety of tentative approaches, each with its own particular subject and point of view dictated by the occasion, to a "diagnosis" of the principal characteristics of the modern industrial type of society. It might have been possible to try to put them into this larger setting by writing, for the volume, a concluding chapter which would attempt to synthesize and generalize their "findings" from this point of view. It seemed better, however, with this brief introduction, to let them "speak for themselves." I have already announced my intention of attempting, in another connection, to present a synthetic analysis of the "case" of contemporary American society and would rather not at this time try to anticipate the outcome of this attempt.

At any rate, the whole collection is meant to be presented as an example of the virtues of theoretical "holism" in attempting to tie together the immense variety of phenomena which, in one way or another, are touched upon in the volume. The essential theoretical background throughout is the theory of the social system, treating the concrete system not as an *empirically* integrated whole, but as a system the *problems* of which must be analyzed in terms of an integrated conceptual scheme. Only by following this path, whatever the specific conceptual content of the scheme, can the various problems associated with the common categories of "structure," of "function," of "process," of "conflict," and of "change" be related to each other in such a way that we can speak of an empirically viable "sociological theory" and not merely of a catalogue of discrete "theories" each relevant only to its particular subject-matter. The underlying question is, is sociology coming to be *a* science, or must it remain a congeries of discrete protosciences?

For the convenience of readers who may be concerned with the relations between the essays included in this volume and my sociological work as a whole, a bibliography of my writings to date is appended. It will be seen from this bibliography that in the same period of approximately five years within which these essays fall there has been considerable concern with two other main lines of sociological work. One of these is the general field of the relation of the personality of the individual to the social system, particularly as developed in *Family, Socialization and Interaction Process* (with Robert F. Bales and others) but also in several papers. The other is the more formal interest in the status of sociological theory as such and its relations to neighboring disciplines, particularly coming to a head in the forthcoming two-volume collection of readings in sociological theory, *Theories of Society: Foundations of Modern Sociological Thought* (co-editor with E. A. Shils, K. D. Naegele and J. R. Pitts) with its considerable volume of introductory analytical materials. These two bases of concern, along with the one which is paramount in the present volume, are conceived as belonging together in the more general context of theoretical "holism" referred to above.

Part I

THE ANALYSIS
OF FORMAL ORGANIZATIONS

CHAPTER I

A SOCIOLOGICAL APPROACH
TO THE THEORY OF
ORGANIZATIONS

For the purposes of this article the term "organization" will be used to refer to a broad type of collectivity which has assumed a particularly important place in modern industrial societies—the type to which the term "bureaucracy" is most often applied. Familiar examples are the governmental bureau or department, the business firm (especially above a certain size), the university, and the hospital. It is by now almost a commonplace that there are features common to all these types of organization which cut across the ordinary distinctions between the social science disciplines. Something is lost if study of the firm is left only to economists, of governmental organizations to political scientists, and of schools and universities to "educationists."

The study of organization in the present sense is thus only part of the study of social structure as that term is generally used by sociologists (or of "social organization" as ordinarily used by social anthropologists). A family is only partly an organization; most other kinship groups are even less so. The same is certainly true of local communities, regional subsocieties, and of a society as a whole conceived, for example, as a nation. On other levels, informal work groups, cliques of friends, and so on, are not in this technical sense organizations.

The Concept of
Organization

As a formal analytical point of reference, *primacy of orientation to the attainment of a specific goal* is used as the defining characteristic of an organization which distinguishes it from other types of social systems. This criterion has implications for both the external relations and the internal structure of the system referred to here as an organization.

The attainment of a goal is defined as a *relation* between a system (in this case a social system) and the relevant parts of the external situation in which it acts or operates. This relation can be conceived as the maximization, relative to the relevant conditions such as costs and obstacles, of some category of *output* of the system to objects or systems in the external situation. These considerations yield a further important criterion of an organization. An organization is a system which, as the attainment of its goal, "produces" an identifiable something which can be utilized in some way by another system; that is, the output of the organization is, for some other system, an input. In the case of an organization with economic primacy, this output may be a class of goods or services which are either consumable or serve as instruments for a further phase of the production process by other organizations. In the case of a government agency the output may be a class of regulatory decisions; in that of an educational organization it may be a certain type of "trained capacity" on the part of the students who have been subjected to its influence. In any of these cases there must be a set of consequences of the processes which go on within the organization, which make a difference to the functioning of some other subsystem of the society; that is, without the production of certain goods the consuming unit must behave differently, i.e., suffer a "deprivation."

The availability, to the unit succeeding the organization

in the series, of the organization's output must be subject to some sort of terms, the settlement of which is analyzable in the general framework of the ideas of contract or exchange. Thus in the familiar case the economic producer "sells" his product for a money price which in turn serves as a medium for procuring the factors of production, most directly labor services, necessary for further stages of the productive process. It is thus assumed that in the case of all organizations there is something analogous to a "market" for the output which constitutes the attainment of its goal (what Chester I. Barnard calls "organization purpose"); and that directly, and perhaps also indirectly, there is some kind of exchange of this for entities which (as inputs into it) are important means for the organization to carry out its function in the larger system. The exchange of output for input at the boundary defined by the attainment of the goal of an organization need not be the only important boundary-exchange of the organization as a system. It is, however, the one most directly involved in defining the primary characteristics of the organization. Others will be discussed later.

The existence of organizations as the concept is here set forth is a consequence of the division of labor in society. Where both the "production" of specialized outputs and their consumption or ultimate utilization occur within the same structural unit, there is no need for the differentiation of specialized organizations. Primitive societies, in so far as their units are "self-sufficient" in both economic and other senses, generally do not have clear-cut differentiated organizations in the present sense.

In its internal reference, the primacy of goal-attainment among the functions of a social system gives priority to those processes most directly involved with the success or failure of goal-oriented endeavors. This means essentially the decision-making process, which controls the utilization of the resources of the system as a whole in the interest of the goal, and the processes by which those responsible for such decisions can count on the mobilization of these resources in the interest of a goal. These mechanisms of mobilization constitute what we ordinarily think of as the development of power in a political sense.

What from the point of view of the organization in question is its specified goal is, from the point of view of the larger system of which it is a differentiated part or subsystem, a specialized or differentiated function. This relationship is the primary link between an organization and the larger system of which it is a part, and provides a basis for the classification of types of organization. However, it cannot be the only important link.

This article will attempt to analyze both this link and the other principal ones, using as a point of departure the treatment of the organization as a social system. First, it will be treated as a system which is characterized by all the properties which are essential to any social system. Secondly, it will be treated as a functionally differentiated subsystem of a larger social system. Hence it will be the other subsystems of the larger one which constitute the situation or environment in which the organization operates. An organization, then, will have to be analyzed as the special type of social system organized about the primacy of interest in the attainment of a particular type of system goal. Certain of its special features will derive from goal-primacy in general and others from the primacy of the particular type of goal. Finally, the characteristics of the organization will be defined by the kind of situation in which it has to operate, which will consist of the relations obtaining between it and the other specialized subsystems of the larger system of which it is a part. The latter can for most purposes be assumed to be a society.

THE STRUCTURE OF
ORGANIZATIONS

Like any social system, an organization is conceived as having a describable structure. This can be described and analyzed from two points of view, both of which are essential to completeness. The first is the "cultural-institutional" point of view which uses the values of the system and their institutionalization in different functional contexts as its point of departure; the second is the "group" or "role" point of view which takes suborganizations and the roles of individuals participating in the functioning of the organization as its point of departure. Both of these will be discussed, as will their broad relations to each other, but primary attention will be given to the former.

On what has just been called the cultural-institutional level, a minimal description of an organization will have to include an outline of the system of values which defines its functions and of the main institutional patterns which spell out these values in the more concrete functional context of goal-attainment itself, adaptation to the situation, and integration of the system. There are other aspects, such as technical lore, ideology, and ritual symbolization, which cannot, for reasons of space, be taken up here.

The main point of reference for analyzing the structure of any social system is its value pattern. This defines the basic orientation of the system (in the present case, the organization) to the situation in which it operates; hence it guides the activities of participant individuals.

In the case of an organization as defined above, this value system must by definition be a subvalue system of a higher-order one, since the organization is always defined as a subsystem of a more comprehensive social system. Two conclusions follow: First, the value system of the organization must imply basic acceptance of the more generalized values of the superordinate system—unless it is a deviant organization not integrated into the superordinate system. Secondly, on the requisite level of generality, the most essential feature of the value system of an organization is the evaluative *legitimation* of its place or "role" in the superordinate system.

Since it has been assumed that an organization is defined

by the primacy of a type of goal, the focus of its value system must be the legitimation of this goal in terms of the functional significance of its attainment for the superordinate system, and secondly the legitimation of the primacy of this goal over other possible interests and values of the organization and its members. Thus the value system of a business firm in our society is a version of "economic rationality" which legitimizes the goal of economic production (specified to the requisite level of concreteness in terms of particular goods and services). Devotion of the organization (and hence the resources it controls) to production is legitimized as is the maintenance of the primacy of this goal over other functional interests which may arise within the organization. This is Barnard's "organization purpose." For the business firm, money return is a primary measure and symbol of success and is thus *part* of the goal-structure of the organization. But it cannot be the primary organization goal because profit-making is not by itself a function on behalf of the society as a system.

In the most general sense the values of the organization legitimize its existence as a system. But more specifically they legitimize the main functional patterns of operation which are necessary to implement the values, in this case the system goal, under typical conditions of the concrete situation. Hence, besides legitimation of the goal-type and its primacy over other interests, there will be legitimation of various categories of relatively specific subgoals and of the operative procedures necessary for their attainment. There will further be normative rules governing the adaptive processes of the organization, the general principles on which facilities can be procured and handled, and there will be rules or principles governing the integration of the organization, particularly in defining the obligations of loyalty of participants to the organization as compared with the loyalties they bear in other roles.

A more familiar approach to the structure of an organization is through its constituent personnel and the roles they play in its functioning. Thus we ordinarily think of an organization as having some kind of "management" or "administration"—a group of people carrying some kind of special responsibility for the organization's affairs, usually formulated as "policy formation" or "decision-making." Then under the control of this top group we would conceive of various operative groups arranged in "line" formation down to the lowest in the line of authority. In a somewhat different relation we would also think of various groups performing "staff" functions, usually some kinds of experts who stand in an advisory capacity to the decision-makers at the various levels, but who do not themselves exercise "line" authority.

It seems advantageous for present purposes to carry through mainly with the analysis of the institutional structure of the organization. Using the value system as the main point of reference, the discussion of this structure can be divided into three main headings. The primary adaptive exigencies of an organization concern the procurement of the resources necessary for it to attain its goal or carry out its function; hence one major field of institutionalization concerns the modes of procurement of these resources. Secondly, the organization will itself have to have institutionalized procedures by which these resources are brought to bear in the concrete processes of goal-attainment; and, finally, there will have to be institutional patterns defining and regulating the limits of commitments to this organization as compared with others in which the same persons and other resource-controllers are involved, patterns which can be generalized on a basis tolerable to the society as a whole.

THE MOBILIZATION OF
FLUID RESOURCES

The resources which an organization must utilize are, given the social structure of the situation in which it functions, the factors of production as these concepts are used in economic theory. They are land, labor, capital, and "organization" in a somewhat different sense from that used mainly in this paper. This possibly confusing terminological duplication is retained here because organization as a factor is commonly referred to in economic theory.

The factor of land stands on a somewhat different level from the other three. If we treat an organization, for purposes of analysis, as an already established and going concern, then, like any other social system, we can think of it as being in control of certain facilities for access to which it is not dependent on the maintenance of short-run economic sanctions. It has full ownership of certain physical facilities such as physical land and relatively nondepreciating or nonobsolescing building. It may have certain traditions, particularly involving technical know-how factors which are not directly involved in the market nexus. The more fully the market nexus is developed, however, the less can it be said that an organization has very important assets which are withdrawn from the market. Even sites of long operation can be sold and new locations found and even the most deeply committed personnel may resign to take other positions or retire, and in either case have to be replaced through the labor market. The core of this aspect of the "land" complex is thus a set of commitments of resources on value grounds.

The two most fluid factors, however, are labor and capital in the economic sense. The overwhelming bulk of personal service takes place in occupational roles. This means that it is *contracted for* on some sector of the labor market. It is not based on ascription of status, through kinship or otherwise, but depends on the specific terms settled between the management of the organization and the incumbent. There are, of course, many types of contract of employment. Some variations concern the agents involved in the settlement of terms; for example, collective bargaining is very different from individual bargaining. Others concern the duration of commitment, varying all the way from a casual relation terminable at will, to a tenure appointment.

But most important, only in a limiting case are the specific *ad hoc* terms — balancing specifically defined services against specific monetary remuneration — anything like exhaustive of the empirically important factors involved in the contract of employment. The labor market cannot, in the economic sense, closely approach being a "perfect market." It has different degrees and types of imperfection according to whether the employer is one or another type of organization and according to what type of human service is involved. A few of these differences will be noted in later illustrations. Here the essential point is that, with the differentiation of functionally specified organizations from the matrix of diffuse social groupings, such organizations become increasingly dependent on explicit contracts of employment for their human services.

Attention may be called to one particularly important differentiation among types of relation existing between the performer of services and recipients of the ultimate "product." In the typical case of manufacturing industry the typical worker works within the organization. The end results is a physical commodity which is then sold to consumers. The worker has no personal contact with the customer of the firm; indeed no representative of the firm need have such contact except to arrange the settlement of the terms of sale. Where, however, the "product" is a personal service, the situation is quite different; the worker must have personal contact with the consumer during the actual performance of the service.

One way in which service can be organized is the case where neither performer nor "customer" belongs to an organization. Private professional practice is a type case, and doctor and patient, for example, come to constitute a small-scale solidary collectivity of their own. This is the main basis of the sliding scale as a pattern of remuneration. A second mode of organization is the one which assimilates the provision of service to the normal pattern involved in the production of physical commodities; the recipient is a "customer" who pays on a value-of-service basis, with prices determined by commercial competition. This pattern is approached in the case of such services as barbering.

But particularly in the case of professional services there is another very important pattern, where the recipient of the service becomes an operative member of the service-providing organization. The school, university, and hospital are type cases illustrating this pattern. The phrase "member of the university" definitely includes students. The faculty are in a sense dually employed, on the one hand by their students, on the other by the university administration. The transition is particularly clear in the case of the hospital. In private practice the patient is unequivocally the "employer." But in hospital practice the hospital organization employs a professional staff on behalf of the patients, as it were. This taking of the customer *into* the organization has important implication for the nature of the organization.

In a society like ours the requirements of an organization for fluid resources are in one sense and on one level overwhelmingly met through financing, i.e., through the provision of money funds at the disposal of the organization (cf. Weber, *Theory of Social and Economic Organization* [1947], ch. iii.) This applies both to physical facilities, equipment, materials, buildings, and to the employment of human services — indeed also to cultural resources in that the rights to use patented processes may be bought. Hence the availability of adequate financing is always a vital problem for every organization operating in a monetary economy no matter what its goal-type may be; it is as vital for churches, symphony orchestras, and universities as it is for business firms.

The mechanisms through which financial resources are made available differ enormously, however, with different types of organization. All except the "purest" charitable organizations depend to some extent on the returns they receive for purveying some kind of a product, be it a commodity, or a service like education or music. But even within this range there is an enormous variation in the adequacy of this return for fully meeting financial needs. The business firm is at one pole in this respect. Its normal expectation is that in the long run it will be able to finance itself adequately from the proceeds of sales. But even here this is true only in the long run; investment of capital in anticipation of future proceeds is of course one of the most important mechanisms in our society.

Two other important mechanisms are taxation and voluntary contributions. In a "free enterprise" economy the general principle governing financing by taxation is that organizations will be supported out of taxation (1) if the goal is regarded as important enough but organizations devoted to it cannot be made to "pay" as private enterprises by providing the service on a commercial basis, e.g., the care of large numbers of persons from the lower income groups who (by current standards) need to be hospitalized for mental illnesses, or (2) if the *ways* in which the services would be provided by private enterprise might jeopardize the public interest, e.g., the provision of military force for the national defense might conceivably be contracted out, but placing control of force to this degree in private hands would constitute too serious a threat to the political stability of the society. Others in these categories are left to the "voluntary" principle, if they are publicly sanctioned, generally in the form of "nonprofit" organizations.

It is important to note that financing of organizations is in general "affected with a public interest" and is in some degree to be regarded as an exercise of political power. This consideration derives from the character of an organization as a goal-directed social system. Every subgoal within the society must to some degree be integrated with the goal-structure of the society as a whole, and it is with this societal goal-structure that political institutions are above all concerned.[1]

THE CONCEPT OF
ORGANIZATION

The last of the four factors of production is what certain economists, notably Alfred Marshall, have called "organization" in the technical sense referred to above. This refers to the function of *combining* the factors of production in such ways as to facilitate the effective attainment of the organization's goal (in our general sense, in its "economic" or factor-consuming aspects). Its input into the organization stands on a level different from that of labor services and financing since it does not concern the direct facilities for carrying out defined functions in a relatively routine manner, but instead concerns readjustment in the patterns of organization itself. It is, therefore, primarily significant in the longer run perspective, and it is involved in processes of structural change in the organization. In its business reference it is in part what J. A. Schumpeter (cf. *The Theory of Economic Development* [1934]) referred to as "entrepreneurship." Organization in this economic sense is, however, an essential factor in *all* organizational functioning. It necessarily plays a central part in the "founding" stages of any organization. From time to time it is important in later stages, since the kinds of adjustments to changing situations which are possible through the routine mechanisms of recruitment of labor services, and through the various devices for securing adequate financial resources, prove to be inadequate; hence a more fundamental structural change in the organization becomes necessary or desirable. This change

---

1. This general thesis of the relation between financing and political power and the public interest has been developed by Parsons and Smelser, *Economy and Society* (1956), especially in chapters ii and iii.

would, in the present frame of reference, require a special input of the factor of organization in this technical sense.

The more generalized equivalent of the land factor is treated, except for the longest-run and most profound social changes, as the most constant reference point of all; its essential reference base is the stability of the value system in terms of which the goal of the organization is defined and the commitments involved in it are legitimized. It is from this reference base that the norms defining the broadly expected types of mechanism in the other respects will be derived, particularly those most actively involved in short-run operations, namely the recruitment of human services through the labor market and the financing of the organization.

THE MECHANISMS OF IMPLEMENTATION

The problem of mobilizing fluid resources concerns one major aspect of the external relations of the organization to the situation in which it operates. Once possessing control of the necessary resources, then, it must have a set of mechanisms by which these resources can be brought to bear on the actual process of goal-implementation in a changing situation. From one point of view, there are two aspects of this process. First is the set of relations to the external situation centering around the problem of "disposal" of the "product" of the organization's activities. This involves the basis on which the scale of operations is estimated and on which the settlement of terms with the recipients of this product is arrived at. In the economic context it is the problem of "marketing," but for present purposes it is necessary to generalize this concept to include all products of organization functioning whether they are "sold" or not; for example, the products of a military organization may be said to be disposed of immediately to the executive and legislative branches of the government and through them to the public, but of course in no direct sense are they sold. The second aspect of the process is concerned with the internal mechanisms of the mobilization of resources for the implementation of the goal. For purposes of the present analysis, however, it will not be necessary to treat these internal and external references separately. Both, as distinguished from the mobilization of resources, can be treated together as governed by the "operative code" of the organization.

This code will have to have an essential basis in the value system which governs the organization. In the case of mobilization of resources, this basis concerns the problem of the "claims" of the organization to the resources it needs and hence the settlement of the terms on which they would be available to it. In the operative case it concerns the manner of their utilization within the organization and the relation to its beneficiaries. We may speak of the relevant value-implementation as centering about the question of "authorization" of the measures involved in carrying through the processes of utilization of resources.

There is an important sense in which the focus of all these functions is the process ordinarily called "decision-making." We have assumed that goal-attainment has clear primacy in the functioning of the organization. The paramount set of decisions then will be, within the framework of legitimation previously referred to, the set of decisions as to how, on the more generalized level, to take steps to attain the goal. This is what is generally thought of as the area of *policy* decisions. A second set of decisions concerns implementation in the sense of decisions about the utilization of resources available to the organization. These are the *allocative* decisions and concern two main subject matters: the allocation of responsibilities among personnel, i.e., suborganizations and individuals, and the allocation of fluid resources, i.e., manpower and monetary and physical facilities in accord with these responsibilities. Finally, a third set of decisions concerns maintaining the *integration* of the organization, through facilitating cooperation and dealing with the motivational problems which arise within the organization in relation to the maintenance of cooperation. The first two sets of decisions fall within the area which Barnard calls the problem of "effectiveness"; the third is the locus of the problem of "efficiency" in his sense. (Cf. Barnard, *The Functions of the Executive* [1938].) Let us consider each of these decision areas in more detail.

Policy Decisions

By policy decisions are meant decisions which relatively directly commit the organization as a whole and which stand in relatively direct connection to its primary functions. They are decisions touching such matters as determination of the nature and quality standards of "product," changes in the scale of operations, problems of the approach to the recipients of the product or service, and organization-wide problems of modes of internal operation.

Policy decisions as thus conceived may be taken at different levels of generality with respect to the functions of the organization. The very highest level concerns decisions to set up a given organization or, conversely, to liquidate it. Near that level is a decision to merge with one or more other organizations. Then the scale descends through such levels as major changes in type of product or in scale of operations, to the day-to-day decisions about current operation. Broadly, this level of generality scale coincides with a scale of time-span of the relevance of decisions; the ones touching the longer-run problems of the organization tend to be the ones on a higher level of generality, involving a wider range of considerations and leading to more serious commitments. An important task for the theory of organization is a systematic classification of these levels of generality of decisions.

As has been noted, the critical feature of policy decisions is the fact that they commit the organization as a whole to carrying out their implications. This area of decisions is the focus of the problem of responsibility. One but only one major aspect of responsibility in turn lies in the fact that all operations of organization to some extent involve risks, and the decision-maker on the one hand is to some extent given "credit" for success, and on the other hand is legitimately held responsible for unfavorable consequences. One of the major features of roles of responsibility is the handling of these consequences; this becomes particularly complicated psychologically because it is often impossible to assess accurately the extent to which success or failure in fact stem from particular decisions or result from factors outside the control or predictive powers of the decision-maker. On high levels of responsibility conflicts of moral value may also operate.

Because of the commitment of the organization as a whole, and through this of the interests of everyone participating in the organization to a greater or lesser degree, authorization becomes particularly important at the policy-decision level. This clearly connects with the value system and hence with the problem of legitimacy. It concerns not simply the content of particular decisions, but the right to make them.

Different organizations, according to scale and qualitative types, of course, have different concrete ways of organizing the policy-making process. Often the highest level of policy is placed mainly in the hands of some kind of a board; whereas "management" has responsibility for the next highest levels, with the still lower levels delegated to operative echelons.

Allocative Decisions

Higher policy decisions will concern the general type and quantity of resources brought into the organization and the more general policies toward personnel recruitment and financing. But the operative utilization of these facilities cannot be completely controlled from the center. There must be some allocative organization by which resources are distributed within the organization, and responsibility for their utilization in the various necessary operative tasks is assigned. This means that specialization in the functions of administration or management precludes the incumbents of these functions from also carrying out the main technical procedures involved in the organization-goal, and hence making the main operating decisions at the "work" level. Thus, a commanding general cannot actually man a particular aircraft or command a particular battery of artillery; a university president cannot actively teach all the subjects of instruction for which the university is responsible.

From one point of view, these mechanisms of internal allocation may be treated as "delegations of authority," though this formula will have to be qualified in connection with various cross-cutting considerations of types of competence and so forth. Thus a general, who by training and experience has been an artilleryman, when he is in command does not simply "delegate" authority to the air element under his command; he must in some way recognize the special technical competence of the air people in a field where he cannot have such competence. Similarly a university president who by academic training has been a professor of English does not merely delegate authority to the physicists on his faculty. Both must recognize an independent technical basis for "lower" echelons performing their functions in the ways in which their own technical judgment makes advisable. The technical man can reasonably be held responsible for the *results* of his operations; he cannot, however, be "dictated to" with respect to the technical procedures by which he achieves these results.

Seen in this light, there are two main aspects of the allocative decision process. One concerns mainly personnel (organized in suborganizations, for example, "departments"), the other financial and, at the requisite level, physical facilities. In the case of personnel the fundamental consideration is the allocation of responsibility. Using decisions as the reference point, the primary focus of the responsibility problem is allocation of the responsibility to decide, i.e., the "decision who should decide," as Barnard puts it. Technical operations as such may then be treated as controlled by the allocation of responsibility for decisions.

The second main aspect of the allocation process is the budget. Though generally formalized only in rather large and highly differentiated organizations, analytically the budget is a central conception. It means the allocation of fluid financial resources which in turn can be committed to particular "uses," namely, acquisition of physical facilities and employment of personnel. Allocation of responsibility is definition of the *functions* of humanly organized subsystems of personnel. Budget allocation is giving these suborganizations access to the necessary means of carrying out their assignment. There is a certain important crisscrossing of the two lines in that at the higher level the decision tends to be one of budget, leaving the employment of the relevant personnel to the subsystem to which funds are allocated. The people responsible at the level in question in turn divide the resource stream, devoting part of it to personnel the employment of whom is, subject to general policies, under their control, another part to subbudget allocation of funds to the uses of personnel they employ. This step-down series continues until the personnel in question are given only various types and levels of control or use of physical facilities, and not control of funds.

Coordination Decisions

Two types of operative decisions have so far been discussed, namely policy decisions and allocative decisions. There is a third category which may be called "decisions of coordination," involving what Barnard has called the problems of "efficiency." These decisions are the operative decisions concerned with the integration of the organization as

a system. Our two types of fundamental resources have a
sharply asymmetrical relation to these decisions as they do to
the allocative decisions. Funds (considered apart from their
lenders or other suppliers) and physical resources do not
have to be motivated to cooperate in organizational tasks, but
human agents do. Decisions of policy and decisions of the
allocation of responsibility still leave open the question of
motivation to adequate performance.

This becomes an integrative problem because the special
types of performance required to achieve the many complex
contributions to an organization goal cannot be presumed to
be motivated by the mere "nature" of the participants independently of the sanctions operating in the organizational
situation. What is coordination from the point of view of
the operation of the organization is "cooperation" from the
point of view of the personnel. The limiting case of noncooperation is declining to continue employment in the
organization, a case of by no means negligible importance
where a free labor market exists. But short of this, relative
to the goals of the organization, it is reasonable to postulate
an inherent centrifugal tendency of subunits of the organization, a tendency reflecting pulls deriving from the personalities of the participants, from the special adaptive
exigencies of their particular job situations, and possibly
from other sources, such as the pressure of other roles in
which they are involved.

In this situation the management of the organization must,
to some degree, take or be ready to take measures to counteract the centrifugal pull, to keep employment turnover at least
down to tolerable levels, and internally to bring the performances of subunits and individuals more closely into line
with the requirements of the organization than would otherwise be the case. These measures can take any one or a combination of three fundamental forms: (1) coercion—in that
penalties for noncooperation are set, (2) inducement—in
that rewards for valued performance are instituted, and (3)

"therapy"—in that by a complex and judicious combination of measures the motivational obstacles to satisfactory cooperation are dealt with on a level which "goes behind" the overt ostensible reasons given for the difficulty by the persons involved.[2]

INSTITUTIONAL FACTORS
IN THE STRUCTURE
OF ORGANIZATIONS

So far two problems have been dealt with, that of the adaptation of an organization to the situation in which it must operate, and that of its operative goal-attainment mechanisms. These prove to be capable of formulation in terms of the mechanisms of mobilization of fluid resources and of the central decision-making processes, respectively. There is, however, another central problem area which is not covered by these considerations, namely that of the mechanisms by which the organization is integrated with as distinguished from "adapted to" other organizations and other types of collectivity in the total social system. This is not a matter of the organization in question treating its *social* situation or environment instrumentally, as a source for the procurement of resources or as the functionally defined field in which it produces its goal-attainment output and makes it available on agreed (or somehow settled) terms to other units of the social structure.

The problem concerns rather the *compatibility* of the

---

2. The famous phenomenon of restriction of production in the informal group as reported by F. J. Roethlisberger and W. J. Dickson (*Management and the Worker* [1939], pt. IV) is a case of relative failure of integration and hence, from one point of view, of failure of management in the function of coordination. It could be handled, from the present point of view, neither by policy decisions (e.g., not to hire "uncooperative workers") nor by allocative decisions (e.g., to hold the shop boss strictly responsible for meeting high production quotas), but only by decisions of coordination, presumably including "therapeutic" measures.

institutional patterns under which the organization operates
with those of other organizations and social units, as related
to the integrative exigencies of the society as a whole (or of
subsystems wider than the organization in question). It is
hence in one aspect a question of the generalizability of the
patterns of procedure adopted in the particular organization
and hence of their permissibility from a wider social point
of view. For example, if a given firm hires and fires on
certain bases, will other firms in the same industry be
allowed to follow this precedent? Or if the security officers in
the Department of Defense follow a given procedure in dealing with alleged security risks, can the same procedure be
tolerated in the State Department? If the two sets of procedures are in conflict, can the two organizations continue
to differ or must they be subjected to a common set of
principles?

It has already been noted that the integrative problem
within an organization most directly concerns the human
agents. This point can be generalized to interorganizational
integration. The central problem concerns the institutionalized norms which can effectively bind the actions of individuals in their commitments to organizations. An important
feature of all complex societies is that the normal individual
is involved in a multiplicity of roles. From one point of view
these roles constitute memberships in or commitments to
collectivities, of which in turn organizations are one principal type. The focus of the integrative problem on a transorganizational level, then, is the problem of the determination of the loyalties of participant persons: on the one hand,
the level of loyalty he bears to a particular organization (in
which, for example, he is employed) and the bases of this
loyalty; on the other hand, the way in which this loyalty
fits into the larger system of loyalties in which his obligations
to a plurality of roles are balanced (for example, to his job,
family, and country). Clearly this allocation of loyalties, not

within the organization but within the society between collectivities, is intimately connected with values. It cannot be only the values of the organization which govern, it must also be a higher-level value system, since the individual cannot determine his loyalties to the organization only on the basis of the values of that particular organization unless in some special sense it claims, and enforces the claim, to absolute loyalty. This is a limiting case, most nearly exemplified in our time by the totalitarian state.

There are three primary complexes of these integrative patterns which have the same order of hierarchical relation to each other that has been sketched for the case of decision-types. Particularly in a society where ascriptive elements of status are relatively minimized, the focal integrative institution is, from one point of view, that of contract. As applied to organizations, this is primarily relevant to the contract of employment. It is the contract of employment—including not only explicitly agreed terms, but "implicit" understandings and also including what Emile Durkheim called the "noncontractual" elements, i.e., the norms governing the making and implementation of contracts which the parties are not at liberty to alter at will—which defines the individual's obligations to the organization. When for any reason the performance of these obligations is brought into question, the problem of loyalty is raised. Limitations on claims of loyalty made by the organization will arise from one or both of two sources, either the personality of the role-incumbent, in that doing what is asked may conflict with his personal values or may otherwise be motivationally distasteful to him, or from other role-obligations, for example, certain requests for overtime work may conflict with obligations to his family. The institution of contract regulates these possible conflicts through patterns which can apply to the organization in question but which at the same time can be motivationally acceptable to most people as "reasonable" and take into account the interests of the other role-complexes in which the same people are involved. Quite clearly the decisions about what particular personnel to hire may be a prerogative exclusively of the organization; the definitions of the institution of contract can in the nature of the case never be the prerogative of one organization, but, with variations, they must regulate the functioning of every organization in the society.

The contract of employment brings out the central significance of contractual relations most vividly. But essentially the same considerations are involved in contracts where property rights rather than human services are the objects of agreement. Where what is transferred is complete ownership, as in the sale of consumer goods or land or capital goods, problems of loyalty are residual. But contracts of investment and the various types of leases involve such considerations directly, since the holder of property claims against an organization is in a position to influence the operations of the organization, sometimes profoundly, through asserting his "rights." Clearly on the interorganization level these contractual patterns cannot be left to the discretion of the particular organization but must be institutionalized on a wider basis.

Both with respect to human services and with respect to property, elements of compulsion may enter to limit "freedom of contract." The case where the role-incumbent is given no choice may be treated as the limiting one. For each category there are two primary types of such limiting cases. With respect to human service one type is that of ascriptive status —for example, on the medieval manor—where the obligation to work a particular plot of land was based on hereditary serfdom to the lord of the manor. On the other hand, certain organizations in the society may exercise powers of compulsion over certain categories of the population in certain contingencies; conscription for military service is a conspicuous example. In the case of property, there may be ascriptive rights and obligations as exemplified by hereditary ownership of land which was inalienable, or there may be powers which legitimize the compulsory relinquishment of property, for example, the taxing power.

The ascriptive case is not of great interest in the present context because it is seldom a feature of organizations in our technical sense. Compulsory contract is, however, of great interest. Essentially it consists of the exercise of authority by an organization of higher-order jurisdiction. It is thus a special combination of the institution of contract, as the definition of the rules under which resources can be made available to organizations, and of the institution of authority, which is the second of the three basic integrative institutions.

The institutionalization of authority may be treated on the interorganization level as cognate with decision-making as a function of the organization itself. Authority is the way in which the binding character of decisions is defined. It is an institutionalized feature of a reciprocal role relationship; there is hence always a double question. First, in what respects and how far is alter bound by ego's decisions and, second, how far and in what respects is ego bound by alter's decisions? We tend to speak of authority only when the relation is relatively one-sided, but the essential elements are present independently of this one-sidedness.

The institutionalization of authority defines, on a basis broader than that of the rules and practices of the organization itself, the ways and their limits in which any given actor, individual or collective, can in a given status in the organization bind others by his decisions and, conversely, the ways and limits in which his action can be bound by the decision of others. Where status in the organization is on a "free" contractual basis, the right to quit is a limiting protection against exposure to authority, and conversely the exerciser of authority is limited in its use by the danger of losing the personnel whose action he seeks to control. Where, as in the military case, the right to quit is severely restricted or altogether eliminated, authority can, of course, go much further.

Although both contract and authority, as institutionalized patterns of the wider society they prescribe, are rules transcending any particular organization, they define obligations which, once entered into, are particularistic. By accepting employment in an organization, an individual accepts a loyalty to that particular organization which, of course, has important limits but which at the same time must be respected within these limits. Authority is also limited, but once in the organization one undertakes responsibilities (i.e., exercises authority) and undertakes to accept the authority of others within the limits of the legitimate range in this organization. These two institutions define the obligations specific to the role in the particular organization which come into force only so far as the incumbent accepts a relation to the organization.

In the conduct of an organization, however, there is a third class of rules or norms which govern conduct independently of any particular organization membership. They are universalistically defined for the society as a whole or for transorganizational sectors of the society's structure. A particularly basic one in our society is the complex having to do with personal freedoms; to take its extreme application, slavery is prohibited not only in that no one may coerce an individual into giving up his personal freedom, but even he himself may not, by however voluntary a contractual arrangement, "sell himself" into slavery. The general rules against the use of force in human relations except under carefully regulated circumstances, against the use of outright fraud in almost any case (not, of course, including the withholding of information to which alter is not "entitled") and a variety of other cases fall here. The essential point is that the conduct of the affairs of an organization must in general conform with the norms of "good conduct" as recognized and institutionalized in the society. The most general principle is that no one may legitimately contract to violate these norms, nor may authority be used to coerce people into their violation.

Thus from another point of view the three complexes of institutionalized rules stand in a reverse relation of hierarchical priority. The most universalistic complex just discussed sets the limits in the treatment of human beings and nonhuman resources within which the conduct of organizations must remain. The institutionalization of authority then defines more specifically how, within these limits, resources may be used within the structure of the organization, while the institution of contract defines the terms on which the resources can be made available at all.

THE PROBLEM OF POWER

As seen in the analysis in the first section of this paper, the development of organizations is the principal mechanism by which, in a highly differentiated society, it is possible to "get things done," to achieve goals beyond the reach of the individual and under conditions which provide a relative maximization of effectiveness, in Chester Barnard's sense. Subject to the over-all control of an institutionalized value system in the society and its subsystems, the central phenomenon of organization is the mobilization of *power* for the attainment of the goals of the organization. The value system *legitimizes* the organization's goal, but it is only through power that its achievement can be made effective.

Seen in these terms, power is the generalized capacity to mobilize resources in the interest of attainment of a system goal. The generation and utilization of power constitutes one of the fundamental functional imperatives of any social system. Like any other major system function, except in the simplest systems, power becomes the focus of a set of specialized mechanisms. So far as these mechanisms themselves become organized to constitute a distinct subsystem of the society, we can speak of the "polity" as the system oriented to the generation and allocation of power.[3] The polity in this sense is parallel to the economy as that concept is ordinarily used in economic theory.

The generation and exercise of power is most conspicuous in relation to a goal which is dramatically and unequivocally a common goal for a whole society, such as victory in war. But in more everyday terms, the goal of the society can be said to be to "get the things done" which are approved in terms of its values as "worth doing" (the term "worth" may, of course, signify varying degrees of urgency). Hence we may speak of power as a generalized societal resource which is allocated to the attainment of a wide range of subgoals and to organizations as the agents of the attainment of such subgoals. Power is comparable to wealth, which, as a generalized societal resource, is allocated to many different societal subsystems for "consumption" or for "capital" use.

The power exercised in and by an organization is generated both outside and within the organization. Every organization, whatever the nature of its functional primacy—for example, manufacturing, or medical care—is part of the polity and a generator of power, but is also a recipient of the power generated at higher echelons in the polity.

The generation of power on any given level depends, as we see it, on four fundamental conditions. The first condition is the institutionalization of a value system which legitimizes both the goal of the organization and the principal patterns by which it functions in the attainment of that goal. The second condition is the regulation of the organiza-

3. The polity in this sense is *not* identical with government, which we interpret to be a complex of *organizations*. Government has other than political functions, and other organizations participate in the polity. We conceive of the relation of polity and government as approximately parallel to that between economy and business. Cf. Talcott Parsons and Neil Smelser, *Economy and Society* (op. cit.) ch. ii.

tion's procurement and decision-making processes through adherence to universalistic rules and to such institutions as authority and contract. It is on these bases that the organization establishes generalized claims to the loyal cooperation of its personnel and of persons outside the organization on whose cooperation it depends. The third condition is the command of the more detailed and day-to-day support of the persons whose cooperation is needed. The fourth is the command of necessary facilities, of which the primary category in our society is financial.

In our society the first condition has frequently become formalized through the privilege and practice of incorporation. This establishes a direct positive link with government and the legal system. Organization for the purpose at hand is formally "authorized," and certain powers and privileges are thereby conferred. The second condition is partly met by the legal regulation of all organizational activity, and partly by an informal reputation for integrity and "good practice" which in itself often becomes an organizational asset. The third and fourth conditions are met by the operative mechanisms of procurement of resources and the operative code previously described. Certain variations in the mechanisms by which this occurs in different types of organizations will be discussed presently.

The mobilization and utilization of power is the central focus of the operation of organizations, but by virtue of the fact that an organization is a social system, it is also dependent on all the other exigencies of such a system. The value component has already been discussed. The other two components are economic resources (centering on the problem of financing) and the command of loyalties (which underlies efficiency in Barnard's sense). Power helps to *command* these essentials, but their availability is not a function only of power but also of the ways in which the cognate activities of the organization mesh with the relevant features of the situation in which it functions. Thus the organization always to some extent "produces" economically valuable goods or services; the marketability of these products constitutes one central set of conditions of its operation. Similarly, the organization is always, through "informal" organization and otherwise, a focus of the relatively noncontingent loyalties of its personnel. The extent to which this is true and the basis on which it rests form another essential condition of the organization's functioning. Power as a factor operates to exploit advantages on these levels and to make up deficits; power never operates alone.

The scheme we have presented is characterized by a certain formal symmetry. The value system of the organization is treated as defining and legitimizing its goal. Each of the other three aspects, the adaptive mechanisms and those mechanisms of operative goal-attainment and the integration of the organization, is regulated by subvalues governing each of these three aspects of organizational functioning. Each primary type of resource input is regulated by a type of contractual pattern, e.g., employment and investment. Each part of the operative code is governed in turn by an aspect of authority, and finally each context of institutionalization is a way of defining, for those participating, the extent of "loyalty" owing to the organization as compared with other commitments.

CLASSIFICATION OF
TYPES OF ORGANIZATION

Organizations are of course always part of a larger social structure of the society in which they occur. There is necessarily a certain variability among organizations which is a function of this wider societal matrix; an American organization is never quite like a British one even though they are nearly cognate in function. Discounting this type of variability, however, organizations may in the first instance be classified in terms of the *type of goal or function* about which they are organized. The same basic classification can be used for goal types which has been used earlier in dealing with the functions of a social system. Thus we may speak of adaptive goals, implementive goals, integrative goals, and pattern-maintenance goals. The reference is always to function in the *society* as a system.

Seen in these terms the principal broad types of organization are:

1. *Organizations oriented to economic production:* The type case in this category is the business firm. Production should be understood in the full economic sense as "adding value"; it is by no means confined to physical production, e.g., manufacturing. It has been emphasized several times that every organization contributes in some way to every primary function (if it is well integrated in the society); hence we can speak only of economic *primacy*, never of an organization as being exclusively economic. This applies also to the other categories.

2. *Organizations oriented to political goals,* that is, to the attainment of valued goals and to the generation and allocation of power in the society: This category includes most organs of government, but in a society like ours, various other organizations are involved. The allocation of purchasing power through credit creation is an exercise of power in this sense; hence a good part of the banking system should be treated as residing in primarily political organizations. More generally, it seems legitimate to speak of incorporation as an allocation of power in a political sense; hence the corporate aspect of formal organizations generally is a political aspect.

3. *Integrative organizations:* These are organizations which on the societal level, contribute primarily to efficiency, not effectiveness. They concern the adjustment of conflicts and the direction of motivation to the fulfillment of institution-

alized expectations. A substantial part of the functions of the courts and of the legal profession should be classed here. Political parties, whose function is the mobilization of support for those responsible for government operations, belong in this category, and, to a certain extent, "interest groups" belong here, too. Finally, those organizations that are primarily mechanisms of social control in the narrower sense, for example hospitals, are mainly integrative.

4. *Pattern-maintenance organizations:* The principal cases centering here are those with primarily "cultural," "educational," and "expressive" functions. Perhaps the most clearcut organizational examples are churches and schools. (Pattern maintenance is not here conceived to preclude creativity; hence research is included.) The arts so far as they give rise to organization also belong here. Kinship groups are ordinarily not primarily organizations in our technical sense, but in a society so highly differentiated as our own the nuclear family approaches more closely the characteristics of an organization than in other societies. As such it clearly belongs in the pattern-maintenance category.

This primary basis of classification can be used as the point of departure for a more detailed one, by further subdividing each of the primary types into lower other subsystems. Thus in the economic case the main bases of sub-classification would include specialization in adaptive functions for the economy (financing), in goal attainment (production and marketing in a narrower sense), etc. Similar considerations will apply in the cases of the other primary types. In each of these cases a primary determinant of the type of organization is the kind of boundary-interchange operating between the societal system in which the organization is primarily anchored and the contiguous subsystem. Thus from the point of view of the economy, production and marketing are the sources of the ultimate production of goods and services to the consumer and of the input of labor services into the economy. Both consumer and worker are anchored in the first instance in the household as part of the pattern-maintenance system. Organizations oriented primarily to consumption interests are necessarily different from those oriented primarily to the financing of capital expansion.

SOME ILLUSTRATIVE CASES

It should prove illuminating to apply the formal analysis presented above to the differentiation between types of organization. For this purpose it seems useful to select the business firm, the military organization, and the university. They belong in three different primary categories and are sufficiently extreme so that the differences can be brought out clearly. Let us contrast them with respect to each of the four main analytical categories which have been sketched in general terms above: values, adaptive patterns, operative code, and institutional pattern.

First, let us look at values. The business firm is governed by the values of economic rationality; the maximization of production with minimal cost in the economic sense. It is *production* which is the institutionalized goal of the firm. In a market economy, however, financial return is both a condition of continuing operation and a central symbol of success. The societal function reference is primary; the market-profit reference is secondary, but very important. In the adaptive context the values of the firm call for independent self-financing and payment of labor on what is felt to be a marginal productivity basis. In the goal-attainment context products are "marketed" on a full payment-of-cost basis involving prices governed by marginal utility, not by "need." In the integrative context, beyond the general commitment to productivity as an ethical obligation, loyalties and obligations to the organization are defined in terms of "self-interest."

The military organization, on the other hand, is organized about the value of technical effectiveness; its primary goal is maximization of power in its particular field. This must be done under a very special set of conditions, since operative exercise of military power is an emergency function and in most societies is not a routine function of social life. Hence the organization must be kept in a maximum state of readiness but for long periods without opportunity to test its effectiveness in combat; and the time when it will be called upon to do so is generally not predictable. Furthermore, the organized use of force in most modern societies is valued only as a necessary evil, legitimized only through the defensive interest of the national society. The functional equivalent of the market in the economic case is extremely precarious because of this ethical ambivalence and because of the high contingency factor. The primary subgoals are the mobilization of support, the authorization of facilities, and the legitimation of the function. Hence there is a high premium on stringency of control over personnel and facilities.

The university belongs quite clearly in the category of pattern-maintenance primacy. Its goal is twofold: it is part of the process of socialization or of education, and it has responsibility for creative modification of the cultural tradition through the processes usually referred to as "research." Its functions for the social system are "expressive" rather than "operative," and its importance is clear in the long run rather than the short run. The university must depend on recognition of its services as "good in themselves" rather than on their short-run utility in the society. It tends to be seen as devoted to "higher" interests which involve self-sacrifice, and it appeals for support on this ground. At the same time it is exposed to attack by those who feel that it is "useless" or worse.

Next let us look at the adaptive factors; for brevity's sake the discussion will be confined to the acquisition of personnel and financial resources. The most striking thing about the business firm in both these respects is that is is expected to "pay its way" on a marginal utility-marginal productivity basis. In the long run it is expected to meet its costs through the monetary proceeds of its operations, with something to spare as a symbol of its success in effective operation. In the short run it may enter the capital market as a borrower, but generally on "investment" terms, meaning that the lender should, discounting the risk, have good prospects, not merely of recouping his investment but of receiving a satisfactory return on it. There are many modifications of this pattern, through the phenomena of direct or indirect subsidies, but for the free-enterprise type of economy the general pattern is clear.

The general principle for the recruitment of personnel to the firm is similar. The employee, both on labor and on managerial levels, is expected to be paid "what his services are worth" in marginal productivity terms as determined on a competitive market. Conversely, adequate or fair remuneration as defined in marginal utility terms is accepted as a standard for defining the individual's obligations to the firm; he will not be blamed for quitting if he can do better (both for himself and in productivity terms) in another job; the presumption is that the firm offering him higher pay is more accurately measuring his productivity. This, as the main context of the definition of "self-interest," is not to be construed as not valuing the goal of production; on the contrary, the level of remuneration is taken as a direct symbolization of contribution to productivity.

Remuneration by marginal productivity is of course an ideal type, and there are many modifications of it. The position of the trade union and the interposition of collective bargaining between the individual worker and the employing organization signify one major focus of limitation on this principle. Another derives from the increasing dependence of business organizations on professional personnel whose occupational status is necessarily anchored in societal functions other than production as such. But by contrast with the other types of organization considered here, this pattern is more closely approached in the business world than elsewhere.

In the case of the military organization, both fields of resource-procurement present a radical contrast. To take financing first, in all modern societies military forces are ideally controlled exclusively by public authority; hence military organizations (with negligible exceptions) do not "earn" any income whatever. Their financing is dependent on a grant by public authority out of funds raised by taxation. The basis for such financing is, therefore, an evaluative judgment, made by certain organs of that authority, of the defense needs of the society. Because of the urgency of the need and the potential seriousness of its neglect, such organizations can command very large resources, but the mechanism of their procurement is nearly as far removed from the economic principle as it is possible to get.

The procurement of personnel by the military also takes place by mechanisms strikingly different from those involved in the business world. Indeed, for military personnel (as distinguished from civilian employees of the military establishment), it is scarcely correct to speak of "employment" at all. There are two basic patterns, namely "volunteering" and conscription. Military service is the only near-occupational role in which compulsory service is sanctioned in our type of society on a basis other than punishment or incapacity. Even military conscription is felt to be justified only as an emergency measure. The volunteer, though not forced into the role, must sign up for a stated term and cannot resign during it; he must also accept contingencies of discipline and personal risk far exceeding those ordinarily accepted in "jobs." The concepts of duty and "service" are heavily emphasized. Remuneration is clearly not regulated by marginal productivity but by some kind of concept of need and of status-dignity. It is thus only in a highly attenuated sense that we may speak of the "market for military employment."

The case of the university is intermediate in both respects. To varying degrees, universities are expected to recoup part of their costs from fees for their services, notably tuition. But this is scarcely a price in the strict economic sense, both because university functions universally are highly subsidized by voluntary contributions and/or taxation, and because tuition is assessed on a modified sliding-scale basis; ability to pay is taken explicitly into account, and many are given scholarship aid. The value of the function therefore is not measured by its capacity to "pay its way" through the market mechanisms. Tuition is justified rather on the ground that since university financing presents difficult problems, it is legitimate to ask those who benefit most directly (though it is usually parents, not students, who pay) to bear as much of the cost as they can.

With respect to personnel recruitment, the university also stands in a position intermediate in most respects between the business firm and the military organization. The key sector of its personnel is clearly the faculty, though various other categories are needed. The faculty member is a highly trained professional person who is also a specialist, often in a highly technical and erudite field. He holds a "job" in that his contract of employment is wholly voluntary, and he enjoys the right to resign at any time. But his role is not defined as "self-interested" in the business sense, and his remuneration is not calculated on a marginal productivity basis, but on a "just price" basis. A particular kind of modification of the market pattern stands in marked contrast with business (though to a degree shared with the military), namely the institution of tenure. In both cases this relates to the fact that the incumbent has renounced the possible advantages of a business career and has devoted himself to an economically unviable source of employment, one in which the remuneration levels generally are, relative to ability, markedly lower than they are in business. Tenure and the sliding scale are institutions emphatically frowned upon in the business world; their clear acceptance in the academic is a measure of the difference between the two types of organization.

Now let us look at the situation with respect to the operative code in each of these three types of organization. In this respect the business firm stands intermediate between the other two. Because of the goal-directedness of organizations generally, we put particular emphasis in this respect on the processes of policy decision. The business firm as we know it is a relatively centralized organization; the main locus of policy decisions is what is usually called "top management," and its procedures are removed from "democratic" norms.

In the tradition which has crystalized in the United States in recent decades, the primary responsibility for decisions is concentrated in a central management, and then both the responsibilities of other personnel and budgetary resources are allocated from the center out by top management. This centralization is legitimized by the expectation that management will be competent, and that there will be an identity of interest between management and other employees in giving management the power it needs to do the job effectively, subject to fair treatment of employees. This expectation is controlled externally, first by competition with other firms so that presumably an ineffective management would not be able to continue in business, and secondly by the free labor market to the extent that its employees are free to quit and seek other employment.

It is notable that the growth of trade unionism in the United States has been accompanied by relatively little demand for managerial prerogatives. It is also notable that there has been a marked diminution in the legitimation of control by ownership of capital assets, and a corresponding increase in control by the effectiveness of a management, most of whose personnel are formally "employees."

The military organization is, of course, the most authoritarian type of organization found on a considerable scale in our society. There is no market standard of effectiveness and no institutionalized right to quit. Legitimation focuses very sharply on authorization from the legally competent source. Once the commanding officer's position is legitimated, he exercises powers of decision and of coercion which would hardly be tolerated anywhere else. This pattern clearly derives from the overwhelming importance of effective coordinated action in dangerous emergency conditions.

It is an important fact, however, that in a modern society the clear predominance of "line" authority as a central principle of operation in either the business or the military version is coming to be seriously modified by the involvement of technical professional services. The strategic significance of such services for the organization comes to be so high that the persons responsible for them must be given high status. But it is the nature of executive responsibility that it must cover the whole range of subject matters relevant to the functioning of the organization as a whole, or to the level of responsibility of the suborganization in question. This diffuseness of responsibility precludes that the executive could be the equal, even on the basis of judgment to say nothing of performance, of the high-level technical expert on his own ground, *in all the different fields of technical expertness* which may be important to the executive's field of responsibility. Hence he cannot supervise the technical expert in detail nor can he have a detailed personal judgment of what the expert does, except from other experts in the same field. He must, therefore, delegate an important share of responsibility to technical experts, or "teams" of them. The multiplication of technical fields, and their differentiation from each other, therefore, leads to an essential element of decentralization in the organizations which must employ them.

This problem seems to be at least one principal key to

the structure of the university, as contrasted with the other two cases. The central personnel of a university organization are its faculty, who are all highly qualified technical experts, spread over a very wide range of different subject matters. It is they who are the main operative performers of the two principal functions of the university—teaching and research.

A university cannot be organized mainly on a "line" principle, with the president issuing orders through his deans to the members of the faculty. The faculty tends, rather, to be a collegial "company of equals" who bear a good deal of corporate responsibility. The "administration" is more a "facilitating" agency responsible for financial resources, physical facilities, and largely for public relations. Perhaps the most important point at which a delicate balance must be worked out is in the field of appointments. The administration cannot simply "hire" a professor without regard to the professional wishes and judgments of his prospective colleagues or to the candidate's standing in the relevant professional field. At the same time, leaving the appointment function solely in the hands of faculty departments also has its dangers. The result is usually a balance of responsibility, with the initiative mainly in faculty hands, and a veto power, effectively if not formally, on both sides. This situation provides another basis on which to explain the institution of tenure. The professor is a technical expert who must take a heavy responsibility in an organization where his administrative superiors are almost always lacking in technical ability to evaluate the quality of his work. Denial to administrations of the right to "fire" him, except for cause involving grave professional or personal misconduct, protects him against arbitrary intervention in his work by persons who inevitably possess great power but who do not possess the competence to exercise it wisely on the basis of their own personal knowledge and experience alone.

The integrative or institutional aspect of the three types

of organizations being compared involves repetition of some of the considerations already stated, since this concerns the institutionalization, on a basis transcending the organization, of patterns of contract and of authority in the society as a whole. It is worth while to sum up the differences.

The business firm relies, and is expected to rely, on "free contract" on the basis of the financially symbolized self-interest of the parties, both for the disposal of its product and, from the proceeds, for the necessary financial and personnel resources for its operation. The contracts are in general balanced on both sides: the right to hire and fire is balanced by the right to accept or reject offers of employment and to quit at will. There are, of course, many modifications of the perfectly "free" market, e.g., collective bargaining, grievance procedures, and regulation of investment, but by contrast with the other types of organization these features stand out clearly. The military stands in this respect in the sharpest contrast, with no "market" for its services in the ordinary sense at all and scarcely a market for its financial or human resources. The university in this respect is in the intermediate position, with a greatly modified market for services, but this is distinguished by a sliding scale, and by the expectation that proceeds will only partially cover costs, the deficit to be made up by taxation and/or contributions. Payment in both military and academic organizations is on the basis of a "just price" system and not of marginal productivity, and the university is characterized by the institution of tenure. (In a modified sense this is also true of military officers.)

In the case of authority the most stringent type is clearly the military, which carries the "line" principle and the use of coercive sanctions further than any other organization in the society. The business firm is in the intermediate position. It has a notable legitimation of authority, but this is limited by the fact that acceptance of authority is voluntary and defined in terms of self-interest and market competition.

Finally, the university is in some respects a peculiarly "anti-authoritarian" type of organization; its "top management" is ordinarily subjected to a conspicuous set of limitations on its authority to intervene in the spheres of competence of faculty members, who in one sense are "subordinates." The case of tenure has been stressed, but another very important sphere in which these limitations operate is that of "academic freedom" in the sense of freedom to teach, discuss, and write without interference over a wide area of tolerance.

CONCLUSION

The principal aim of this paper has been to relate the analysis of "formal organizations" more closely than is customary to some categorizations available in general sociological theory. There is a tendency in our society to consider different types of organizations as belonging in the fields allocated to different academic disciplines; thus students of business organization are likely to be economists, those of governmental and military organization, political scientists, and so forth. This tendency to divide the field obscures both the importance of the common elements, and the *systematic* bases of the variations from one type to another.

The procedure of this paper has been first to attempt to define an organization by locating it systematically in the structure of the society in relation to other categories of social structure. It seemed appropriate to define an organization as a social system which is organized for the attainment of a particular type of goal; the attainment of that goal is at the same time the performance of a type of function on behalf of a more inclusive system, the society.

It proved possible to bring to bear a general classification of the functional imperatives of social systems and with this to identify the principal mechanisms necessary to bring about the attainment of the goal or the organization purpose. The classification used has proved its applicability both for the level of the total society and for that of the small group. The present application to an intermediate level further increases confidence in its generality.

The classification distinguishes four main categories: the value system which defines and legitimizes the goals of the organization, the adaptive mechanisms which concern mobilization of resources, the operative code concerned with the mechanisms of the direct process of goal implementation, and finally the integrative mechanisms. These four categories are specifications of categories which, as noted, have been used in a variety of other contexts for the analysis of structural differentiation and phases of process over time in social systems.

These categories were first used to analyze the main components in the structure of an organization—its value system defining the societal commitments on which its functioning depends; its mechanisms of procurement of resources; its operative mechanisms centering about decision making in the field of policy, allocation, and integration; and its institutional patterns which link the structure of the organization with the structure of the society as a whole. It has proved possible to spell out these considerations in ways which link directly with the well-known ways of dealing with the problems of organization in the relevant literature.

The same basic classification of the functional problems of social systems was used to establish points of reference for a classification of types of organization, and the broadest outline of a proposed classification was sketched. The capacity of the conceptual scheme to account for variations in the important features of organizations was then tested in a preliminary, illustrative way by a rapid survey of some of the principal features of business, military, and academic organizations.

In the nature of the case this essay has been subject to severe limitations. Such limitations are partly involved in the space available. More important, however, is the fact that the essay constitutes a preliminary attempt to approach this range of problems systematically in terms of this order of general theoretical analysis. The results seem to justify the hope that carrying such analysis further will help to codify our knowledge of organizations more systematically than has been the case before, and to link it more closely with knowledge of other types of social systems and of the social environment within which formal organizations must operate in a society like our own.

CHAPTER II

SOME INGREDIENTS
OF A GENERAL THEORY
OF FORMAL ORGANIZATION

Most of the recent literature in the field of formal organization has tended to deal with internal structure and processes: such problems as line authority, staff organization, and the process of decision-making. I have therefore selected for comment three fields which have been less in the center of attention. The first of these is the set of differences which arise at various levels in the hierarchy of control and responsibility in systems of organization. The second concerns analysis of the *external* relations of organizations to the situations in which they function, and the third is the variation in *types* of organization which is related, on the one hand, to their technical functions, on the other, to variations in their external relations. These three problem areas are closely interdependent. It would not be useful to deal with them entirely independently; it will be necessary to interweave them. But I would like to build the main structure of the paper on the distinctness of these three themes and at the same time their interdependence.

The theory of "bureaucracy" has been so strongly influenced by the conception of "line" authority that there has been a tendency to neglect the importance of what in some sense are qualitative breaks in the continuity of the line structure. There is much sound observation and comment on many relevant problems but little direct attempt to analyze them in a more formal way. I would like to suggest a way of breaking down the hierarchical aspect of a system of organization—of examining, for example, the line within a school system that runs all the way from the chairman of the school board to the teacher of most junior status, or even to the non-teaching employee in the humblest position. I make this breakdown according to three references of function or responsibility, which become most clearly marked in terms of the external references of the organization to its setting or to the next higher order in the hierarchy. These three may be called, respectively, the "technical" system, the "managerial" system, and the "community" or "institutional" system.

Three Levels in the Hierarchical Structure of Organization

In the first place, every formal organization has certain "technical" functions. In an educational organization these are the actual processes of teaching; in a government bureau, the administrative process in direct relation to the public (e.g., tax collecting by the Bureau of Internal Revenue); in a business firm, the process of physical production of goods, etc. There is, then, always a type of suborganization whose "problems" are mainly those of effectively performing this "technical" function—the conduct of classes by the teacher, the processing of income tax returns and the handling of recalcitrants by the bureau, the processing of material and supervision of these operations in the case of physical production. The primary exigencies to which this suborganization is oriented are those imposed by the nature of the technical task, such as the "materials"—physical, cultural, or human—which must be processed, the kinds of co-operation of different people required to get the job done effectively.

I assume, however, that on the level of social differentiation with which we are here concerned, there is another set of "problems" which becomes the focus of a different order of organizational setup. In the area where parents teach their own children, for example, to speak 'their language, there is no problem of the selection and appointment of teachers, or even of their qualifications; the status of parent *ipso facto* makes him the appropriate teacher. But in a school system teachers have to be especially appointed and allocated to teach particular classes. Moreover, classrooms have to be provided; the teacher does not automatically control adequate facilities for performing the function. Furthermore, while it is taken for granted that a child should learn to speak the language of his parents, what should be taught in what schools to what children is by no means automatically given.

In a complex division of labor, both the resources necessary for performing technical functions and the relations to the population elements on whose behalf the functions are performed have become problematical. Resources are made available by special arrangements; they are not simply "given" in the nature of the context of the function. And who shall be the beneficiary of what "product" or "service" on what terms is problematical; this becomes the focus of organizational arrangements of many different kinds.

When the division of labor has progressed beyond a certion point, decisions that pertain to this division must take precedence over those on the "technical" level. Thus it does not make sense to set up classrooms without having decided what children should be taught what things by what kinds of teachers, or without knowing whether specific teachers and specific physical facilities can be made available. Similarly, the Bureau of Internal Revenue does not just "collect taxes" in general; it collects specific taxes assessed by a higher authority, from specific categories of persons. And the plant does not just produce goods without anyone's worrying about how the materials will be procured, who will do the actual work on what terms, and who wants the goods anyway—again on what terms. In the case of a subsistence farm family there is no problem: its members have to eat; they have access to soil, seeds, and some simple equipment; and they work to produce their own food. But this is not the typical case for a modern society.

We may say then that the more complex technical functions are performed by suborganizations controlled and serviced—in various ways and at a variety of levels—by higher-order organizations. The higher-order organization is sometimes called an "administration." In the business case it is usually called the "firm," whereas the technical organization is called the "plant." In the field of government, "bureaus" are mainly technical organizations, while the "political" parts of government are, literally, the "policy-making" parts (in our system, principally legislative[1] and higher executive). Perhaps a good name for this level of organization is, as suggested above, a "managerial" system.

The relations between such a managerial system and the technical system can be divided into two categories: mediation between the organization and the external situation, and "administration" of the organization's internal affairs. Both involve the "decision-making" processes which have been the center of so much recent attention.

At the level I have in mind, there are two main foci of the external reference and responsibility. The primary one is to mediate between the technical organization and those who use its "products"—the "customers," pupils, or whoever. The second is to procure the resources necessary for carrying out the technical functions (i.e., financial resources, personal, and physical facilities).

In one set of connections, decisions made in the management system control the operations of the technical system. This is certainly true for such matters as the broad technical

---

1. The legislative function may, however, be placed mainly at the still higher level, which I call "institutional" and which will be discussed below.

task which is to be performed in the technical system—the scale of operations, employment and purchasing policy, etc. But, as in other cases of functional differentiation, this is by no means simply a one-way relation, for managerial personnel usually are only partially competent to plan and supervise the execution of the technical operations. The managers present specifications to the technical subsystem, but vice versa, the technical people present "needs" which constitute specifications to the management; on various bases the technical people are closest to the operating problems and know what is needed. Perhaps the most important of these bases is the technical *professional* competence of higher personnel in technical systems, a professional competence not often shared by the administrative personnel who—in the line sense—are the organizational superiors of the technicians.

In its external relations, the managerial system is oriented to the "markets" for the disposal of the "product" and for "procurement" of the resources required by the organization to perform its functions. But those "lateral" external relations do not exhaust the "external" problem foci of a managerial system. The organization which consists of both technical and managerial suborganizations never operates subject only to the exigencies of disposal to and procurement from other agencies (which stand on an approximately equal level) as "customers" or as sources of supply. There is always some "organized superior" agency with which the organization articulates.

A formal organization in the present sense is a mechanism by which goals somehow important to the society, or to various subsystems of it, are implemented and to some degree defined. But not only does such an organization have to operate in a social environment which imposes the conditions governing the processes of disposal and procurement, it is also part of a wider social system which is the source of the "meaning," legitimation, or higher-level support which makes the implementation of the organization's goals possible. Essentially, this means that just as a technical organization (at a sufficiently high level of the division of labor) is controlled and "serviced" by a managerial organization, so, in turn, is the managerial organization controlled by the "institutional" structure and agencies of the community.

The ways in which the managerial system fits into the higher-order institutional system vary widely according to the character of the managerial system's functions and the organization's position on both the "lateral" and the "vertical" axes of the larger social system. But it is a cardinal thesis of this analysis that no organization is ever wholly "independent." In terms of "formal" controls it may be relatively so, but in terms of the "meaning" of the functions performed by the organization and hence of its "rights" to command resources and to subject its "customers" to disciplines, it never is wholly independent.

As noted, this third level of organization, which articulates with the managerial, may take many forms. In the educational field, for instance, I would put school boards with their representative functions in the local community in this category; similarly with trustees of the various types of private, non-profit organizations and, indeed, under the fully-developed corporate form, with the boards of directors of business corporations.[2] These, and possibly other agencies, are the mediating structures between the particular managerial organization—and hence the technical organization it controls—and the higher-order community interests which, on some level, it is supposed to "serve."

Without attempting to be more circumstantial and formal at this stage, I may merely suggest that the foci of these higher-level controls which stand "over" the managerial organization are of three main types, which often appear in combination. One control is universal: the operation

---

2. For the business case one may thus designate the three organizational levels as plant, firm, and corporation. The "central office" may be thought of as the "plant" of the administrative organization of the firm.

of the organization is subjected to generalized norms, valid throughout a wider community. These range from the rules formally codified in the law to standards of "good practice" informally accepted. So far as control is of this type, the distinctive thing is that no organized agency continually supervises the managerial organization; intervention is likely only when deviant practice is suspected—such control is exerted, for example, through litigation or by law-enforcement agencies, trade and professional associations, and relevant "public opinion."

The second type of control mechanism is some formal organization which is interstitial between the managerial structure and a more diffuse basis of "public interest." The fiduciary board which supervises the typical private non-profit organization is the type case, though in many respects the directors of business corporations also belong in this category.

Finally, the third type is that which brings the managerial organization directly into a structure of "public authority" at some level. In our society this is usually "political" authority, i.e., some organ of government; but in the past, religious authorities have also performed this function, and even now, for example, the Catholic school system should be treated as belonging to this type. The relation to superior authority may in turn be "administrative" or "regulative."

THE POINTS OF ARTICULATION
BETWEEN THE THREE SYSTEM-LEVELS

I have emphasized these *three* different levels of the organization hierarchy because at each of the two points of articulation between them we find a qualitative break in the simple continuity of "line" authority. School boards, boards of directors, or trustees and political superiors do not, in the nature of the case, simply tell the people at the next level down "what to do." This is essentially because the people "lower down" typically must exercise types of competence and shoulder responsibilities which cannot be regarded as simply "delegated" by their "superiors." This again is because the *functions* at each level are qualitatively different; those at the second level are not simply "lower-order" spellings-out of the "top" level functions.

In the case of the technical organization, I illustrate this by the case of the higher level technical functions. When the personnel of the technical organization reach a full professional level of competence, a crucial problem of organization appears. For no matter how far removed these professionals may be from certain levels of concrete "operations," they must necessarily have the last word in planning and evaluating these operations (i.e., setting the *criteria* of effective operation in technical terms), simply because their managerial superiors are seldom, if at all, equally competent in the technical field. Organizational arrangements are extremely varied; sometimes such people have important positions in the "firm" or other managerial organization, and they should be regarded, like the foreman, as interstitial. In any case, their position cannot be a simple "line" position. Nor, indeed, is it adequate to assign them to the "staff" and say that their function is to "advise" the "lay" executive. This implies that it is the executive who *really* makes the decisions. But this is not correct. The technical expert must, in the nature of the case, *participate* in the technically crucial decisions. He does not simply lay the alternatives with their consequences before his "boss" and say, "Take *your* choice." The technical expert takes responsibility for *his* judgment, and when the decision has fallen a given way, he must assume his share of responsibility for the consequences. Hence, if he feels that he cannot take this responsibility, his recourse is to resign, exactly as in the case of an executive. A decision is arrived at not by the executive's deciding in the light of the expert's advice but by a process of weighing the considerations for which each is responsible and then reaching some kind of a balance of agreement. Because of the functions of the managerial organization, the executive has some kind of "last word." But this is a veto power, not a capacity to implement, because the executive is powerless to implement or plan implementation without the competence of the expert. The most the executive can do is to fire one expert and hire another in his place.

This leads to another crucial point. The technical expert at the professional level may be a member of the managerial organization, and of the technical system under it, but his allegiance is never exhausted by these two. Though degrees of formal organization vary greatly, the expert is typically a member of one or more collectivities of specialists sharing a type of competence which cuts across the structure of managerial and specific technical organizations. Thus no one industrial firm employs all the engineers, nor one hospital all the doctors, nor one school system all the teachers. The "reference group" to which the expert looks in connection with his competence and the definition of its standards is not his "managerial" boss but his professional peers and colleagues.

Similar considerations apply at the point of articulation between the managerial and the institutional system. But the qualitative break in line authority at this point is obscured because we have tended to describe organizational situations according to one of two extreme types. One is exemplified by the business firm where the "top man" is thought of as beholden to no one; he is "on his own." He is thought of as responsible only to his own conscience, and everyone else in the organization is under his orders. The other type of organization is that in which the managerial unit is incorporated in a "political" structure, so that the nominal head of the unit is thought of merely as a subordinate of his political superiors.

The essential focus of the qualitative break in line authority I have in mind here is the managerial *responsibility* assumed by the executive and the managerial organization which he, in many cases, heads. This also is not a mere "delegation" where the executive is commissioned to carry out the "details" while his superiors decide all the "policies." This is because it is not possible to perform the functions of focusing legitimation and community support for the organization and at the same time act as the active management of it—that is, when the differentiation of function in the structure has gone far enough. The "board," or whatever structural form it takes, is a mediating structure between the affairs of the organization at the managerial level and its "public." It can become absorbed in the managerial structure only at the expense of its primary function.

Of course the degree to which legitimation and support are essential functions varies from case to case. In some cases, most nearly approached but by no means reached in the business world, the "automatic" institutional controls constitute the main regulatory mechanism. Perhaps near the extreme in the other direction is the case of the school board in a community where a great many issues touching the operation of the school system are politically "hot." Then the superintendent may be sorely in need of a buffer between himself and various "pressure groups" in the community, but by the same token the board itself may be "bent" by the pressures of these groups. Its failure to protect the "professional"[3] element in the school system is not, however, an adequate measure of its dispensability.

Not least of the reasons why the board does not merely delegate functions to the managerial executive is the type of relation the latter must maintain with the technical personnel. The same holds, however, for the executive's external responsibilities. The essential point is that the executive must perform his functions by coming to terms with categories of other people—experts, customers, and resource

---

3. Note the ambiguity of the term "professional." Ordinarily I use the term in a sense denoting *technical* competence. When used otherwise, I shall put it in quotation marks.

people—who are in a position (within limits) to exact their own terms independently. Therefore, to be effective, the executive must have considerable freedom to use his own judgment as to what terms are good for the organization. He can be reasonably bound by broad policies and rules laid down from above, but these cannot be too restrictive. Certainly he cannot be regarded as the mere implementing agent of other people's decisions. Furthermore, he must be in a position to present *his* problems to his board and to negotiate with them from a position of relative strength, not just to go to them for "instructions."

I may generalize about the nature of the two main breaks in line authority which I have outlined by saying that at each of the two points of articulation between subsystems there is a *two-way* interchange of inputs and outputs. What has to be "contributed" from each side is qualitatively different. Either side is in a position, by withholding its important contribution, to interfere seriously with the functioning of the other and of the larger organization. Hence the *institutionalization* of these relations must typically take a form where the relative independence of each is protected. Since, however, there is an actual hierarchy, since in some sense the "higher" authority must be able to have some kind of "last word," the problem of protection focuses on the status of the lower-order element. Accordingly, we find that such institutions as tenure serve, in part at least, to protect professional personnel from pressures exerted by management—pressures that are often passed on down from board levels.

THE DISPOSAL
AND PROCUREMENT FUNCTIONS

Let us now take a brief look at the second main topic in my outline: the relation between each of these systems—the technical, the managerial, and the community—and the "lateral" elements of the society with which they have to deal.

First, what I have called a "technical" process must be carried out in relation to some "materials" or to an environmental situation; facilities are required to do this, and many of these resources must be secured from outside the organization.

With respect to what I have called materials, the first important distinction is whether they are or are not "physical" objects whose "motivations" do not need to be taken into account. Physical production in the sense of modern technology is the type case involving the physical object. Complex organized co-operation is generally necessary to carry out the technical process of production, but it is not necessary to secure the "co-operation" of the raw materials or of the partly finished products at any stage. Nor is it necessary to get the consent of the finished product to dispose of it to users outside the organization in any way the management sees fit. In economic terms this is the type case of a "commodity."

In another very large class of cases the "materials" on which technical operations must be performed are human individuals, or collectivities. This is pre-eminently true of education, but also of health services, of the practice of law, and of "administration," which may be defined as the processes by which persons and collectivities and categories of them may be brought actually to fulfil the obligations imposed by the decision of a "legitimate authority"—e.g., paying taxes, teaching the classes assigned, or observing traffic regulations. Here the conditions under which the "objects" of the technical process will co-operate satisfactorily and the kind of social relationship structure required under these conditions become matters of paramount importance.[4]

The important point to which I wish now to call atten-

---

4. There is a third category, namely, where the technological problem concerns attainment of results in a cultural realm, the solution of scientific problems through research being a type case. The valued result is in this case neither a physical object or class of them, nor a state of social objects, i.e., of

tion is that the second case, where the object is a "social" object, necessitates a special link at the managerial level between the technological process and the disposal process. In the physical cases the technical production process can be completed, and then, quite independently, those responsible for sales can take over; the customer need have no relation at all to the technical production process, though of course there are cases of "custom" production where he supervises phases of it quite closely.

In the case of the social object, however, a *prior* relation to the recipient or beneficiary of the "service" is a prerequisite for undertaking the technical process at all. Teaching presupposes pupils in the school, and therefore settlement of the terms on which pupils go to school is a prerequisite for the teaching process. Similarly with the practice of medicine and law—there have to be patients or clients "on whom" to practice, and there has to be a basis on which they have "come to" the doctor or lawyer. In the case of administration, finally, the law or policy which has to be administered must designate the categories of persons or collectivities to which it applies, and only when this has been specified can the administrative agency even *begin* to administer.

Even within the category where the object of processing is a "social" object, a wide range of variation is found. At one extreme is the case where a rule simply forbids certain actions; then the administrative agency is involved only when the prohibition is violated; its only "customers" are offenders. At the other extreme is the case where the organization, or agency, must establish a long-continuing and in some sense "intimate" relation which affects the most vital interests of the recipients of the organization's service. Education belongs in this category. There must be a long-standing relation between a pupil and a succession of teachers, and

---

persons or collectivities, but an addition to the body of *knowledge,* which is a cultural object. This may, of course, impose very special exigencies upon the technical process. For simplicity's sake I shall ignore this third case in the discussion which follows.

both the structure of the pupil's personality and his future position in the community depend heavily upon the process of education.

In this type of case it is common for the recipient of the service to be taken into an important kind of *membership* in the technical organization which provides the service. The school class is a social system with an important degree of integration between teacher and pupils. Teaching cannot be effective if the pupil is simply a "customer" to whom the "commodity" of education is "turned over" without any further relation to its purveyor than is required for settlement of the terms of transfer—as in the case of the typical commercial transaction. An even further stage of variation is given by the case of the boarding school or residential college where the main focus of the recipient's everyday living is brought within the organization. The same is true of hospitals, but of course for periods of different duration.

From one point of view, the *technical* necessity of establishing a prior and special link between the organization and its recipients imposes an important set of constraints on the managerial system. It is not free to "bargain" with its "customers" in ways which might jeopardize the conditions essential for carrying out the technical functions of the organization. Circumstances such as these strengthen the position of the technical personnel vis-à-vis the managerial, because the former are in a position to insist upon the conditions they think essential for doing the job adequately if management, in turn, *wants* it done adequately.

Looked at from a slightly different point of view, the performance of "services" requires the *co-operation* of the recipient of the service. This co-operation cannot always be taken for granted; it has to be motivated. Witness, for example, the problem of truancy in schools, to say nothing of passive resistance to learning and the commonness with which patients leave hospitals contrary to medical advice. Since sheer coercion is not adequate, the service-performer must *offer* something to induce adequate co-operation, and the readiness to do this has to be included in the terms by which the co-operative relationship is set up in the first place. But the physical producer does not have to offer his raw materials anything.

This difference between the processes of physical production and various types of "service" has much to do with the fact that the *products* of physical technology in our society tend to be disposed of through the process of commercial marketing, while services—with many variations, of course—are much more frequently purveyed within different kinds of non-profit contexts.

These problems also have an important relation to the problems of "payment" for the products of organization function, and hence to the procurement side at the level of financing the operations. Again it is no accident that it is the business firm—an agency most frequently concerned with physical production—which is expected, in the long run, to finance its operations *wholly* from the sales of its products—in the long run, because borrowing for investment purposes is common and essential. Some services are provided on this same basis, but examples range from these cases to those where the service is provided to the recipients entirely without charge, and the organization must therefore be financed from other sources, notably private contributions or taxation.

One aspect of the "meaning" of the payment emerges from the above discussion: in the commercial case, all the "contribution" to the process of production has been made by the producing organization; the customer has typically "done nothing" to make the result possible. But in cases like education, the pupil and his parents have obviously done a great deal; without their co-operation, the result would not have been possible at all. Probably along with the problems of equality in access to benefits, this is the principal reason why "full payment" is not expected for many services. If payment is expected, it may well be a matter of "noblesse oblige," as in the case of medical patients at the upper end of the sliding scale paying considerably *more* than the service costs to provide. They are contributing to a worthwhile societal function in proportion to their financial capacity to do so.

THE MANAGERIAL CONTRIBUTION
TO SOCIAL FUNCTION

If there is a meaningful set of interchanges between the output of "technical product" and what is in some sense "compensation" for that output—on the model of the sale of the commodity and full payment for it—we may now ask whether this account of things is adequate to account for the importance of the *managerial* level of organizations in its relation to the lateral aspect of its external situation. Is the managerial organization, then, nothing more than a "facilitator" of the process of technological production?

I am conceiving the problem in direct relation to its formulation for purposes of economic theory. It has seemed possible on the levels already dealt with to relate the prototypical economic case to others in a fairly specific way, and I should like to attempt this for the managerial level. Here the point of reference is the "double interchange" which has served as a central paradigm for treating problems of equilibrium in the economy and hence in its suborganizations.

One of these two interchanges is the one just reviewed, the output of commodities or goods in exchange for money payment. In the case of the business firm, this payment is expected—in the long run—to cover the whole cost of production. But in the economic paradigm there is a second interchange, that of the wage output of the firm for labor input from outside. In part this duality is necessitated by the division of labor and is facilitated by the monetary mechanism. The typical customer of a firm is not also an employee.

But there is not merely a difference of agency; there is also a difference of level. We might say that the firm "pumps" purchasing power into the market system. This is not an instrumentality of consumers' "want-satisfaction" but of *control* in the allocation of resources within the community. In return, the firm receives a share of an essential societal resource—what in technical terms I have called the "performance capacity" of the community. Some economists have called it "labor power." This performance capacity represents the human agent's commitment—within the limits of his competence and skill—to co-operate in the productive process. By treating performance capacity as an input to the firm, we mean that *this* firm has been allocated this share of commitment through the contract of employment.

The next question is whether the firm's output of purchasing power in the form of wage payments is more than an instrumentality for securing an indispensable facility for its operations. Of course it *is* such a facility, but it is also more. It is a contribution to the total pool of purchasing power in the community. The firm "makes money" in a double sense; it is the recipient of the proceeds of sales, but it also contributes to the flow of commodities and to the community's purchasing power. This is the main mechanism for the *generalization* of facilities, for increasing the community's level of economic effectiveness. This has been a commonplace to economists since Keynes.

In the system as a whole there must, of course, be a balance between the flow in marketing commodities and the output of purchasing power; imbalance in one direction results in deflation; in the other, inflation. But the main point here is that the output of purchasing power is not merely an "instrumentality" for purchasing labor; it is an essential part of the functional *contribution* of the firm, and of course the same is true on the consumers' side. The famous oversaving is the counterpart of undue hesitancy about production commitments.

The output of commodities is primarily the work of the technical subsystem of the organization — of the plant. But the output of purchasing power is the work of the managerial organization. Hence this distinction of "levels" in the structure of organizations corresponds to the differentiation between the two interchange processes which have figured so prominently in economic theory.

This set of relationships is not peculiar to organizational contexts where the primary technical output is commodities. In many respects education is the antithesis of the commodity case. Here the technical output is the change in the character, knowledge, and skill levels of *individual* pupils. But the school *system* may be treated as responsible for another category of output: its contribution to the general level of performance capacity in the community. Just as "wealth" is not a simple aggregate of physical commodities but one which includes the specifically *economic* element of generalized disposability through the mechanisms of purchasing power, so the capacity of a community to get valued things done is not, so far as it depends on the performances of individuals, simply an aggregate of the individual qualities of its members; it includes a factor of allocation relative to need and generalized disposability — through the "labor market." Through such decisions as what to teach to what categories of pupils, the school system decisively influences this pool of usefully disposable performance capacity in the community; it adapts the technical education process to the conditions of the community, how effectively is, of course, an empirical question in the individual case. These decisions are the result of "ideas" and "plans" on the part of school authorities and of the "demand" for trained performance capacities in the community—not, of course, only in an economic sense of demand.

The "input" at this higher level from the community may be said to consist in the community's *support* for education as a function, in its commitments to the maintenance or improvement of the capacity-level of its population. Here, in a sense parallel to the economic case, the effectiveness of a particular individual's education is a function not only of what he has acquired in the process but also of the educational *level* of the community as a whole. Hence various units in the community, but particularly families and interest groups oriented to educational goals, are concerned with this *level*. What I am speaking of here is a set of relationships focused not on the community as a whole, but rather on those members who are direct "clients" of the educational system. But this is one of the essential foci of responsibility for the managerial subsystem in education. This should be distinguished from the superordinate (e.g., "political") support of education to be discussed later.

A few words about the parallel in the political field may extend the picture a little. Here the technical process is the administrative implementation of "decisions" reached at higher levels. "Compliance" or the necessary "co-operation" is perhaps the relevant input category. This compliance must, however, be "motivated" by some sort of "demands" in the community that the measures in question be carried out; if this is in deficit, the administrative process runs into all sorts of difficulties (such as, shall we say, tax evasion) which coercive powers alone are often not adequate to cope with. But there is also a higher-level output of political systems which may be called the assumption of leadership responsibility. This is the system's contribution to the community's general level of political effectiveness; this involves more than satisfying particular interests and demands for decisions.

For this generalized contribution to take place, there must be a counter-input to the political organization from outside. The primary mechanism seems to be that the citizen, especially through his vote but in other ways also, contributes to the *generalized support* without which effective leadership in the political system would be impossible.

In a democratic system this operates above all through the mechanism of parties. Only a party supported by a majority of the electorate can take the leadership responsibility required for making important decisions and can implement them over a wide enough range. The support on which a party depends cannot be specific to a particular issue or interest, except in a limiting case. But without both generalized support (at least at the party level) and the assumption of leadership responsibility, the political system's capacity for effective action in the public interest is impaired.

The Procurement of Personnel

In discussing the functions of the "managerial" level of organization in mediating the organization's relations to the external social situation, I have concentrated on the "disposal" function. Its monetary aspects have necessitated some discussion of the "procurement" functions because of the relation between them. There is, however, one part of the procurement function which requires special discussion because it is so fundamental to all types of modern organization: namely, the procurement of personnel. It is fundamental to modern society that a large range of its functions are performed in *occupational* roles by persons who have no ascriptive or associational connection with the organization but are *employed* by it through a formal or informal contract of employment.

From one point of view, the contract of employment is a special case of the settlement of terms for the selling of a service. Its distinctive feature is that the service is performed in the context of organization, and the "customer" is the organization in a managerial capacity. Of course, the kind of contract and the expectations of the occupational role will vary enormously as a function both of the kind of organization and of the type of role within it. There is thus the closest sort of link between the procurement of personnel and both the technical functions and the internal organization of the employing unit. Very broadly indeed, it may be useful to distinguish three basic types of role, and hence of personnel: "operative" at the technical levels; "administrative" or "executive," having special responsibilities for the functioning of the organization at the managerial level; and "professional," characterized by some special competence which roots in a generalized cultural tradition focused outside the organization as such. These are "ideal types," and there are plenty of mixtures among them.

Economists have long discussed the standard of "marginal productivity" for determining the rewards available to an employee of an organization. Similarly, most economists tend to assume that the "reward-value" of a job will be exhausted in monetary terms.[5] This reference is to an equivalence between the economic value to the firm of an employee's contribution to its functioning and the value to the employee — which really means to his household — of the goods and services which can be purchased with his money wage. This also tends to go with a form of "contract" according to which the relation is terminable at will on both sides, with no "justification" needed for discharge or "laying off" other than that it does not seem profitable for the firm to continue the employment. Of course this actually is not the typical pattern for employment at operative levels by business firms, but it is more closely approximated there than elsewhere. Variations from this pattern may be looked at under three headings: first, the pattern of monetary reward itself — whether it focuses on what the service is "worth" in monetary terms; second, the balance between monetary and non-monetary components in the reward; and, third, the terms for continuance or termination of the relation.

The closest approach to this marginal-productivity, ter-

---

5. Alfred Marshall was an exception to this tendency, since he insisted on the importance of "activities" valued "for their own sake." See *Economy and Society*.

minable-at-will pattern seems to be the operative technical role in the business firm, namely, the ordinary industrial worker or clerical employee. This seems in turn to be closely related to the fact that such firms to such a large extent produce commodities. This circumstance minimizes the non-economic element in the firm's relation with its customers and eliminates overlap between the customer role and the employee role. This relatively unobstructed orientation to the market facilitates internal cost accounting and exerts a pressure toward maximizing the use of cost criteria in contracting for the factors of production (in terms of what he is *worth* to us, not of what we can afford). Accordingly, the terminability of the contract at will protects management's freedom to rationalize its employment procedures from a cost accounting point of view.

This pattern has been both an ideological ideal for the businessman and a highly convenient reference point for the economist; if this pattern were tenable, it would greatly simplify the economist's problems. But it has in fact been greatly modified, most conspicuously by the development of trade unions. The union seems to modify the situation in two directions. First, and most obviously, it greatly restricts the employer's freedom to hire and fire. Unions in general do not impose formal rules of tenure; "layoffs" are permissible for purely economic reasons, e.g., when the company, for market reasons, "needs" to cut down its scale of operations. But these cuts must be made according to well-formulated rules, not simply at the employer's discretion. Furthermore, the closed shop ideal of unionism would restrict hiring to members of the union or would at least require union membership of all who accept employment. The second main focus of the union's effect is to compress the spread of wage rates among its members, so that in unionized industries there is a greater concentration near the average.

The union seems to root in two circumstances that are predominantly non-economic in significance. The first of these is the power discrepancy between the employing organization and the individual employee, particularly when so much is at stake for the employee both as an individual and as the representative of his family. Here the union has not only acted on its own but has also been supplemented by the government in assuring workers a measure of "social security." The second context is the associational solidarity of union members, to some degree constituting a company of equals banded together for mutual benefit and protection. There is some inhibition on their differing too much from each other in individual performance or interest because of the impact this differentiation would have on the structure of the union. Of course, patterns such as strong emphasis on seniority also enter into union practice.

But the farther the function of an organization moves away from the production of commodities for a market, the more the pattern of employment and remuneration of "operatives" tends to move away from the "marginal productivity" standard. The largest-scale example of a very different type is provided by the civilian operative employees of governmental agencies. Here two patterns are particularly conspicuous, namely, the seniority principle and the institutionalization of tenure. More generally, there is regulation by a complicated civil service code. Within the limits of effectiveness, it may be said that one main emphasis is on security. Negatively, this seems to be associated with the virtual impossibility of effective cost accounting, since the value of the service provided by the agency is generally not measurable in money terms. Furthermore, the code protects a group in a weak power position from arbitrary action by administrative superiors and from "political" intervention. Positively, however, in a field where achievement cannot usually be very high, the code seems to be related to the need for enlisting loyalty to the employing organization by emphasizing the sense of "belongingness." In general, a direct appeal to "self-interest" does not accord well with the "public service" orientation of government.

It is of great importance that government stands in competition with private employment for personnel. There is, however, a persistent lag between the salary levels for civil servants and of those for comparable jobs in the business world. This may mean that there are non-financial components of the reward pattern in government which are not present in business to the same degree. Security is probably one of them, but the sense of contributing directly to the public welfare may well be more important than much of our current ideology would allow.

Among different types of organizations we find a wide range of policy about administrative personnel, especially in regard to remuneration and tenure. However, we can identify the practice in two main types of organizations. At one end of the range is the American business executive. Here the pattern is to emphasize very high financial rewards but to minimize anything like tenure. The executive assumes his responsibilities at his own risk, as it were. He is highly rewarded if he is regarded as successful, but he is subject to being cashiered if he fails to satisfy his organizational superiors. The other type is found in most non-profit organizational contexts, including government.[6] Here the pattern is one of very moderate financial reward, much less than in business and comparable to many professional levels. On the other hand, such positions generally contain elements of security which the business executive does not enjoy. This security is either explicitly recognized by the organization itself, or— as in the case of "policy" level political appointees — is provided by the cushion of the party's indebtedness to them, if not through tangible recognition of this indebtedness.

These two types of practice for administrative personnel —for the business executive and for the government executive —may be considered alternative reactions to the assumption of *responsibility* in the sense discussed above and to the meaning of its assumption for those agencies on whose "be-

---

6. Elective office is, however, too special a case to be considered here; it is not technically "employment."

half" it is done. The relevant agencies are usually not "customers" but the superordinate organization on the institutional level; i.e., a business executive is "responsible" in the most direct sense to his board.

In the case of the managerial executive of a business firm, I think that his high salary-bonus remuneration is not to be interpreted mainly in terms of the marginal productivity of his services, as many economists would argue, and much business ideology too. Nor is it primarily entrepreneurial profit, e.g., in Schumpeter's sense. It is rather the "wages of responsibility," the symbolic recognition of the importance of executive responsibilities. Since the success of the firm tends to be measured in terms of its "profits," it is *symbolically* appropriate for managerial responsibility to be remunerated in terms cognate with the measure of the firm's success. This is not, in the sense that economists have used this concept with reference to entrepreneurial profit, primarily a reward for "risk-taking," since it is fundamental to the structure of modern business that the typical executive does *not* risk his personal property. He takes responsibility in situations where other people risk their property, which is a very different thing.[7]

The executive in a non-profit organization, on the other hand, receives a different order of financial remuneration in the first instance because profit is not the primary measure of the success of his organization, be it governmental or private. On the contrary, money to finance the organization's operations has to be "raised" in whole or in part. Hence it becomes a question of what remuneration, usually a salary, is "fair" in terms both of the resources of the organization and of the interests of the individual. (These interests in-

---

7. The aspect of executive remuneration I have just discussed cannot be the result of a sheer assertion of "power" on his part. There is a power factor in this as in all other cases of remuneration, but there is an institutionalized factor as well. Business executives as a group are far less organized than either operative employees or professional people; they are clearly neglecting an opportunity to assert their power.

clude an adequate standard of living and status-dignity.) In this case there are other components of reward than the financial; recognition of service is in some sense a very important component. The non-profit executive is also likely to have some form of tenure.

In the society as a whole there is a delicate balance between these high-remuneration and low-remuneration sectors of the administrative class. I think it likely that in recent times the balance has tipped unduly in favor of the business group and that a readjustment is likely to come, indeed is already in process.

In the case of professional services, a convenient point of reference is the sliding scale which typically operates in the situation of individual fee-for-service practice. Here the practitioner can cover his total expenses and make a good living from professional fees. But his patients or clients pay by "capacity," not by the value of the service as if it were a commodity. I have noted above that professional service very generally (not, for example, for engineering) involves establishing a co-operative solidarity between performer and recipient. From this point of view, the fee is a "contribution" to the *joint* performance of the valued function.

When professional services are performed in the context of organization, the sliding scale principle does not disappear, but it is typically moved up either one or two organizational levels in the focus of its application. This is to say that recipients pay the *organization*, not the practitioner, on a sliding-scale principle. Thus in the case of college or university, though there are standard tuition fees, "needy" students are given scholarships, and well-to-do alumni are expected to contribute to the college in some sort of proportion to their resources. Or, where support is by taxation, a still "higher" organizational level is involved, in which case the assessments to support the organization are made on a "progressive" principle. But in this instance the service is a public responsibility independent of whether the individual taxpayer is or has been a recipient of the particular service.

The professional practitioner in an organization, however, typically works on salary. Salary levels, then, are typically those prevailing in non-profit organizations and are usually below executive salaries, but not too much. Special problems are raised by professional personnel employed in business firms; there clearly is a tendency to lift their remuneration levels up toward those of executives in the same organization. But with the exception of this and of certain elite private-practice groups, the level of remuneration for the professional practitioner is similar to that for the non-business category. Again, this suggests the importance of a non-financial component in the rewards of professional workers.[8]

Along with government employees, professional workers in organizations—notably teachers—provide the type case of the institution of tenure. I interpret this, above all, as a mechanism for protecting these workers from pressures by the administrative authority to which they are necessarily subject. This gives them some assurance of professional independence and integrity.

The marginal productivity model of economic theory and the "liberal" idea of a contract of employment governed by simple mutual advantage of the moment ("freedom of contract" in one version) thus provide a convenient reference point. But this model is more nearly descriptive of an industrial than, say, of a feudal society. However, this pattern of employment is only approximated even for the operative employees in a business firm; as we go to other types of organization and to other types of occupational role that cut across organization types, we find increasing deviation

---

8. Some component of this kind must provide part of the explanation for the well-known findings of the North-Hatt study that professional occupations tend to outrank business in prestige in the community, with physicians ranked in the highest regular category of all. It also has something to do with the pressure by many marginal groups to secure recognition as "professionals."

from this pattern. It is a *limiting* type of contract of employment, not a model type for the general occupational structure, even within an industrial society.

DISPOSAL AND PROCUREMENT
AT THE INSTITUTIONAL LEVEL

To complete this review of the principal set of factors that account for differences between types of formal organizations, we need to examine further what happens at the "institutional" level. So far, I have dealt with this level mainly in its relation to the managerial level — particularly, I have noted how the institution or community provides legitimation and support to management and why management cannot secure this support through its relation with the recipients of its product—whether commodity or service —or through its relation with its resources of procurement. It should be clear that the importance of these legitimation and support functions mounts rapidly as we move from the case of the "pure" commodity to those categories of service which require a strategic, long-term relation of solidarity between performer and recipient.

It should also be clear that where financial resources must be "raised" in order to finance the function of the organization, the responsibility for this generally rests either at the institutional level or, as in the case of many tax-supported functions, at a still higher level in the organizational scale. In this respect, the administrative head of a non-profit organization (like a university) often has a key role in money-raising. However, a university president, like an industrial foreman or a non-commissioned officer in the military, occupies an interstitial position between two organizational system-levels. He is *both* the top executive of the managerial subsystem of the university *and* a member and representative of the trustees. In his role as money-raiser, he acts predominantly on behalf of the trustees, not as manager of the university.[9]

An institutional system, however, has not only vertical relations to the managerial subsystem for which it takes some order of responsibility but also lateral relations. It has a "product" to "sell," and it has procurement problems. Of course it also must be integrated with still higher levels of organization, of which just a word presently.

What order of "product" can an institutional organization be conceived to "sell" which is not already covered in the previous discussion? The answer lies in the proper use of the concept of function at different levels in the structure of society as a system. The economist's typical commodity is a contribution to the functional needs of the consuming unit, which is typically though by no means exclusively the household. The same is true of the types of service which have been reviewed above. For example, education, especially elementary, and medical practice are, at the *technical* levels, services to the family household. This is why there is a "parent-teachers' association" but no teacher-prospective employers' association of comparable significance, and why the doctor who is treating an adult male will often deal directly with the patient's wife but seldom, if ever, with his employer.

At the managerial level, I have argued that there is also a function, namely, contribution to the *generalized* capacity of the society to perform that category of function. For example, the economic process produces both commodities and wealth; the educational process, both character, knowledge, and skills of individuals, and generalized performance capacity at the societal level. However, the production, even of the generalized capacity to perform the relevant function effec-

9. Similarly, it is significant that most universities have a treasurer or chairman of the finance committee who clearly acts as a member of the governing board, and this office is clearly distinguished from that of the bursar or comptroller, who is an *administrative* officer at the managerial level.

tively, does not settle the *position* of that function in the society, does not in itself determine the "public's" evaluation of it, nor the proportions of resources which are to be devoted to it in comparison with and hence in competition with other functions. It is in this sphere that the outputs or products of institutional organizations are to be found.

A striking example is the business corporation's policy on what proportion of income will be distributed in dividends and what proportion will be "ploughed back" into the company. This is a decision between two alternative uses of financial resources, consumption[10] or economic investment. In the classical theory of the corporation this was a decision made by the *owners* of the property rights in the business, but this position has become radically unrealistic. The decision has tended to become the responsibility of a *fiduciary* board who, to a degree, represent owners, but not simply in the sense of the owners' financial "self-interest." (Similarly, the *institution* of property itself is not, as one ideological version would have it, a simple matter of protecting the right of an individual to "do what he will with his own.") Insofar as individual owners have ceased to be primary,[11] these decisions have tended, in the "private" sector, to be shared between banks (and other fiduciary financial organizations) and producing corporations. But in the latter case is is above all at the board level that such decisions focus: they are not, in the sense of this paper, "managerial" prerogatives.

Cognate things can be said in the case of education. The teacher's role is primarily to educate in the *technical* sense. That of the school administration, i.e., the superintendent's office and the principal's, typically is to *organize* the educational process in the community, to make it, within the

---

10. Consumption refers to any use of funds *other* than investment. Of course, the stockholders are free to invest their dividends in other lines of production, too.

11. They have usually represented *kinship* property interests.

framework of community commitments to education, as effective as possible and thereby to contribute to the level of performance-capacity in the community. But the superintendent is not the focus for determining the community's commitments to education in relation to other competing demands on its total resources. In community terms this is a "political" problem. In organizational terms this problem focuses on the school board; in the case of the university, the trustees. In this context it is essential that the membership of such bodies should not consist predominantly of "professionals," meaning persons with a full occupational commitment to education, since their role is to *mediate* between the "professionals" and the more diffuse community. To constitute such boards principally of "professionals" would be to make the profession judge in its own case, a privilege which a pluralistic society obviously cannot grant as a general rule.

From this point of view, then, the primary "disposal" function of the institutional organization is to contribute to the *integration* of the higher-order system within which the function at the managerial level is placed. Its role is to mediate between the claims of this function on community resources and legitimation, and the exigencies of effective performance of the function on the "lower" levels. Of course, just as the university president is generally involved in financial responsibilities, so is the school superintendent involved in "politics," because he also occupies an interstitial status.

On the procurement side, something has been said of the financial responsibilities of institutional organizations. The salience of this responsibility is a function of the failure of "automatic" market mechanisms to provide for the problem through generating adequate proceeds. But even the business corporation is not, as I just tried to show, a case of full "automatization" because decisions have to be made about the allocation of proceeds—presuming the firm is "in the black" — between further investment and consumption, and the investment decisions of the board hence are—in our sense — procurement decisions at the institutional level. On the other hand, where the financial question becomes too difficult, there is a tendency to shunt it to the next higher level of organization, as in the case of financing public education through taxation (but, it should be clearly noted, so far mainly through *local* taxation). In the middle is the case, typical of private non-profit organizations, where the proceeds, if any, are clearly inadequate to finance the essential services, and hence the responsibility for meeting the deficit rests squarely at the board or trustee level. The function here is essentially that of persuading those who control financial resources in the community that what the organization is doing is important enough to merit their financial support (this includes the self-persuasion of wealthy trustees). The number of dunning letters in the mail of persons who by no current standard could be considered wealthy is an index of the great importance of this factor in American society. There is almost as intensive a competition for the citizen's contributory dollar as there is, through advertising and other aspects of salesmanship, for his consumer's dollar.

The prominence of the financial aspect of the procurement responsibilities of institutional organizations is in the first instance a result of the fact that money is the generalized facility par excellence. It is also particularly prominent in a society so heavily oriented to economic values and functions (properly understood) as the American is. But it is by no means the only relevant input at the institutional level. Perhaps second in importance in most cases is the factor of power, in a technical political sense which cannot be fully explained here. The essential point is the "subsumption" of organization goals under the more generalized goal-structure of the still higher-level social structure and therefore the explicit or implicit "authorization" to embark on the organizational activities in question and to "take them seriously" to the degree to which that is done. A very important aspect of what is sometimes called the struggle for power in a society consists in this competition for support and authorization among the many different organized interests of the society.

"Organized" here, as so often, has a double reference. One is to the organizations which have interests in their power position in the larger society. The other is to the ways and extent to which units with common interest in this sense have organized to promote their interests. I suggest two primary points about this situation. First, the unit of the *organization* of "interest groups" in the political sense is not the managerial system but the institutional system. The "board" must have the primary concern for the position of the *category* of organization for which it is responsible within the power system of the community as a whole. Second, the category of interest group is on quite a different level from that of economic interests; to identify them is the "Marxian fallacy." The Catholic church is an interest group par excellence, as is the National Association of Manufacturers. The point is that there is a problem of allocating power to *all* significant organized units in the society, *whatever* their primary functional significance. The assertion and mediation of the claims of this interest necessarily focus at what I have called the institutional level.

What I have said about wealth and power applies equally to other societal resources. To give only one more illustration, what above I have called performance capacity is a resource which has to be allocated among different fundamental functions in the society. Given a high level of differentiation, perhaps one of the worst tendencies of organizational practice is for trustees or boards to attempt to control specific appointments in the organizations under their trusteeship. This function rests between the managerial and the technical aspects of organization. But trustees *must* be concerned with the question of how far and under what conditions their organization (and, at the next level up, their type of organization) has access to the type and quality of performance capacity which is essential for the proper functioning of the organization. To take a current example, the concern of university trustees with faculty salaries is not a simple "financial" problem. Discrepancy between salary levels in the academic profession and those in other occupations in competition with it—and the same goes for teachers—can be a serious threat to access to the essential capacities without which the fiduciary responsibilities in question cannot be discharged. It is therefore important to distinguish two levels of the financial responsibilities of institutional organizations. The first of these is the responsibility for adequate financial resources to perform the function of the organization. The second is the policy about the kind and amount of performance capacity which, in the societal interest, *should* be made available for this function and hence the price, financially speaking, which *should* be paid for this performance capacity. For instance, thinking of university trustees only as "businessmen" interested in driving the best bargain they can in the labor market ignores the importance of the second financial responsibility. They cannot escape a responsibility for the *level* of faculty salaries as well as for the conservation of the university's necessarily limited funds.

It is directly in the logic of our whole analysis that the institutional organization, as well as the managerial and the technical, will necessarily have connections and interchanges "upward" as well as laterally and "downward." These "upward" connections fall above all in the area of legitimation and support. One context in which these problems have repeatedly come into the discussion here is where the function is treated as a "public" or political responsibility, most conspicuously, where the organization responsible is made an integral part of governmental structure itself. Here not only the responsibility but also conversely, the claim to legitimation and support is sharply focused for the collectively organized segment of the society—i.e., from local to national levels of government. So long as the responsibility is accepted as a *public* responsibility, there is an obligation on government to "do justice" to the exigencies of discharging it effectively. From this case, there is a shading-off to the ideal type of the purely laissez faire sectors of economic organization, where public responsibility is confined to protecting the freedom to produce for the market and reap the rewards, setting up the necessary regulatory system of legal rules, etc. This is clearly a limiting case and is really only approximated. But even here it is essential to note that this is a mode of organizing and institutionalizing societal responsibility for effective economic production. This case does not reflect the absence of any such responsibility. Else why should a President of the United States continually emphasize the duty of the government he heads to facilitate the functioning of a private enterprise economy? The clear implication is that the welfare of the society, not just of individual business men or firms, is thought to be dependent on this system.

THE VARIABILITY OF ORGANIZATIONAL TYPES

Co-ordinate with the heavy emphasis on the unbroken continuity of "line" authority which I noted at the beginning of this chapter, there has been a tendency to think of "bureaucracy" as a kind of monolithic entity which can vary in degree of development but not significantly in type. A major purpose of the present discussion has been to question this assumption and to help lay the basis for a more sophisticated analysis of the variation we find in types of formal organizations and in the factors on which these variations depend. All the essential considerations I have in mind—at the present stage of development in my knowledge of the field—have already been brought up. However, it may be useful to try to pull some of these together in summary fashion.

Perhaps the appropriate type of organization will be determined by the type of function the organization performs in the system of which it is a part. But though true, this formula by itself is wholly inadequate, for it fails to discriminate the various levels of differentiation from subsystem to subsystem which inevitably exist in a complex society. What is by a conventional designation, like "economic" or "educational," the "same" function does not lead to the same type of organization at all levels. This is obvious—no one would seriously suggest that the United States Office of Education can be treated as if it were a classroom, though both this office and a classroom have educational functions— but the point is often overlooked. My distinction between technical, managerial, and institutional levels of formal organization has been designed to help make discriminations of this order in a useful fashion. I have argued that there are important uniformities which are primarily a function of the *level* at which the organization or suborganization operates but which are independent of the functional *content* of the organization at any level. In general, the theory of bureaucracy has concentrated at the managerial level and has emphasized the uniformities most appropriate to it, across the board.

Another equally important and independent set of considerations, however, are those which differentiate organizations according to their functional type. In a sense, the most obvious of these concern the technical functions themselves and the exigencies to which they are subject. But these considerations are so various that there is a great temptation to jump to the managerial level and talk as if the imperatives of good organization—whatever the function in technical terms—are always the same. I hope I have adequately indicated that this is not true; a good organization for the physical production of goods at the technical level would inevitably be a bad one for the educational process.

I have then attempted to show that organizations at all

these levels are subject not only to technical exigencies but to those of disposal and procurement at each level and that these exigencies—even at the same level—are sources of profoundly significant differences in organizational type. Thus I think it safe to say that no organization dependent on highly trained professional personnel can employ them typically on the basis of a marginal productivity, terminable-at-will contract of employment. Or, on the other side, the organization which produces commodities for a market must be very different in structure from the residential college which takes its "customers" into a special type of membership status.

Next, I have emphasized the relative independence of the three level-types of organization, an independence that constitutes my main objection to the continous line-authority picture of formal organization. This relative independence means that there is, at each linkage point, a range of possible *different* types of articulation. Thus the professional personnel of military organizations are much more rigidly subjected to line authority than are those with the same professional qualifications in, let us say, the professional faculty of a university. There are limits to how far the military can press its professional personnel into the line pattern, but it does not follow that the university pattern is the only possible one. Similar considerations hold at the articulation point between managerial and institutional systems. An important special case of this problem is the very top of the three-stage hierarchy with which I have been working, namely, the articulation of the institutional system with the still wider society.

This is not the place to attempt a classification of types of formal organizations. If such were to be attempted, however, it would be necessary to build into it many of the distinctions that I have reviewed and illustrated here. Even within the same society—to say nothing about a comparative perspective—the range would be wide and the significantly different types numerous. Only along such a path as this, however, can even the structural aspect of a theory of organization reach a modicum of scientific maturity. And a sophisticated understanding of the range of structural variation is essential to any high-level attempt at analyzing the dynamic processes that take place within organizations.

I do not mean this last note to be one of discouragement. Much fine work has been done in this field. But its range has been rather severely limited. There are many insights which social scientists have developed in this field which can be highly useful to the practical administrator here and now. But the field is one of immense complexity at the scientific level and is only at the beginning of its scientific development. An immense amount of work will be required before we can have anything that deserves to be called a theory of formal organization. We have, however, made some very important beginnings. For administrators, the great importance of social science theory lies in the future, when these beginnings will have grown into a mature science.

Part II

SOCIAL STRUCTURE
AND ECONOMIC DEVELOPMENT

CHAPTER III

SOME REFLECTIONS ON
THE INSTITUTIONAL FRAMEWORK
OF ECONOMIC DEVELOPMENT

INTRODUCTORY REFLECTIONS

By the latter part of the nineteenth century in the Western world, problems of the economic organization of society had come to the forefront of intellectual discussion, displacing the religious and political emphases of earlier times. This discussion of economic problems combined attempts at scientific interpretation of the social situation with attempts to provide an ideological rationale for political action; to our day has fallen the task of distinguishing more clearly between the two. Although in *ideological* terms Karl Marx has emerged as the most influential social thinker of that movement, the modern sociologist is more likely to look to Max Weber's work as a major point of reference, and this is what I propose to do in this paper.

Weber's thinking provides a particularly suitable point of reference for a number of reasons in addition to its high intellectual quality. Weber's interpretation, far more than that of any other writer, was based on extensive comparative study, especially in his monographs on the sociology of religion, of the West to the other great civilizations. His sociological work was mainly an interpretation of what he called "modern capitalism" in the light of the total institutional structure of Western society. The phenomenon, as he saw it, had come to a fruition at about the turn of the twentieth century.

Weber's empirical concentration on the turn of the century is useful because this was perhaps the last point at which it could be said that "modern capitalism" was essentially a Western phenomenon; even then Japan had already made great strides toward economic modernization, but elsewhere outside the West the impact of the Western social system had been felt mainly through the role of the colonial powers and the peculiar combination of trade and cultural and political influence which had grown up in the relations of the West to the rest of the world. Particularly since the close of World War II this relation has come into a complete flux bringing the extensive breakdown of the colonial system and the rise of national independence movements everywhere. Weber's concern was with the conditions which made it possible for "capitalism" to develop in the West, and why this did not occur in other societies. Now it can perhaps be said that attention must be centered on the conditions of its spread from the West to other societies all over the world.

At the same time, the "capitalism" of Weber's concern has not remained static. Indeed the half-century since the time of which Weber was writing has, particularly in the United States, seen immense changes, which were only very partially foreseen by Weber, to say nothing of Marx. Weber did, however, strike a major keynote with his emphasis on the factor of *bureaucracy* in the business enterprise—this, it will be remembered, was one of the main bases on which he distinguished the "rational bourgeois capitalism" which he felt to be the central modern Western phenomenon, from the many other types which he discussed.

I have noted that Weber, in common with the Marxists and many others then and since, used the term "capitalism" as the overall term designating the modern Western economic order. There are two principal senses in which this designation might be justified. The first is the technical economic one in which the modern "industrial" system is very much a "capital-intensive" as distinguished from a "labor-intensive" and/or "land-intensive" mode of economic organization. From this point of view, however, Soviet industrialism also is obviously "capitalistic." The other sense concerns the fact that in the Western world the industrial system grew up mainly—in spite of a variety of qualifications—under the aegis of "private enterprise," which has been defined above all as meaning through agencies which are controlled through property holdings and are not identified with "public authority." This, of course, is the basis on which partly scientifically, but even more ideologically, capitalism is opposed to socialism.

It seems to me that the development of Western economic organization since Weber's day has greatly reduced the significance of this second consideration. Looked at both in value terms and in organizational terms, the differences between the "public" and "private" modes of structuring an economy are secondary in the sense that preference between them becomes a question of *relative economic efficiency* which, in the nature of the case, will vary with concrete conditions; it is not a simple question of "principle."

In value terms, the striking fact is that virtually the whole world has, within our time, come to assign to economic productivity a very high value indeed. The essential differences are not over productivity as *value,* but over the most effective means of implementing this value. Even the difference between American and Soviet orientations, which some feel is the deepest difference in the world, is not primarily a difference over the valuation of productivity.

In organizational terms, it can be said that the differences are somewhat, but only somewhat, greater. Essentially they concern the *top* levels of the organizational structure, namely whether control should be implemented directly from above by administrative mechanisms or whether there should be heavy reliance on the more "automatic" controls which operate through the market mechanisms. But at the level of the producing unit or "firm," the differences are decreasingly significant. That the typical large-scale firm must be a "bureaucratic" organization now goes without saying. In the United States as well as the Soviet Union, proprietorship has ceased to have primary significance, for such firms must employ highly qualified technical and managerial personnel on an occupational, not a proprietorship basis. Obviously in *both* countries the average "worker" is "expropriated" from ownership of the means of production, simply because the firm is a large-scale organization under unitary management, not a loose federation of independent craftsmen.

I would like to suggest that in the "socialist" societies the insistence on the importance of political controls at the top levels of economic organization is at present (in the sense of an observer's explanation rather than the actor's "rationalization") probably far more due to their stage and pace of economic development than to a belief that such political controls are best, on principle, for the operation of a highly developed industrial economy. The justification of socialization rests mainly on the conditions of getting quick and effective new development, not of effectively operating, even in the "public interest," a relatively "mature" industrial economy of the American type. This primarily explains the appeal of "socialism" to the economically "underdeveloped" areas of the world.

Conversely, however, I would like to contend in this paper that the *original* development of industrialism in the Western world not only *did* but *had to* take place in "capitalistic" forms. This is because political organization in a preindustrial situation without outside pressures would put usually insurmountable obstacles in the way of such economic development, unless there were features in the social structure which could put institutional restraints on the exercise of political power and which *independently* of the political structure would provide special impetus to economic development.

It is only because the essential structure of modern industrialism has already been in existence in the Western world that political initiative has been able to take the main lead in its promotion elsewhere—starting with Japan and Soviet Russia. This view, I think, is supported by the fact that, contrary to Marxian expectations, a socialist revolution has not occurred in a single society which already had a highly developed economy.

Some Highlights of
Western Institutional Development

The keynote of my analysis is consideration of the process of structural differentiation in societies. My thesis will be that a *primary* orientation to economic productivity on the part of a major sector of the total social structure, which modern industrialism requires, could not emerge until a relatively advanced stage of the process of differentiation had been reached. A variety of institutional and cultural features of Western society have tended to press this process of structural differentiation further and faster than it occurred in other parts of the world, both by providing positive impetus to the process and by neutralizing the inhibiting effects which seem to inhere in most pre-industrial types of religious and political organization.

Weber specifically emphasized the importance of the ethic of ascetic Protestantism, a view which I hold to be essentially correct. But this influence was not an isolated phenomenon; it represented a critical phase of a more general development which involved both culture and social structure in the Western world.

On the cultural side, it was clearly Christianity which was the most important single heritage. In Christianity the rationalizing trends and cognitive universalism of Greek thought were fused with post-prophetic Judaism's special combination of transcendentalism and actively oriented ethical universalism. The fact that Christianity, in spite of the late Roman establishment of the Church, stood on the whole aloof from secular society in a sense in which this was true neither of Judaism nor of Greek religion, was also of great importance. The Greek element was also semi-independent and could emerge in the Renaissance as the focus of secular Humanism.

The other most important cultural heritage centered about the Roman law, as a fusion of Greek intellectualism and Roman practicality. The three basic keynotes, then, were transcendentalism, universalistic rationality, and a kind of practicality. Transcendentalism provided the central leverage for motivating change in a given social order, while rationalism provided a basis for the generalization of changes throughout society, and this was a strong counterforce to the type of particularism which was as strongly entrenched in the European Middle Ages as in so many other societies. There was also a strong individualistic strain in Christianity, which dissociated the religious fate of the individual from the organized secular community of which he was a part. In the Catholic phase the Church claimed to control the individual's access to salvation, but that was a very different thing from defining his religious welfare as bound up with the fate of a social community as such.

Turning to the institutional side, it may be suggested that there were two crucial heritages from the ancient world. The first is the differentiation of Church and State, a state of affairs unique to the West. It grew essentially out of the fact that a transcendentally oriented religion spread within a society which was in a sense "alien" to it: Christianity never became fused with the social structure of the Roman Empire. The essential difference, in this respect, between the situation in Antiquity and in the Middle Ages was that, in the latter period, as Troeltsch has shown, the Church had accepted a role as part, but *only* part, of a Christian society conceived to be permanent. The secular arm was not, except by certain Papal extremists, conceived to be a mere branch or administrative agency of the Church, but an authentically independent ordination of God.

The second basic institutional heritage from Antiquity was the consequence of the structure of Greco-Roman society as a network of *poleis* or *municipiae*. In the areas of Europe which had been parts of the Roman Empire, notably Italy, France and Spain, the semi-independent urban community remained on some level continuously in existence through the "dark ages" and could serve as a model for its extension into other territories such as Germany. It was never completely absorbed in the rural-feudal structure of power and authority, so the towns constituted important independent centers of political organization, and indeed of military force. If they were to grow beyond the level of a mere village refuge for the tiller of surrounding fields, they had to subsist in important part from commerce and industry involving trade beyond their walls.

The essential point is that with this institutional heritage from Antiquity, medieval Europe did not become socially polarized between a "ruling" religio-political upper class and a broad mass of predominantly peasant common people, as over so much of the world. Instead, the various structurally independent elements *could* checkmate each other in situations where one of them had an interest in inhibiting new developments. Let us now attempt to see in what general ways different types of religious and political organization would tend to inhibit economic growth beyond certain points.

First, with respect to religion, it seems clear that there are two principal ways in which religious interest may tend to oppose economic development. The first of these derives from the dichotomy of wordly and other-worldly interests which inheres in transcendentally oriented religion. From this point of view, very strong interest in economic productivity cannot fail to be interpreted as a threat to the primacy of the religious interest itself. Wealth, power, and erotic gratification have always been the primary centers of the religiously defined dangerous "things of this world"; it is perhaps not fortuitous that their neutralization seems to be the focus of the famous vows binding an individual to the monastic life, namely poverty, chastity and obedience. The second religious barrier to economic development is the general religious tendency to favor traditionalistic stereotyped behavior. This is most prominent where the religious tradition itself is strongly permeated with magical and ritualistic elements, but is also true wherever much of secular life is endowed with direct sacred-symbolic significance. A relatively extreme non-primitive case is orthodox Judaism. Economic development inevitably involves a "process of rationalization" which is upsetting to such religious traditionalism.

In both these contexts it was of the first importance to economic development in the West that the sphere of religious jurisdiction was *specifically* delimited to the Church and thus could not too grossly invade the sphere of secular jurisdiction without arousing strong resistance from the institutionalized rights of the secular sphere. Such a sphere of immunity from religious "interference" has not been something to take for granted in all "civilized" societies.

This negative aspect of the matter is not, however, sufficient to account for the place of religion in Western economic development. In addition to a relative degree of noninterference, Western Christianity has, in varying degrees, provided positive encouragement, though not without frequent and severe internal religious conflicts. This encouragement was possible largely because of the combination noted above of a strong rationalizing tendency, a transcendentalism hostile to idealization of a social status quo, and a practical orientation of action which gave positive religious sanction to good conduct *in the world*. The ultimate Calvinistic conception of the Kingdom of God on Earth was the last of a series of stages, starting with the place given to useful labor in the Benedictine Rule, by which the importance of constructive work in this life was increasingly emphasized. It is particularly essential to recognize that it was the *combination* of transcendentalism and orientation to the importance of worldly tasks which was most important. The two have too often been interpreted to be mutually exclusive alternatives. In sum, it can be said that the Western world combined a relation between religious and secular organization and a type of religion which were both relatively favorable to economic development.

Let us now turn to the political side of the question. The central reason for the inhibition of longer-run economic development by political considerations is that political power-holders and power-aspirants are oriented to relatively short-run goals of the social system. This in turn goes back to the fact that political power rests on the support of important elements in the collectivity in and for which leadership elements assume responsibility. Such support acts as a process of *integrating* the social system for the attainment of its goals through the action of its leadership elements. The essential problem concerns the mechanisms by which support of such leadership elements can be brought about and/or maintained. This support can be unproblematical only when it rests on a "traditionalistic" basis. And a traditionalistic basis of support is one which can readily be jeopardized by economic innovations which involve changing the main institutional structure of the society in question. The main point is that a traditionalistic political authority is almost in the nature of the case committed to the bolstering of economic vested interests, if these interests can advance a strong claim to legitimacy in terms of the traditionally established order.

If the basis of political support is *not* traditionalistic, then it will tend to involve an appeal to relatively immediate interests and to the emotions of the strategically situated groups in the population. Political influence as such, then, seems either to be oriented to relatively short-run "constituency" interests, or to fall readily into traditionalistic stereotyping. These seem to be the reasons why Weber spoke of the "economically irrational" influence of political interests.

Of course this is by no means to say that the political area has not involved a very important amount of rationalization, particularly in law, administration, and military organization. The principal elements of rationalization, notably in administration and law, seem, however, to go back to cultural points of reference other than the political interest constellation of a given time. In the Western case these reference points are found in the universalistic rationalism of Greco-Roman culture and law, and the transcendental individualistic universalism of Christianity. Much of this influence had been built into Western political structures. But it may still be doubted that there could have been a general breakthrough in economic development without severe restraints on political authority.

In the first instance, these restraints were, as noted, found in a balance of social power, particularly the balance between feudal-monarchical power and church, and of both of these vis-à-vis the independent towns. Within this balanced system, particularly in the towns, there was a positive cumulative development of productive capacity both through handicraft industry and through mercantile commerce. Furthermore, and just as important, there was the gradual development of an institutional framework within which such activities could have a chance to grow. This development was the result of a combination of what we would now call "business practice," of law relatively independent of the non-legal political authorities, and of positive measures by political authority. Thus in both the revived Roman and the Common Law traditions, the law of contract, of property and of "master and servant" came to be progressively clarified. Roscoe Pound has strongly emphasized the influence of Puritanism on the common law in England, which attests to the cultural component in this institutional development. It was thus not a matter either strictly of political action or of economic interests alone. A gradual rationalization of monetary practices was of course another major thread in the developmental process.

Such a development was never of course simply "linear." Relatively stabilized states were attained—such as the urban guild system and the mercantilist system—which in turn proved to be obstacles to further development, so that a breaking out of the restrictions imposed by them was necessary for further steps. For the reasons sketched above, it proved possible for such controls to be broken through, though not without severe struggles, whereas in many other areas comparable situations remained frozen for very long periods.

Coming back to our problem of "capitalism," it can be said that until this century the organizational core has been mainly the "family firm." This, one might say, has been a kind of petty economic monarchy governed on "legitimist" principles. It started with the actual operation of the enterprise exclusively or mainly by family members themselves, helped, in the guild system, by one or two apprentices and/or journeymen. Gradually, but on occasion only after violent conflict, the size of such units grew, and it became possible to employ increasing numbers of people other than family members themselves. But very generally the relation of the employing family to employees has tended to remain "paternalistic," covering actually, if not legally, far more than what we now understand by a contract of employment. Only with the quite large enterprises of the nineteenth century did this paternalism begin to be broken through on a large scale, and of course much of it still exists today.

The decisive thing about the family firm, seen in our present perspective, was its "emancipation," *in the sense of structural differentiation,* from the political system. The starting point of this process seems to have lain in the fact that the producing units, usually guilds and below them full guild members, already possessed from the beginning a certain independence rooted in a peasant-like control of their petty enterprises. As in the peasant case, family, operative work, and capitalization were fused in a single small social unit. With the growth in scale of operations, the role of the "head" of the family firm inevitably shifted in the direction of managerial functions. His position vis-à-vis the rest of the community could not rest simply on the fact that he, like the old-fashioned shoemaker, was the one who directly made the desired goods. In his relations to the "public" his position inevitably focused at two points, namely marketing and financing. In marketing, where the purchaser has some choice as to whether to buy or not, there is an inherent risk in the position of the firm; hence it was essential to its adaptive security that it should have a certain degree of control over the factors of production required for its products.

This control has of course been achieved through the institution of property, and increasingly the decisive kind of property has come to be money funds. This, in turn, is directly connected with the extension of the market system by which factors of production—land, labor, and essential items of equipment and materials—have become available through purchase to whoever was in a position to pay for them.

It is essentially on this basis that the association of private enterprise with capital has developed. If security of access to the essential means of production is not *directly* provided, and it can *only* be so provided on a large scale by political authority, then the only alternative is to leave control over those means to the firm or to some organized aggregate of firms. The institution of property in the modern Western sense does not guarantee any particular unit success in gaining access to adequate resources, but once that access is gained, e.g. by selling goods acceptable to customers, it guarantees the "entrepreneur's" security in control of these assets, and hence their disposability for the purposes of the firm. It seems to me that this structural connection between the family unit and the institution of property as the basis for control of the factors of production is the essence of "capitalism" as ordinarily understood.

In assessing the historical role of this type of structure it must be remembered that anything like fully "bureaucratic" organizations independent both of the church and of the political structure simply did not exist before the nineteenth century. Furthermore, the social structure was heavily oriented to ascription of status, and hence of powers and privileges, on the basis of kinship relations. In a society in which the political organization itself was so directly bound up with royal and aristocratic lineages, it is difficult to conceive how any economic organization independent both of the lineage principle and of political organization could possibly have come into being. It is my view that the historic role of the family firm has been to establish the independence of economic from political organization, to bring about a structural differentiation between these two major functional aspects of the society.

THE TRANSITION TO
MODERN BUREAUCRATIC INDUSTRIALISM

Max Weber, perhaps more than any other social scientist, has emphasized the importance of the structural differentiation between the household and the organization in which the members of the household perform occupational roles. In Western economic development this differentiation of firm from household started at the bottom of the status and responsibility scale and diffused upward from there. The first approximation to a modern type of occupational role was the journeyman of the handicraft system. With the emergence of larger scale units, particularly of factories, the typical role of the propertyless wage laborer emerged, of course much more prominently in industry than in agriculture. There were also, even as early as the later eighteenth century, some cases of the differentiation of managerial roles from those of ownership. But by and large the fusion of the two remained the dominant pattern of "classical" capitalism, and it was only after the turn of the twentieth century that structural differentiation on the upper levels took place. It is striking that Marx, writing after the midpoint of the nineteenth century, seemed to postulate a simple dichotomous structure of the typical firm as between the owning-managing family on the one hand and the employed propertyless workers on the other.

So far, then, as this pattern prevailed, there was a fundamental structural asymmetry in the firm, between the achieved-occupational component at the bottom, and the ascribed-kinship component at the top. To a degree this paralleled the structure of the political organization, with developing administrative bureaucracy in the lower reaches, and royal families buttressed by hereditary aristocracies in the upper. From a sociological point of view this was a temporary and unstable structure; further development was bound to challenge the status of the ascriptive lineage component in the upper reaches of the organization.

In the first place, the labor element never was simply a mass of equals in misery, but was always to some degree differentiated in terms of skill and subsidiary executive responsibility (e.g. at the foreman level); this differentiation below the level of "top management" has occurred as a function of increasing size of the organization. The importance of this internal differentiation below the level of "top management" has enormously increased as a function of the increasing complexity of technology and certain other processes. It is, above all, significant that professionally trained personnel have been employed in increasing numbers at strategic places in industry, pushing the occupational achievement principle to the high levels of prestige and responsibility in the firm.

This development could, within limits, coincide with the preservation of family-owner control at the top, as in the case of the Ford Motor Company in its first generation. But from the mid-nineteenth century there was a cumulative erosion of family-ownership control. In the limited liability company, for instance, a body of stockholders was created who were only nominally participants in managerial responsibility and who had no kinship relation to the actual management. This is connected in turn with the development of a genuine capital *market*. Access to capital then no longer required the commitment of personal property by the owning-managing kinship units and the automatic flow of all proceeds back to these units. A capital market meant that capital as a factor of production was mobilized from holders of funds wherever they might be found. This included both "private investors" not interested in assuming managerial responsibilities, and increasingly, "institutional investors" such as banks, insurance companies, endowment funds, etc.

At the same time the *corporate* unit came to be more and more dissociated from the private property interests of an "owning" kinship lineage. "Ploughing back" of profits into expansion not only remains but if anything has increased in importance as a mechanism for financing industrial development, particularly perhaps in the United States. But in the large-scale sector of the economy it is no longer the ploughing back of *family property*, but of *corporate property*, before it becomes the private property of any family. The other side of this process has, for the large firms, been the elimination of the lineage as such from any primary control of the enterprise, just as truly as republicanism and constitutional monarchy have eliminated royal lineages from real control of political organizations.

In short, the principle that the firm is a structure of occupational roles has now been generalized to the higher reaches of the organization; its structural fusion with the owning lineage has been broken for the larger-scale, pace-setting sector of modern "capitalistic" industry. In structural terms this is probably the most crucial change in the economy since the Marxian diagnosis was made.

Indeed, this structural change seems to me to be so fundamental that it is of dubious value to continue to speak of the "free enterprise" sector of the industrial economy as "capitalistic" at all. At the very least, the differences from the institutional structure dominant around the mid-nineteenth century are so great that most of the dynamic generalizations drawn from the facts of that situation simply cannot be applied. Above all, industry and government have assumed formal similarities of pattern to a far higher degree than before; in their operative sectors they have both become *bureaucratized.* That is, functions are performed overwhelmingly in occupational roles, structurally segregated from the household of the incumbents, arranged in a hierarchy of executive authority and differentiated in function on bases of technical competence, with selection by appoinment, often involving tests of competence. In both industry and government Weber's broad model of bureaucratic structure fits correctly if sufficient allowance is made for the role of technical competence in the higher ranges, i.e. at professional levels, and the ways in which this modifies the structure of "line" authority. It is because of this similarity that I suggested at the beginning of the paper that the balance between governmentally-controlled and free-enterprise industry is, much more than is generally held, a pragmatic question and not one of fundamental "principle." Consider the analogy of higher education. In the United States, both government (state and local) and private universities and colleges exist in large numbers. It does not seem to be necessary to engage in bitter ideological controversies as to whether one or the other pattern is the *only* right and ethically acceptable one.

Clearly both contribute to essential functions in the society, and the *balance* between them may be of considerable importance.

But it must not be forgotten that, as Weber so often insisted, the top of bureaucratic structure cannot itself be bureaucratic. In the West the formerly "legitimist," monarchical-aristocratic political top has been "democratized"; that is, top political authority has been placed in the hands of popularly elected officials. In private industry, the change typically consists in the replacement of the legitimist owning-lineage by a *fiduciary* board of directors. Though they are nominally elected by stockholders, thus indicating that control is legally in the hands of the *owners* of the enterprise, in most cases this clearly has become a fiction. The main tendency is toward a fiduciary role, in which, besides the central responsibility for production itself, responsibility is assumed for the administration of "other people's money" and for the ramified public interests which attach to large industrial enterprises. In this respect the government of industrial enterprises is approximating that of universities, hospitals, and other "nonprofit" organizations in our society.

Associated with this trend is one toward the "professionalizing" of business management which, since their funtions are so largely administrative, may best be compared with the development of civil services. This is evident in the growth in the United States, not only of formal training in Schools of Business Administration, but also of a "managerial ideology," as it is sometimes called, which tends to place an emphasis on responsibility above the older pattern of the "rational pursuit of self-interest."

This restructuring of the "capitalistic" economy has gone farther in the United States than in most of Western Europe, not only because of the scale of economic development, but also because of the difference in social stratification and in political structure. Above all, the United States has never had a hereditary aristocracy, and therefore no clear-cut *lineage* dominance of its political and social life through such an upper class. The "Virginia dynasty" in the early days of the Republic was the closest approach, and it was thoroughly broken in the Jacksonian era. This meant that the "feudalization of the bourgeoisie," such a prominent pattern all over Europe, could not take place. Above all, the business success of the highest groups, which was so great as to leave few if any business fields to conquer, left no structural support for maintaining the lineage principle in the control of business enterprise. In this situation a universalistic valuation of occupational achievement had a far better chance of dominating the situation than it did in European conditions.

In the United States of the mid-twentieth century there has thus emerged a type of industrial organization of the economy, and of its integration with the rest of the society, which is very different from that of a century ago in Europe. It is a "bureaucratic" industrialism, nearly completely dissociated from lineage-property controls in the higher reaches. It is successfully integrated, though not without strain, with the democratic-bureaucratic political organization. A strong and independent trade union structure has developed. Perhaps above all, the hereditary lineage basis of the upper class structure has very largely disappeared. An old landed aristocracy of the European type has not been replaced by an industrial-lineage aristocracy of great owning families, but by an *occupational* élite composed of business management personnel, political and administrative leadership, and the various professional groups. It is not the *property* interest of owning classes which is the dominant control-focus of the private enterprise economy, but the *organizational* interest of the firms themselves, with managers having the same type of "stake" in the firm that a professor has in his university. The trend of European development seems to be clearly in this general direction. It is this new bureaucratic industrialism, not the "classical capitalism" of a century ago, which is the essential reference point for analyzing the problems of economic development in the non-European world.

THE PROBLEM OF
THE "UNDERDEVELOPED" AREAS

At the beginning of this paper I mentioned that among those groups which are self-conscious about the larger issues confronting their societies, there is an apparently world-wide consensus on the valuation of economic productivity. Whatever the values of different societies outside the Western world, and their roots in different religious and philosophical traditions, as "first order of business" there are clearly two basic commitments (not always fully compatible with each other) to political independence and economic development. In this section of the paper I would like to attempt a broad diagnosis of the conditions necessary for economic development to reach the industrial level. This diagnosis is parallel to the sketch of the principal conditions involved in the economic development of the West. My main thesis will concern the differences in the role of government in the two cases. In the case of the *original* development of industrialism I have argued that it could not have occurred without the freeing of private enterprise from certain types of political control. But in the *present* case I shall argue that political authority is usually a necessary agency and that under certain conditions, far from obstructing, it is likely strongly to facilitate the process.

The primary point for the present situation is that an industrial system is already in full-blown existence. This means two things: first, that the presence of an industrial economy in some parts of the world sets the conditions under which any nation must now exist and develop; and second, it presents a model which others can follow and a resource on which, in varying ways, they can depend.

As a set of conditions, the industrial economy is fundamental to the political power structure of the world; it is obviously no accident that the two great powers around which the world political system has been polarizing since the end of World War II are the two leading industrial nations and that Britain's loss of relative political status coincides with her much smaller scale of industrial production. Thus world industrialism must affect the problem of political independence for former colonial areas. It is also the primary source both of markets for many of their products and of competition for their own attempts at new lines of production. It can also be a source of technical and managerial help and financial support, and the degree and nature of control which may go with such help is always a complicated and touchy problem.

In those areas which are not, like the English-speaking British Dominions, primarily overseas offshoots of European society, social structures vary enormously of course in many respects, but I think one major axis of structure is sufficiently general to serve as the major point of reference for this analysis. This is the dominance of a two-class system, with the upper group enjoying prerogatives of political power and usually also religious prestige, and the lower consisting predominantly of peasants and some craftsmen and petty traders. The situation is, with important exceptions, one in which economic production is controlled but not actively "managed" by the upper groups. That is, through taxation or through property rights, economic production provides the "surplus" which has made possible the activities and life-styles of the upper groups, but the upper groups have not participated importantly in the productive process itself, either in technical or in managerial capacities. They have been devoted to other functions, notably of a political and cultural-expressive character. It is this *dissociation* between the functions of economic production and the other functions which is the focus of the economic development problem in such societies.

This generalization must of course be qualified in a number of respects. In many societies in the past, essential economic changes *have* been undertaken through political agency. An important case is that of the irrigation and water-control projects of so many river-valley civilizations, notably Egypt, Mesopotamia, and China. But once these projects have been carried through and stabilized, the tendency has been for the productive process to become routinized, again primarily in the hands of the common people. Thus in China, in spite of drainage, canal-building, and dike-building on a grand scale, the broad social structure, revolving about the peasantry-gentry differentiation, has not been disturbed until this century.

Another important qualification must be made for the role of "interstitial" elements which do not quite fit into this neat dichotomy. A notable case is the combination in Japan of some of the Samurai and some of the mercantile elements which grew up in the towns and cities. It was this combination which formed the main spearhead for overthrowing the Tokugawa regime and initiating the process of modernization in Japan, under the stimulus of foreign pressure. Thus the Japanese upper class in the nineteenth century was very far from monolithic. Another case is the way in which the Santri Muslim group in Indonesia have formed a kind of middle class having considerably stronger tendencies toward economic function and rationality than does either the upper class or the peasantry. They have both a position and an ethical orientation which could become one focus of an economic development.

Still another type of variation is provided by the case of India. Here the caste system has operated in the past primarily as a powerful sanction for the traditionalistic fixation of economic behavior. But the caste system, with its complicated criss-crossings of class, ethnic groupings, occupation, and local solidarities, is not a simple two-class system. It seems quite clear that this structure has been a primary obstacle to the appeal of communism in India—and it is quite possible that it might provide some points of initiative for economic development. Indeed, this has already happened to some degree. Unfortunately I am not sufficiently well informed in this case to have a further independent judgment.

With these qualifications, let us take the broad two-class pattern as the standard one for economically "underdeveloped" societies. We must then consider the ways in which economic production in such societies is tied in with these two classes and with their interrelations. We may expect to find a structure of vested interests operating as obstacles to change.

The obstacles at the lower levels seem to be the simpler ones; they may be summed up as a combination of "traditionalism" and a strong pressure to reproduce the existing pattern of economic organization wherever opportunity exists for its expansion. Let us take up the latter first.

All over the oriental world labor-intensive peasant agriculture occupies an exceedingly prominent position. It is integrated with the kinship system in such ways that an expansion of opportunity can very readily and directly be taken up through the multiplication of segmental units which take over the new area of opportunity, at about the same level of productivity—a process generally associated with population increase. This occurred, for instance, in Indonesia when, after the 1930s' depression, the war-time Japanese occupation, and the subsequent revolution, the large-scale plantation agriculture begun under Dutch auspices collapsed and there was a complete reversion to the situation existing before the change, only on a basis of increased population and even greater labor-intensiveness, so that the situation had become more difficult to change than it was before.

It may be suggested that for this type of lower-class economic organization to be changed, there has to be a combination of favorable circumstances. One is obviously *opportunity* presented either (a) by a situation within the agricultural system which can give real—i.e., locally meaningful—incentives to increase the investment in agriculture, thereby reducing the labor per acre and increasing the individual unit's scale of operations, or (b) by opportunity for non-agricultural employment which is again locally meaningful. Indeed, both seem necessary, because any improvement in the agricultural system alone is almost bound to intensify the overpopulation problem on the land, creating counterpressures which can only be reduced by a considerable draining off of people into other occupations. Failure for this to happen on a large enough scale may, if industrialization develops successfully apart from it, create a seriously unbalanced situation in other respects. One may suspect that this has indeed been the case in parts of Europe such as France, where the old-style peasant agriculture is still sufficiently intact to constitute a very solid block of opposition to the forces for economic development.

In the cases under discussion the peasant complex is probably so firmly institutionalized that no fundamental changes could be gotten under way through the provision of opportunity alone. There needs to be considerable shaking up of the set of adjustments existing under the old system. This can probably occur most effectively through the production of a considerable labor shortage. But with the general tendency to overpopulation, a labor shortage would seem to be the very change most difficult to bring about. Presumably the most promising possibility is rapid development in other sectors of the economy. Another important process, however, is the upgrading of the population through education. The educated young man, it is hoped, will in a sufficient number of cases not be satisfied to continue in the ancestral pattern of peasant life, but will either actively seek his fortune in the towns or will seek to improve the agricultural organization. This seems to be occurring on a considerable scale, for example in Indonesia.

The cultural traditionalism of the peasant masses is closely bound up with the economic organization of agriculture and small handicrafts. Shaking up that organization will almost inevitably have considerable cultural repercussions. For a new cultural structuring, the most effective pattern will almost certainly stress nationalistic political ideology. The Western ideology of "private enterprise" is excluded from prominent appeal by two circumstances; first, it is associated with the primary negative symbol, "colonialism," and second, it lacks resonance in *either* of the two main indigenous classes, the peasant masses or the upper groups.

So far as the upper groups of these societies are concerned, one of the main conditions for getting a process of structural change going is clearly a far-reaching disturbance of the status quo. More than anything else, this disturbance is structured about that previous relation of political and economic dependency on the Western powers which has commonly been called "colonialism." Whether full national independence has already been achieved or is still developing, the status quo prior to World War II clearly cannot be restored. This means that an active seeking for a restructuring has been initiated everywhere, and that the first responsibility falls on the indigenous upper groups.

It is also clear that nationalism and the search for a new independent status necessarily activates *conservative* elements in the indigenous social structure. Independence inevitably tends to be interpreted, to some extent, as "restoration" of a pre-colonial system, with renewed freedom for the implementation of the *traditional* values of the society. Such restorationism is, however, directly inimical to economic development. The essential question, then, is where impetus and leadership can be found to counteract the restorationist conservative trend and set the society on a path of positive economic development.

It seems clear that the two-class structure I have posited greatly favors the Marxist definition of the situation, and that the restorationist tendency further plays directly into its hands. It is indeed this dominant two-class system, with religion associated with the upper classes as an obstacle to development, which is the primary explanation of the ironical fact that Marxism has appealed in almost directly inverse proportion to the level of a society's economic development.

An organization like the Communist Party could step into this type of situation, and mobilize the opposition both against "colonialism" and against this restorationist trend of the local upper classes. The Party is obviously committed to economic development and it has at its disposal many of the incentives for such a program. Indeed, if the situation is allowed to polarize too much around the restorationist problem and if the Party is helped from the outside, possibly by the blundering of Western powers suspected of wanting to restore the old colonialism, this is a very likely outcome.

If development is to be under Communist auspices, perhaps the most important question for its success is how far the movement can succeed in mobilizing nationalist sentiments behind it. One of the many important questions underlying this one concerns the prospects of bringing in enough educated and technically trained personnel, most of whom will necessarily have to come from the higher groups in the earlier stages. This did succeed in Russia and apparently to a considerable degree in China. It is an open question whether the exposure of the Communist movement's new imperialism, and hence its conflict with the interests of underdeveloped areas in their own political independence, will soon place very serious obstacles in the way of this possibility.

What then can we say of the possibilities of mobilizing

elements of the older upper groups in such societies to seize the opportunities leading to economic development on a non-Communist basis? Presumably in the current world situation this could not be in radical opposition to the *whole* indigenous upper class, but would have to lead to a splitting of it, to the development of a subgroup who were strong enough to oppose and eventually to overcome the restorationist subgroup.

In discussing Western socio-economic development I have emphasized the extent to which religion under unfavorable circumstances may serve as a primary obstacle to economic development. There is a particularly strong probability that following liberation from colonialism, a combination of nationalism and religious fundamentalism will set up very powerful obstacles to development. Here one of the strengths of the Communist movement, in the short run at least, is its uncompromising hostility to traditional religious groups and symbols. Whatever the longer run costs—and they may be very great—if Communism achieves political control it will very likely be able to break immediate religious resistance to major economic changes.

It is probably in this connection that one of the most important roles for the "intellectuals" is to be found. It seems to have been a worldwide feature of hereditary aristocracies that they have had a disdain, first of manual labor, but then by generalization, of any economic pursuits. By contrast, they have emphasized "spiritual" values and highly sophisticated, refined "styles of life." At the same time, however, such upper groups, with certain exceptions, have been deeply concerned with political power. This, I think, is the primary basis of leverage for change.

Since these upper groups are associated with a structure in which religion has been directly fused with both political power and upper class status, they fear the symbol of "materialism" in the Western system. This symbol clearly has a restorationist reference to a situation in which the freedom of "gentlemen" from contamination with "material" interests could be taken for granted. But it also refers to a fear that the "materialistic" interest of the West could lead to the erosion of the central national community by the "economic individualism" of the West. The classic formula of the "rational pursuit of *self*-interest" seems to them to present a threat to the all-important social solidarity of the nation.

On general sociological grounds it can be argued that a society which is deeply oriented to the problem of its own identity and internal solidarity will, when the pressure of its external relations is strongly salient, be above all concerned with problems in the *political* area. It will be highly sensitive to any symbols which might suggest the freedom of elements within it to disregard the national interest. For this reason economic individualism is unlikely to have a strong ideological appeal in underdeveloped areas; on the contrary, it is, if pushed, very likely to "backfire" to the disadvantage of development under non-Communist auspices.

Furthermore, some sort of "socialist" ideology of economic development allows intellectuals to oppose restorationism, precisely from the point of view of national interests because restorationism is unrealistic as a program under the conditions of the modern world. Unless the intellectuals have secular political support which taps nationalistic motivations, it is difficult to see how this argument against fundamentalist restorationism could be successful.

But besides religiously motivated restorationist sentiments, in different societies there are, as noted above, varying degrees of positive religious motivations pointing in the desired direction of change. The case of Japan has been noted, as has the case of the Indonesian Santris.

Let us now turn to the most important elements of the social structure itself. I am presuming here that the primary impetus to change will come from the political sector of the society. In this connection what I have called above the bureaucratization of modern Western industrialism is particularly important. Here, that is to say, there is a relatively direct model of organization available which need not, like the family firm structure of an earlier period, clash directly with the present trend to predominant political control in the earlier stages of economic development.

The situation will, in some respects, be favorable to change in proportion to the "bureaucratization" of government in a country. Thus, to take one example, Indonesia is more favorable than was China because of the relative weakness of a landlord interest independent of the governmental structure. In China the whole social structure could be polarized about the peasant-landlord conflict, with a Communist government taking the side—temporarily—of the peasant. But in Indonesia, government, if kept out of Communist hands, can serve as a source of leverage on the system as a whole, strengthened by the mobilization of nationalistic sentiments. Another essential point is how far government controls the machinery of education.

Various aspects of such bureaucratic governments may, however, present serious problems. Their tendency is to incorporate a diffuse social class superiority, of a type inimical to concern with economic affairs. This has, for instance, been the case with the *prijaji* governmental elite in Java. An essential problem, then, is where to find a sub-group of such a governmental class which can split off from the older tradition. The strongest impetus here seems to come from the nationalistic-developmental complex of ideology and the groups most drawn to this, who are presumably "intellectuals."

Prominent among these are bound to be those who have had direct contacts with the West, particularly through education abroad or under Western auspices at home. This makes their position delicate since they can readily be accused of sympathy for, or even alliance with, "colonialism." This is one of the reasons why "socialism" as opposed to "capitalism" is such an important symbol, since adherence to it helps to dissociate people from the dangerous contamination with colonialism. It may be surmised that the effect of this ideological situation is to place primary emphasis on the problem of economic development as a "technological" rather than a "managerial" or "entrepreneurial" problem. Then it can simply be taken for granted that the primary auspices will be governmental. Furthermore, the "engineer" is not vulnerable to the charge of self-interest to the same degree that the "businessman" is, and thus has a better chance to escape being impaled on the horns of the restorationism-colonialism dilemma.

It is probably within this broad ideological definition of the situation that the impetus to economic development under non-Communist auspices will have to come. It is ironic that even though the United States is the industrial country of the West in which the older-style, "capitalistic," economic structure has been most fully outdated, and it is also least tarred with the brush of a colonialist history, it is at the same time the country which for internal reasons has been most prone to emphasize the antithesis of capitalism and socialism on the *ideological* level. There cannot but be serious danger that this emphasis will only further the polarization of the situation in the underdeveloped areas between the restorationist type of conservatism and the Communist movement. There can be little doubt, so far as this happens, where the longer run advantage will lie. It is of the greatest importance for the United States not to allow the situation to be defined in this way, and not to allow itself to be maneuvered into the position of all-out support for the restorationist elements against the masses, or above all, of alienating the intellectuals who see their problems in a nationalist and "socialist" framework. So far, we have taken much better account of the sensibilities of nationalism than those of "socialism."

Although in this discussion I have broadly located the center of developmental initiative in a bureacratic political structure, and outlined an ideological setting within which development is likely to take place, this is still a long way from describing an institutional framework within which the process can in fact take place. When we get to more detailed levels, the variations from one local case to another necessarily become wider and it becomes more difficult to generalize across the board. I shall attempt to mention only two important sets of conditions.

The first is the provision of leadership for *specialized* bureaucratic organizations, and support for such organizations within the larger governmental structure. This is peculiarly important because of the diffuse general character of the authority and superiority traditionally enjoyed by the dominant governmental groups in most of these cases, a superiority very generally associated with *devaluation* of economic and other specialized functions. The general goal of this institutional development must be the building up, under the "umbrella" of government, of a strong, highly educated and—in the requisite proportions and fields—technically-trained class of people whose primary social status is bound up with *occupational* careers of the modern type and who thus come to be dissociated from any traditional élite groups in their society. It must in some sense be a functional equivalent of the Western "middle class."

The second broad condition I wish to mention is the stability of the political system itself, under which economic development must take place. One very obvious possibility is a Communist takeover, which has already been commented upon, and the short-run consequences of which are relatively clear. But apart from this possibility it is essential to note that in the Western world the bureaucratization of industry has been accompanied by the democratization of government. They are essentially parts of the same general process.

In the nature of the case the process as a whole will undermine the older bases of traditional political legitimacy, notably, of course, the power of royal lineages and of hereditary aristocracies. However important these may be in some places as stabilizing factors in the short run, in the longer run they cannot serve as the mainstays of a bureaucratically industrial type of society. Indeed, once processes of economic development have gotten fairly under way, I should regard the instabilities inherent in such a political situation as the most serious source of threat to their smooth continuance. Here again the fundamental importance of nationalism as a focus of solidarity and, under favorable conditions, of responsibility, comes out. But at the same time the potential instability is so great that it is to be hoped that the introduction of the inevitable changes will be gradual. Beyond this it is not possible to go in the present essay.

CONCLUSION

In conclusion, I would like to summarize my main argument briefly and then make a very brief application of it to Israel. There is a perhaps understandable common-sense presumption that the conditions under which an important social phenomenon has once developed are the same as those which will be most favorable to its repetition at a later time. My main argument has been that for the case of an industrial economy this is probably not true. I have argued that in the first place industralism *had* to develop, as in fact it did in the Western world, in essential independence from the main political organizations of the society. In the present situation, however, for the "diffusion" of this organizational type from the Western world to other areas, it seems clear that the most favorable conditions will center on the right type of political initiative.

There are two basic reasons for this. The first is the fact that an industrial system already exists and does not need to be created from the beginning; it is both a model to imitate and an active economic and political influence on all nonindustrial societies. The second is the fact that, the system itself, particularly in the United States, has changed structurally since the time when it stood in the sharpest structural antithesis to the more advanced governmental systems. The predominance of the family firm has given way to a "bureaucratization" whereby, even in the private enterprise sector, there is only at the very top any clear structural difference between private industrial and governmental organization. Governments could not very well have taken over family firm capitalism, but they can take over many of the functions of modern industrialism.

The political and social urgencies of a recently emancipated ex-colonial world make for great haste in development. Because of this and of the inherited antagonism to colonialism, it is unlikely that private enterprise on the nineteenth century model can have much prospect of spreading widely very soon. Governments, acting in the name of "nationalism" and of "socialism," are likely to be by far the most important agencies. Because of the inherited social structure, there is a possibility of polarization between the predominantly peasant masses and the relatively monolithic religious and political upper classes. In such a situation, with the necessary reactivation of what I have called a "restorationist" pattern, the Communist movement has a good chance to gain control. The main alternative for the time being is a development in the direction of "democratic socialism," in which intellectuals who have an important contact with Western culture are bound to play a prominent part.

There is good prospect of this broad alternative to Communism succeeding if it is given opportunity, though the probabilities will of course vary with conditions in different areas, since these are by no means uniform. Perhaps the most important forces to bank on are the *vested* interests of the local upper groups in a *continuity* of change to avoid their drastic liquidation, which would be likely with Communist ascendancy, and the *general* interest in national independence which, it cannot fail to become evident, is far from secured by accepting membership within the Communist system. The example of Hungary should not be altogether lost on many countries.

At the same time, it should not be forgotten that the changes involved in industrialization are in almost every respect socially *drastic* changes, and they cannot be painlessly accomplished, especially if they take place rapidly. Above all, it will not be possible to industrialize and at the same time to retain or restore an idealized version of the indigenous traditional society which includes the privileges of hereditary aristocracies. Particularly because of the severity of these inevitable strains, special account needs to be taken of the ideological sensitivities which have been reviewed, since these are symptoms of the strains in question.

Israel, it may be noted, occupies a very special position in relation to the problems discussed in this paper. In location it is an extra-Western society, but populated with enough people of European origin so that its overwhelming tone is and will, I think, continue to be that of a Western society. But because of the special historic status of the Jewish people, it lacks the traditional aristocratic classes associated with the political structure in Europe—in this respect it resembles the United States.

Furthermore, the people of Israel are characterized by a special concern with and talent for economic development, and by a special respect for intellectual values, especially as they underlie the technological and organizational impera-tives of industrial society. Still another notable institutional feature is their special type of agricultural settlement through which they have established a social pattern for the land which, whatever the utopian elements in the *kibbutzim,* is a very different pattern from the peasant organization so prominent elsewhere, and which clearly avoids the vicious circle of resistance to modernization which is characteristic of so much peasant organization.

Israel is thus a thoroughly modern state, committed to a

program of modern industrial development. Important among its other virtues is its infusion of European socialist ideological tradition. It is thus a living example that a developing society does not need to be either Communist or fanatically anti-socialist in its orientation, but that there is a middle ground.

At present Israel is involved in an acute conflict with Arab nationalism. But if this conflict can be kept from erupting into explosive forms, the example of Israel, standing as it does at the crossroads of the Middle East, may prove to be of the greatest historical importance as a lever in helping to bring about the social and economic changes which throughout most of the world today are deemed both desirable and necessary.

CHAPTER IV

SOME PRINCIPAL CHARACTERISTICS
OF INDUSTRIAL SOCIETIES

INTRODUCTION

The task of this paper is to delineate, in the light of general sociological theory and of comparative and historical empirical knowledge, some of the principal features of the structure of that still small, but growing group of societies which can be called "industrial." Naturally this will include consideration of some of the principal sociological conditions which seem to be necessary for the development of such a society, but the emphasis of the present paper will not be on accounting for the *process* of development, but rather on structural characteristics as such. These two problems are by no means identical.

These structural characteristics are both economic and noneconomic. Analysis of the economic characteristics is not the task of this paper, and I shall therefore attempt to outline only a few main economic points of reference for the classification and analysis of the important *noneconomic* factors with which the main discussion of the paper will be concerned. Here I will be outlining precisely those aspects of an industrial society which, I think, cannot be adequately dealt with in technical economic analysis. After making one preliminary point, I shall proceed to a very broad outline of the essentials of an industrial economy, and in the course of that discussion introduce a classification of the essential noneconomic factors.

The one preliminary point which needs to be made is that, by contrast with all previous type of society, an industrial society must at some time have given *special emphasis* to the development of the economy, and therefore either is or has been one in which economic considerations have a certain primacy over others. This, in turn, means that relative to concerns "internal" to the society, such as its own values, religion, personality interests, or its own integration, such a society must have been pronouncedly oriented to mastery of the *external* environment. This emphasis is difficult to identify within a single culture, but stands out sharply in contrasts such as that between modern Western society and India or China. Economic emphasis is not, however, the only type of orientation to situational mastery. Political emphasis is also possible, in which politically organized societies, or "states," contend for positions of power. By contrast with concern for power position, the economic emphasis is on mastery of the *physical* environment and economic advantage through *trade* with other societies.

Here it is essential to distinguish between a society's possible *political* emphasis in mastering the external situation, and, *within* an *economic* emphasis, the role of political agency in developing and managing the economy. I shall argue below that the main differentiation of type, at least in the early stages of industrialism, is between that which does and that which does not rely most heavily on political agency for industrial development and management. The Soviet Union is the paradigmatic example of such reliance, while the United States approaches the extreme in the other direction at present. Formerly Great Britain was an even purer type.

THE INDUSTRIAL ECONOMY

In dealing with the main features of an industrial economy I shall adopt the Marshallian pattern of classification and attempt to fill in the main rubrics with broad empirical-typological characterizations. The first essential distinction is between consumption and production. Since in an industrial society there is a highly elaborated division and specialization of labor, any one "firm" or producing unit must draw from many different households for its labor supply, and reciprocally, any one household must draw from many different producing units for its supply of consumer goods. Hence there must be some structure of markets, both a consumer's goods market and a labor market. Such a market system must be mediated either by money or by some functional equivalent, an "accounting" system.

It is essential that for any given productive purpose the supplies of the factors of production should not be fixed, but should be capable of mobilization. From the point of view of the economy as a system, then, there should be flexible, economically sensitive mechanisms for allocating the factors. According to Marshall these factors are land, labor, capital, and organization. Let me discuss each of these in turn.

Land. Through most of economic tradition land has been treated as a natural resource, the supply of which is, for purposes of economic analysis, seen as *given*. Consequently the total quantity of such a resource available to the economy is not a function of its price. What is open to the operation of "economic forces" is only the *allocation* of this fixed quantity of resources. There are, however, other components which behave, from the point of view of the economy as a whole, like the physical resource land. These components comprise the main interests of the sociologist, consisting of cultural resources and institutional structures. The cultural resources are 1) technological knowledge and 2) commitment to cultural values, both of which are of particular significance for economic analysis.

So far as technological knowledge is produced by economic organization it becomes a form of capital, but generally it seems safe to say that the more fundamental framework of the "state of the arts" is the outcome of noneconomic processes, and for economic purposes should be treated as a given. This may be treated as an empirical problem. It seems correct to say that technological development becomes a product of productive processes rather than a given factor far more in the later than in the earlier stages of industrial development. With reference both to technological knowledge and to natural resources it is quite clear that relatively high levels are necessary for an industrial economy, simply because it is, by comparison with other kinds of economy, characterized by high levels of productivity. There is, however, the one crucial difference between the two: usable knowledge is "produced" by two processes which, though economic factors play a part, are clearly *predominantly* noneconomic, namely research and education.

The second cultural component I have referred to as value-commitments. Empirically it influences the economy through the channel of human services, including those of "entrepreneurs." But from an analytical point of view, it should be considered to be a given. We may divide the motivation of human services in production into two components, 1) that which we would think of as responsive to economic sanctions as rewards, and 2) that element which, psychologically, we would call internalized values. It is this latter component which is at issue here. In industrial terms it may be called high motivation to achievement in directions which can be utilized for economic production. This component therefore articulates with the value system of the society and the mechanisms of its institutionalization.

Labor. In empirical terms "labor" usually means to the economist the concrete activities of an individual human being engaged in production, including all the factors which determine these activities. In the present analytical sense, however, it must refer to one of the components determining such activities, namely, given the individual's value-commitments, that other motivational component mentioned above, which determines what portion of his energies will become available for particular productive purposes. It is this component the supply of which can, under certain conditions, be treated as a function of economic sanctions, i.e., of its price. Clearly "wages" constitute a prime determinant of the allocation of a given labor supply among economic uses, and is an important factor in attracting people, or portions of their energies, into the "labor force." Now an industrial society will require both an adequately *large* force and a *flexible* or mobile labor force. And though the quantity of labor is not a given from the point of view of economic analysis, the *institutional* framework within which labor services become available *is* a given. Hence the degree and kinds of flexibility or mobility of the labor force will be determined by institutional patterns which are noneconomic givens. The levels of *skill* of that force I should treat also mainly as a given for economic analysis, namely the "internalization" of technological culture through educational processes.

Capital. The factor of capital is from the point of view of production a special one because it is not, in the same sense as land or labor, independent of production itself. Capitalization is essentially the diversion of the product of past production to form an instrumentality for future production. Clearly, to be built up from a preindustrial level, an industrial economy requires a very large capital investment, either from internal sources or from outside. And the industrial economy requires not only high capitalization, but flexibility in the market structures so that the quantities of capital devoted to production can be large, and flexibly allocated both within the economy and relative to other competing claims upon them. The *quantity* of capital, like the quantity of labor, may vary with economic forces, but similarly, the *flexibility* of its allocation will be given by the institutional framework within which the economy functions.

Organization. Marshall's factor of organization must, like labor and capital, be broken down into two components: an economic variable and a noneconomic given. The given component concerns the institutional structure of the collectivities or "organizations" which carry out production by combining the factors of land, labor, and capital. In the strict *analytical* sense this is what I shall call a "political" area of institutionalization, distinguishing this analytical sense from that of "government," which I shall treat as political organization at the level of the total society. From this institutional component of organization it is also necessary to distinguish the "entrepreneurial" component. This is a flexible, allocable resource which can be attracted into given fields of production by economic opportunity. An industrial economy requires the appropriate institutional framework for the establishment of organizations or "firms" which can operate in terms of a clear primacy of economic, i.e. productive, functions, and which are allowed a high degree of internal control over the factors of production as well as access to supplies of them from outside.

The factors of the social system which must be treated as given from the point of view of economic analysis will, so far as they have been reviewed so far, be treated under two main headings in what follows: namely 1) commitments to values, and 2) the structure of institutional systems. The latter will be discussed first on the level of the general character of normative institutions, particularly that of law, and then in more detail concerning a) a primarily "economic" complex (relating to labor and capital as factors) comprising contract, property, and occupation, and b) a primarily "political" complex (relating to organization as a factor) comprising what I shall call leadership, authority, and "regulation."

There is, however, another major subject too vital to omit and also primarily noneconomic, though it may be "harnessed" to productive goals, namely political organization at the societal, i.e. governmental, level. This does not relate specifically to any one factor of production, but is most closely connected with organization. It is significant above all in two connections, as presenting first, through administrative mechanisms, a set of alternatives to the mechanisms of the market; and second, an alternative to independent entrepreneurship. In connection with the latter it may be a particularly important instrumentality of new and rapid industrial development.

COMMITMENTS TO VALUES

As I noted at the beginning of this paper, the relevance of value-commitments is in part relative to the stage of a society's development. In general, however, a society's industrialization is possible only through a relatively strong orientation to the problems raised by the exigencies of the situation *external* to it, whether the main focus of this orientation be economic or political. Therefore as a first step it may be said that industrialization implies either a strong emphasis in this direction built into the longer-run institutionalized value-system, or a recent shift in the direction of this greater emphasis. At the same time industrialization is related to the level of structural differentiation of the society. Hence one would not expect that societies below a given level of such differentiation would respond readily even to outside stimulus in this respect, whatever their values.

It can also be stated as a generalization that, whatever the causal factors, spontaneous development of a major value-orientation from within a society is always expressed in its religious tradition, which therefore constitutes an important index and partial determinant of its values.

From this point of view the Judeo-Christian tradition has from early times tended, with certain periods of "recession" from it, to be highly activistic in relation to the external environment. By contrast, the great civilizations of the Orient, notably China and India, have had a quite different character. But there have been a number of different phases in this Western tradition, and the one most directly relevant as underlying the development of industrialism is certainly that phase associated with what Max Weber called "ascetic Protestantism," in north-western Europe and North America in the two centuries immediately preceding the Industrial Revolution.

The essential point here is that the institutionalization of a system of values, when internalized in the personalities of individuals, can motivate sufficient "drive" for economic production to carry through the immense labor of industrialization, and can "legitimize" the institutional arrangements and political structures associated with this process, which often involve quite radical changes from previous states of affairs.

The requisite system of values need not, however, arise "spontaneously" within the society. It may become institutionalized through processes which are analogous to the internalization of adult culture by children, namely by what anthropologists would call "diffusion." This is likely to be the main process in societies which have been industrialized at a late period after important models which were already in existence impinged on them in important ways. Here, however, the relative "hospitality" of the value-system of the society undergoing industrialization is a factor of the first importance. Japan, for instance, seems to have had a value system more favorable to such reception than did China, where a more radical change in values was necessary. At the very least, however, it would have taken very much longer for Japan to develop an industrial type of organization had not both the model and the economic and political pressure of the West existed. Quite clearly this influence of the external model is the most crucial factor at present in the widespread attempts at industrial development in the "underdeveloped" societies, whether their industrialization is proceeding under communist or "democratic" auspices.

Let me return for a moment to the role of such internalized and institutionalized values. The essential point at the motivational level is the motivation to *achievement* in occupational roles devoted to productive functions. The relevant tasks may manifest a very wide variety of technical content, and also of course be located over a wide organizational range in terms of technical and organizational status and responsibility. But there are above all two major characteristics that define the core of the motivational problem: 1) people must be motivated to serve the goal of *production* beyond the levels previously treated as normal, desirable, or necessary in the society, and 2) they must perform such tasks to a far higher degree than before, in organizations specifically differentiated from other, nonproductive functional contexts, i.e., labor must be "alienable."

Most preindustrial societies have not had the cultural or structural basis for a value system which would motivate this type of activity over a wide range. Very often economic production has tended to be treated as a function definitely inferior to aristocratic or gentlemanly pursuits and thus fit only for persons of low if not servile status. Another great uniformity in preindustrial societies is the fusion of most productive functions with other functions that have primarily noneconomic significance, or at best only very partial economic significance. Peasant agriculture may serve as a type case of this latter phenomenon.

In this connection it should be made quite clear that internalized values constitute a quite different component of motivational systems from that "economic rationality" which the main tradition of economics has tended to emphasize. They differ in that the expression of an internalized value is not primarily dependent on any specific level of reward for its motivation. This was Weber's fundamental point as against the economic-utilitarian interpretations of "capitalism." Market mechanisms, and with them monetary rewards, have played an enormously important *allocative* function in the development of industrial societies, but money income should not be held to account for the main direction and intensity of the deeper motivational "drives" underlying high production.

Similar considerations apply to the importance of values in legitimizing institutionalized norms. This is above all the case with the mobility of the factors of production, as well as on the consumption side of the economy. The barriers to the mobilization of resources for production have been so fundamental as to involve the value level at many points. This is evident from the strong strain of *moral* indignation which has very generally been aroused by large-scale attempts to increase such mobility. It is a gross error to suppose that the predominant problem of economic development which would involve major structural change in the society is that of finding more efficient ways to produce more goods. The principal barriers to industrial development today are resistances to changing the values and institutionalized norms which form the main structural framework of the society.

Where the primary process of value change involves borrowing from a model external to the society, I suggest that ideology tends to serve functions analogous to those of religious movements in the case of internal value change. The necessary changes in the structure of the society are "justified" in terms of a system of beliefs which are held with high emotional intensity and are indeed, in their sociological characteristics and functions, far removed from "technical" considerations of economic efficiency and political effectiveness. The function of these ideologies is not to define technologies of economic organization, but to legitimize change in values and in institutional structure.

Seen in this perspective, a remarkable thing has happened in the world in the last generation or so. In spite of the immense range of variation in values and other elements of culture, as in social structure, there has come to be almost a world-wide consensus in approving of high, i.e. industrial-level, economic productivity. Ideology is the main expression of this. Essentially it means the general acceptance of Western industrial models as providing at least *one* essential part of the "good society." The intense emotionalism accompanying the assertions of ideology and the clear ambivalence involved, e.g., an intense "anti-colonialism," at the same time indicate serious strains which, in many cases at least, are occasioned largely by incomplete institutionalization of the new values and norms. The broad ideological division between the "capitalistic" and the "socialistic" models of the industrial society reflects the ways in which the role of government is differentially conceived, which will be discussed further later on.

THE STRUCTURE OF INSTITUTIONAL SYSTEMS

The legal system. In the modern Western world the essential institutional prerequisites of industrialization, with respect notably to markets and to the mobility and organization of the factors of production, have rooted in the first instance in legal systems whose main outline antedates the industrial revolution, namely modern Roman Law and English Common Law.

The important thing about these bodies of law is that, far more than any other legal systems, they have institutionalized principles over wide areas of human relations which are congruent with the institutional requirements of an industrial organization of the economy. Of course there are important differences between the Roman and Common Law systems, but broadly they are comparable in the relevant respects, while in Islamic, Chinese or Hindu legal systems there is nothing comparable in the same respects.

Perhaps the most important general characteristic of these Western legal systems is that they have institutionalized firm patterns of rights and obligations which, within politically organized units of society, have *cut across* the lines drawn by the traditional "primary" bases of social solidarity, and hence have become in certain respects independent of them. The most important of such lines of primary solidarity would be kinship, the "feudal" types of political allegiance, and the solidarity of smaller territorial communities. Ethnic solidarities may be regarded in certain senses as extensions of kinship.

Over against such bases of solidarity these legal systems have embodied principles of *universalism* and of *specificity*. By universalism I mean that rules have been formulated and held to apply to categories of persons or collectivities on the basis of generally defined characteristics independent of their statuses in these "lower-order" particularistic solidarities. Thus there have been rights to enter into contractual relationships, the consequences of which were defined as independent of the kinship or local community relations of the contracting parties. Or, in a political context, certain obligations have been applied to citizens as such, again independently of their differentiation by these particularistic subsolidarities.

By specificity in this connection I mean the definition of legal rules in such a way that the rights and obligations thereby created could be abstracted from the status and expectations of certain particularistic solidary memberships, without destroying that membership. The primary solidary structures would therefore be "insulated" from the crosscutting relationship.

The most relevant areas of legal institutionalization for present purposes are the ones which may in the present analytical sense be called economic and political and I shall turn presently to a sketch of the principal sub-areas of each. Before that, however, it should be noted that a very important feature of the place of these Western legal systems in the societies in which they have functioned is their

relative independence of governmental structure and processes. It is in the nature of the place of law in societies that
there should, especially with reference to jurisdiction and
sanctions, be a close integration between the legal system and
government. Law must be the law of "politically organized
society" as Dean Pound put it. But this is not to say that the
law is simply an "agency" of government. Its involvement
in the social structure is far more complex than that. Even in
relatively centralized or "absolutist" situations there has been
relative independence of the judiciary from both executive
and legislative organs of the state. A "government of laws and
not of men" in the American sense, a *Rechtsstaat* in the
German, implies this. I suggest that in the Soviet case and
even more in Oriental cases, the relative weakness or near-
absence of such an independent legal system is one major
condition making for predominance of governmental agency
in the process of industrial development.

Economic institutions. What I am calling the "economic
complex" can be broken down into three subcomplexes,
namely those of contract, property and occupation. Of these
contract is the more general and central institutional focus,
while property and occupation, through the contract of employment, may be treated as derivative from it. The broad
connection of contract with both the market complex and
the mobility of resources should be nearly obvious. Contract
makes possible the freedom of individuals and collectivities
to make ad hoc agreements to exchange goods and money,
and to enter into mutual obligations involving future performances. But these freedoms could not be institutionalized
within a stable system of social relationships unless there
were adequate general rules defining, among other matters,
the content of permitted contractual relations, and the limits
of such permission. Without attempting to justify such a
statement here, I would like to suggest that there are four
essential fields in a contractual system which must be adequately defined and regulated if the system is to be stable.

The four fields are: 1) definitions of permitted and prohibited *content* of contractual agreement; 2) definitions of legitimate and illegitimate *means* of securing the assent of the other party to a contract; 3) definitions of the situations of *risk and uncertainty* which are considered, and of the normative consequences of certain unforeseen changes in circumstance; and finally, 4) definitions of the *societal interest* in contractual relations, particularly interest in their consequences for third parties.

For defining the institutional prerequisites of industrialization, the crucial problem of contract concerns the freedom of consumers' markets and of the supplies of the factors of production, hence freedom of mobilization *for* combining these factors in accord with individual or collective economic interests. This, in turn, involves freedom *from* anchorage in other ties which would impede such structuring. Once industrialization is an important societal interest it can, therefore, provide the main criterion for the fourth category above. But a system of norms governing contractual relations must function as a system and must therefore adequately cover the other three fields which were enumerated above: 1) In Western societies we not only permit contractual freedom in many fields elsewhere barred to such treatment, but we also prohibit it in certain very important areas; the most important perhaps is contracts which would infringe the freedom of the individual by any form of "involuntary servitude." 2) In the field of means, the crucial prohibitions outlaw coercion and fraud as means of gaining assent. 3) In the field of risk and uncertainty, the most general principles concern relieving contracting parties from crippling obligations whose seriously onerous character could not have been foreseen at the time the obligation was assumed.

Property. These general principles can be more fully specified with reference to property. Where the objects of possession are physical objects, the key institution is ownership, which was clearly developed in Roman law. This has two main aspects. The first is the gathering together of *all* property rights regarding the same object into *one* bundle to be held by a single owner, whether the owner be individual or corporate. This clearly was not the case in medieval law, where several holders could have different kinds of property right to the same piece of land, for example. The essential rights may be classified as those of use, of control (specifying who shall use and for what purposes) and of disposal. Some of these elements may of course be kept out of the contractual context altogether by ascriptive restrictions, as in the common case of inalienability of land. Indeed in the medieval manor even use was to a considerable extent "traditionalized."

The second aspect concerns the differentiation of property rights from other rights in the same object. The most obvious case here is political jurisdiction and the most obvious example is land. Again in European medieval law it was impossible to have property rights in land without carrying with them elements of status in the political structure, e.g., the land-"owner" was at the same time the land-*lord* in the sense of holding jurisdiction over the land—the manorial court being one expression of this. Ownership thus involves the *differentiation* of the previous bundle which included both property and jurisdictional rights.

A particularly important special case of property rights is of course to be found in the institutionalization of money and other monetary instruments involved in contracts. This is in detail a highly complex matter. Suffice it to say that in modern Western societies property in monetary assets is, from a certain point of view, the center and focus of the whole property system. From that point of view property is the right to acquire possession and to alienate for monetary consideration. This right, that is to say, tends to "govern" the lower-order rights of control of physical objects and use of them. Money from this point of view is an institutionalized standard for the evaluation of commodities and services in terms of their *economic* significance, and is itself an object of possession in which property rights are institutionalized.

Occupation. The second main aspect of contractual rights and obligations concerns the use, control, and "disposal" of human services, individual and collective. The most important case is the contract of employment resulting, in the case of the individual, in an occupational role, where for the duration of the contract he assumes obligations of performance within the employing organization, and in certain respects, recognition of the legitimacy of the control exercised over this performance by that organization. I shall argue presently that this means that economic and "political" patterns of institutionalization interpenetrate at this point. The "formal organization," which is the most important type of collectivity employing persons in strictly occupational roles is a system with political primacy on its own level, though not necessarily in the society as a whole.

The important point here is the mobilizability of human services for economic production, and hence their freedom from ties and imperatives which would interfere seriously with economic production. There is a set of components of the occupational role which corresponds to use, control and disposal in the case of property. First, there are rights to specify and supervise the tasks of occupational activity, independently of traditionalized specifications. Second, there are rights to control such activity in terms of the decisions as to who shall act in the interest of these task-goals, and what procedures they should use. Finally, corresponding to disposal, there are rights to transfer services from one employing organization to another. The wider the scope of contractual freedoms on each of these levels in turn, the greater the mobility of labor as a factor in production.

The structural tendencies in the institutionalization of occupational roles have, in the Western world, paralleled those of the case of property. On the one hand the tendency has been to tie all of these components of the control of human services into one bundle, so that employment, once accepted, gives the employing organization rights of control and of "use," i.e. specification of particular tasks, as well as of disposal of one's services when no longer needed. The parallel also holds in the other principal respect, namely that the occupational role comes to be sharply differentiated from other roles in which the same individual is involved. Perhaps the most important case is the differentiation between occupational and kinship status and expectations. There has been a strong tendency for industrialization to be associated with increasingly sharp differentiation in this case, but it has had to go through a number of stages, and it has taken long periods to approach completeness.

A particularly important example of incomplete differentiation, for the history of industrial development, has been managerial position in a "family firm." Here, three components, which ordinarily would be analytically distinguished, are fused in the same status-role unit. The first is what I should call an occupational role-element in a strict sense. This concerns managerial responsibilities within a formal organization devoted to some phase of economic production. The second component is that of kinship organization. The individual has a status in his kinship group which certainly involves expectations and responsibilities which on occasion may not coincide with the productive interests of the firm. The third component, in turn, is the property component. The manager, in his familial role usually, is also a *proprietor* of the organization. Legally his managerial control has usually rested mainly on the property element. There is no doubt that the family firm played a crucial part in the early industrialization of the West; indeed I think it can be argued that it was indispensable, largely because it was the only way in which, at one stage, responsibility for production independent of governmental authority could be institutionalized. Thus it could focus entrepreneurial responsibility beyond the interests or lifetime of a single individual, it could accumulate and safeguard capital, and it could establish a solid reputation in the community. But at later stages it can become a serious source of obstruction to further development. The more recent tendency has been clearly toward differentiating these components from each other. The typical occupational manager in the larger firms is no longer in his position by virtue of kinship ascription, and property ownership is not a significant factor in his leadership and authority within the firm.

Political institutions. Let us turn now to what I called above the "political" complex of institutionalization. This concerns the normative structure of those aspects of collectivities which bear most directly on their effectiveness of operation in achieving goals. Defined in this way the category "political" applies at any level of the social structure. It is particularly relevant to those "formal organizations" which are organized about some particular "goal-attainment," of which economic production is one particularly important case. Seen in these terms, government is a special type of "politically" oriented collectivity, that one which organizes the society as a whole in the interest of collective goals. But because of the imperative of consistency in a normative system, the same basic principles of institutionalization tend to apply both to government and to many "private" organizations within the society.

I would like to treat the "political complex" of institutions as involving, in a sense parallel to the economic, three subcategories; one of them, which I call "leadership" is, like contract, more general, while the other two, which I shall call "authority" and "regulation" are, like property and occupation, more specific.

Leadership. By the institutionalization of leadership I mean the pattern of normative order by which certain subgroups within a collectivity are, by virtue of the "positions" they occupy within it, permitted and expected to take initiative and make decisions about attaining the goals of the collectivity, which bind the collectivity as a whole. It is in leadership roles that the more active functions of collective goal-attainment are institutionalized. This basis of differentiation is, in certain respects, cognate with the division of labor in the economic sense.

Leadership can be broken down into a series of functional contexts which are cognate with those set forth for the case of contract. We may speak first of the *societal interest* in leadership. This is essentially what Max Weber meant by "legitimation" in his treatment of the concept which has been translated as "authority" *(Herrschaft)*. Legitimation in this sense includes the question of incumbency, i.e., *who* is permitted to exercise the functions of leadership, on the basis of what process of selection for this role. Among the alternatives are hereditary succession, appointment, election, etc. Secondly, there is the problem of the *goals* in the interest of which leadership is institutionalized. Certain goals, like forcible seizure of governmental power, are often prohibited. Third is the question of the *means* allowed in the exercise of leadership. As in the case of contract, there is general exclusion of fraud and of coercion, except in imposing negative sanctions for resistance to legitimate authority. In industrial organizations not only the law of the state, but union contracts are important foci for the definition of these rules. Finally the orientation to *risk and uncertainty* may be thought of in reference to the problem of collective responsibility. This applies both to the leadership and to the followership elements of a collectivity. Leaders may pay certain penalties if things go wrong even though it could not clearly be said to be "their fault," and conversely they "get the credit" for good fortune. For the rank and file it means above all that they are bound by the consequences of the leaders' action, even though these consequences could not have been foreseen or approved in advance.

Again, for industrial organization leadership must have freedom to organize human services in the interest of production goals, without being impeded by the non-relevant commitments and ties of the persons involved. It is quite clear that such organization cannot be brought by purely egalitarian processes to a level capable of coping with complex technological tasks; there must be institutionalized leadership, whether by private "entrepreneurs" or by public agencies. This leadership pattern then can be spelled out in each of two directions, which I should like to call "authority" and "regulation."

I would like to use the much-controverted term "authority" here for a special subcategory of leadership in which the leader has the right to make *specific* decisions which are binding on the members of the collectivity. By regulation, on the other hand, I mean a set of controls over activity where the regulating agency specifies only *limits* of acceptable action on the part of the units under its control. One of the main contexts in which regulation instead of authority operates is that in which the content of roles or of suborganizations is *technical* in a sense which precludes detailed supervision by agencies which are not technically qualified.

Authority. Authority, like property and occupation, may be said to involve three elements of direct concern here. The highest of the three levels is the general power of making binding decisions which commit the organization to one among several alternative directions of action. This is cognate with the right of disposal in the case of property. The other two are different cases of authority to implement this general decision-making power. One of these is the power to allocate responsibilities of subunits within the organization. This is the crucial point at which the institutionalization of authority and that of occupation converge. The other is the power to allocate facilities, which in modern societies primarily means budgetary control. As in the economic cases these three constitute a control hierarchy. In general, he who holds the more general decision-making power controls the allocation of responsibilities within the organization, and he who controls these responsibilities controls the allocation of facilities to their functions. There may of course be various restrictions on such control as through seniority and tenure rules.

The tendency in the modern Western world has been more and more to tie these three components together in a single "package." This, I think, is the central point about what Weber called "rational-legal" authority. It is the condition of maximum disposability of human resources in the productive, as in other processes. It is the focal institution in the ideal type of "bureaucracy."

As in the other cases, however, this consolidation has occurred through a process of *differentiation* of the authority complex from other, nonpolitical patterns with which these have previously been fused, such as kinship ties in monarchical regimes or in family firms. Another type of differentiation which has had to take place at the governmental level is from elements of "political" interest which, though of great social import, have often been in conflict with interest in effective attainment of the specific organizational goal. The whole spoils systems, the use of administrative appointments as rewards for "deserving" Democrats or Republicans, is a case of this type.

Regulation. Regulation may also be broken down into a cognate set of three components. The first is again at the task level. The distinction from authority here involves the range of discretion in allowing access to the specific facilities required or to the funds necessary to acquire them. A good example is the provision of facilities through monetary funds rather than controlling access to specific physical objects. Hence from the point of view of leadership, i.e. the regulating agency, it is budgetary control. The second component is at the role level and concerns *function* or responsibilities within the collectivity. Here, as contrasted with authority, the function is performed with reference to some kind of standard which is beyond the control of the regulating agency. One of the most important types of standard is technical, e.g., with reference to engineering, research, medical procedures, etc. Or from the point of view of public regulation of independent business, the standard of profitability within the institutional framework is such an independent standard. Finally, the third level concerns the basis of commitment to the interests of the regulating collectivity, e.g., to the "public interest."

There has, in Western institutional development, been the same general tendency in this as in the other fields to bring these components together in a single package, and therefore to make it possible to "tie in" with the interests and goals of important collectivities those complexes of activity which could not be controlled through direct authority. This has been particularly important in areas where higher level technical processes were concerned. Under the guilds of the medieval economy the artisan's skills were very closely bound in with a special type of social organization so that they could not be used in the contexts which foreshadowed the industrial revolution. For this to happen, a differentiation had to take place, making his services more widely disposable. But this in turn meant differentiation *from* the solidarity of the guild system. The most important examples of full differentiation in this sense are such organizations as university faculties, hospitals, and industrial research laboratories, where an individual works at a "full-time" occupation and the organization exercises all three levels of "regulation" over him.

It is, however, important to be clear that if the attempt were made to institutionalize such services on the basis of what I have called "authority," this would probably fail, because it would interfere too much with the necessary order of independent responsibility. Such institutions as academic tenure are ways of protecting high-level professional personnel against "arbitrary" interference by administrative authorities. Similarly governmental civil service tenure may be said to protect the civil service against the spoils system; there is a sense in which an administrative bureaucracy is a "technical" subsystem which can only be "regulated," not "administered" by the top political authority.

Failure to deal adequately with the field I am calling regulation and distinguish it from authority constitutes, it seems to me, the most serious defect, in the present context, of Weber's famous analysis of bureaucracy. With this sort of qualification, however, there seems to be little doubt that bureaucracy is a very central feature of institutional structures which are favorable to industrialization.

It should also be clear that it is considerably more difficult than in the case of property to realize an ideal type in this whole area involving the overlapping patterns of occupation, authority and regulation. This is essentially because in the case of property either the physical object or the monetary funds can be fully dissociated from long-term involvement in other organizational contexts. Human service, however, has a fundamentally different character. If it is to be specialized at all, the specialized service must be differentiated out from a matrix of many different interests and role-commitments. Only within very severe limits can a *total* human being be specialized to a particular occupational function. There must, therefore, be a dynamic equilibrium between the occupationally involved elements of the personality and the rest of it, and the more specialized the occupational function, the greater the relative importance of these other parts.

It is for reasons such as these that authority over human beings in specialized roles never approaches the absoluteness of control that is characterized by ownership of property, and that the extremer types of authority seem to be unstable. Trade unions are a response to this problem to a large extent, as is the development of regulatory forms of leadership instead of authority.

The Problem of "Social Control." This point leads over into another area of institutionalization, that which the sociologist tends to call "social control." What I have called the economic and the political institutional complexes define patterns of legitimized behavior and structure of sanctions for such behavior. They presuppose motivational commitment of the individual to "conformity" with such normative patterns, so far as such conformity is not a function of "expediency." Within this "motivational" area there is another whole set of institutionalized mechanisms for the control of tendencies to deviant motivation. In a modern society like our own I would include in this context an important part of the functioning of such professions as medicine, law or social work. Probably more important for the larger outlines of structural development, however, are certain aspects of religion and ideology. In some respects religion and ideology serve as mechanisms of value-"indoctrination" and maintenance, but they also operate at lower levels in the normative structure of the society. The revivalistic movements in a good deal of the Protestant Western world can be interpreted in this light, and it seems that the aspect of Soviet ideological manipulation which is analyzed by Inkeles as "agitation" also belongs in this category.

I shall not attempt to go into these mechanisms at present, but only call attention to their existence and importance. Perhaps the most important single brief statement which can be made about their relevance to industrialism is that they must somehow reinforce motivation to participate in higher-order, more mobile types of organization than would be the case in a more highly "traditionalized" and particularistic society. Hence the more general themes in ideological slogans may be of great importance because attachment to them serves to emancipate the individual from attachment to too specific loyalties.

THE ROLE OF
GOVERNMENT IN INDUSTRIALIZATION

As my last main task I should like to take up briefly the relevance for industrialism of political organization at the *societal* level as distinct from the level of the producing organization. It is quite clear that the political organization of European feudal society was intimately involved with its economic organization and that feudal "governments" could not have sponsored and carried through processes of industrialization without fundamental structural alteration not only in their own organizations, but also in the institutional patterning for the society as a whole. The same is equally clear for the governmental structures of, say, China and India about 1700. This is not to imply that any particular form of government is required, above all not that it must be a "democratic" government. It means only that government must be sufficiently stable and also sufficiently *differentiated* from institutionalized structures in the society which are incompatible with industrialization, so that either it does not interfere too drastically with factors favorable to industrialization which are independent of government, or that it is itself sufficiently independent to be able to exert a strong leverage on the society to create more favorable new structures.

Indeed it seems clear that the main differentiation of types of industrialization must be made with respect to the role of government. Futhermore, it seems to be true that the appearance of an industrial economy for the *first* time required a predominance of "private" initiative and therefore an important set of restrictions on the intervention of government in the economy; whereas once an industrial system is in existence, the adoption of its patterns by other societies can proceed effectively through predominant governmental initiative. Indeed at the very least there are two further arguments to be made in this area: first, that governmental initiative provides the most rapid way to achieve significant industrialization and, second, that in the societies in question, this is the path most likely to be *institutionally*, rather than narrowly economically, feasible.

In the West, where industrialization took place first, perhaps the most crucial barrier to government intervention was a legal system, to which governments were committed, which institutionalized the *rights* of private initiative in this area. Of course, once the process was under way, governments derived great advantages from it, in revenue, in a basis of power in foreign relations, and in other respects. But this does not mean that governmental initiative could have brought it about. A crucial factor needed was the motivation of people involved in the value-commitments sketched in an earlier section of this paper. These could operate, however, only where the proper constellation of factors of *opportunity* was also given. I think the institutions focusing on the legal system were the most fundamental of these opportunity factors because they *underlay* the "extent of the market" and the availability of mobile resources.

In the cases of governmental initiative in industrialization, as in Japan, the Soviet Union, and more recent cases, especially in Asia, one might say that the opportunity factor was *external* to the society, in the existence elsewhere in the world of industrial systems and the networks of trade and communications associated with them. Here the analogue of the "individual" level of value commitments, as delineated by Weber, is the *national* commitment to the development of industrial productivity as fundamental to enhancement of national power and prestige. Given then the combination of the model and the pressures of the external industrial systems, the necessary patterns can, under favorable conditions, be institutionalized. These conditions include the seriousness of the national commitment, to which ideological mechanisms are obviously relevant, but also the possibility of creating the essential *internal* opportunity factors of the sort which have been sketched in the preceding section.

This general pattern seems to have been repeated twice on a major scale. Great Britain took the leading role in the first major process of industrialization, which started in the later eighteenth century. On the continent of Europe, but also to some degree in the United States, the response to the British example was generally characterized by a much more active role of political agency, e.g. in railway building (and subsidization), than was the case in Britain. Thus, in the first great phase, the polarization was about laissez-faire vis-à-vis the less "individualistic" parts of the West, with the non-western world little touched; the second great phase has become the "capitalistic" West vis-à-vis the more "collectivistic" "underdeveloped" areas of the world.

While on the most general level, the same framework of analysis is applicable to cases of industrialization both through governmental initiative and through private initiative, on more concrete levels there are important variations between and within each of these two major types. For example it seems clear that in the Soviet case there has been a far sharper emphasis on the authority component than in the Western cases. This has been tolerated, I am inclined to think, for three primary reasons: First, the cultural tradition of Russia, ultimately rooting in Eastern Orthodox Christianity, seems to make the exercise of sharply defined authority more tolerable than in Western Europe and the United States. Second, nationalistic interest has been very closely identified with successful industrialization and hence the whole complex of sentiments involved in nationalism has been mobilized behind it. Third, there has been the *élan* of a revolutionary movement, which was able to fuse with the nationalistic components through basing the national position of Russia on its position of leadership of the world Communist movement. Without some such fusion of components it is difficult to see how it would have been possible for the Soviet system to get over the problem of the "take-off," as Rostow calls it.

There may, however, be serious factors of instability in the Soviet case which are not readily visible. One I would particularly like to call attention to is the problem of the balance between what, above, I have called authority and regulation. It is clear that within the Soviet system organizational leadership has been heavily skewed in the direction of authority. In its relevance to industrial efficiency, as distinguished from the stability of the governmental system, the problem would seem to focus at two points. One of these is the problem of whether and how far allocation of *accounting* responsibility to the firm has, as some of Berliner's material suggests, set up a tendency for it to acquire such a large sphere of genuine managerial independence from higher authority that the authority system itself may in time be jeopardized. This is to say that an element of market freedom would have to be permitted and eventually legitimized. The second and perhaps more crucial focus is the problem of the status of highly trained technical personnel. It is likely that attempting to keep them within a rigid system of control through line authority involves serious strains. These are in part mitigated by recruiting "engineers" for administrative positions, so that the operating technical people do not feel they are being bossed by "laymen." Also I suspect that there is a good deal of informal leeway granted in actual operations. But the question remains whether this leeway will not sometime have to be institutionalized, with considerable repercussions on the general system of authority.

One more remark about the Soviet case may be in order. Apparently because of tsarist "despotism," there were remarkably few "middle-level" structures in the society which were in a position to offer serious resistance to the Soviet dictatorship. The church was already highly centralized and politicized and could almost directly be "taken over." The middle classes were weak, and, such as they were, could either be liquidated or absorbed in the new occupational system. This case stands in marked contrast to Great Britain, for instance, where the preindustrial class structure and church have remained strong and have considerably influenced the present outcome. So the main problem with respect to the old Russia seemed to be the "socialization" of the population in the values of high-productivity industrialism. Ideology and education plus a realistic opportunity of great magnitude have been the main instruments of this process, and it seems to have been highly successful. It therefore seems reasonable to suggest that the main sources of instability and change in the Soviet system should be looked for, not in the strains entailed by the problem of integration with pre-Soviet social structures, but in the internal dynamics of their type of industrial society itself, including of course not only the economy, but perhaps above all the governmental system.

A note about Japan may also be in order. Abegglen has called attention to the persistence, in middle-sized Japanese industry, of "particularistic," especially kinship-type bases of organization of the labor force, which has often been thought to be incompatible with industrialization. When such phenomena are found, I think they should be used as clues to look for other compensating factors. In Japan one of the most important of these seems to be the very high pressure to achievement which has been developed *within* the kinship context. I should therefore expect the organization of services in the Japanese economy about kinship to be more nearly compatible with industrial conditions than would be the case for all but a few other kinship systems. Even here, however, I would expect the situation described by Abegglen to be seriously unstable and to show a marked tendency to change in the more expected direction with further industrial development. The case would be partly parallel with the strains involved in the rigidity of the Soviet authority system.

I have introduced these very cursory comments on the

Soviet and Japanese cases, not in any way to claim a general understanding of them, but to illustrate that this paper's view of industrial societies is not meant to imply rigid uniformity at the empirical levels. At the same time, it is not legitimate to conclude that there are no important common elements, that an industrial economy would be compatible with *any* set of values, any institutional structure, and any governmental system. As these things go in comparative sociology, the specifications for successful industrialism are relatively narrow and definite.

SUMMARY

This paper has been concerned with the problem of what kind of *society* is compatible with an industrial economy. It first pointed out that though the focus of the characteristics of industrialism is in the economy and not in the political organization of the society, the question should not be begged of what role governmental *agency* might or might not play in the development and maintenance of such an economy. Indeed two main types of industrial society could be distinguished: the one in which the main focus of agency has been in "free enterprise" relatively independent of governmental control, and the one in which governmental agency has had primacy.

I then attempted to outline the most essential features of an industrial economy as such. With respect to the structure of the society in which such an economy exists, these features could then be said to be dependent on the economy's relations of relative compatibility with three other "primary subsystems" of the society—which I called the "cultural" system, including societal values and their internalization in personalities; the "institutional" system, referring to the institutionalized norms formulated in legal systems but also extending to private and informal levels; and the "political" system focusing, at the societal level, in government.

The most crucial noneconomic factors underlying the industrial type of economy may be classified as 1) "drive" as a cultural value, and 2) "opportunity" provided by the institutional system. There must be widespread motivation to active achievement in instrumental, "worldly" activities, essentially the type of pattern which Weber classically delineated for ascetic Protestantism, though it is now clear that Protestantism is not the only cultural base on which such a value-orientation can develop.

The institutional prerequisites center on the mobility of commodities and access to them through markets, on the mobility of the factors of production, and on effective organization for their utilization. Institutionally considered, all of these factors go back to *differentiation* relative to preindustrial institutional systems. I paid special attention here to what I called the "economic" complex of contract, property, and occupation; and the "political" complex of leadership, authority, and regulation. In both of these cases and their subtypes, the essential pattern is a dual one. On the one hand components of the institutional category which in other systems have been segregated from each other, have come to be put together in a "package." On the other hand each of the components has been differentiated out from previous "fusions" with functionally different components, such as kinship. The modern institution of property ownership is the paradigmatic case, seen on the background of feudalism. These processes of institutional differentiation have proceeded to different levels in different societies, but the general trend in relation to the industrial economy is clear.

It was possible only very briefly to call attention to the possible importance of what sociologists call the "mechanisms of social control," particularly, in this case, religion and ideology. It would be expected that cognate processes of differentiation have taken place in this field.

Finally the relevance to the industrial economy of political organization at the societal, i.e. governmental, level was dealt with very briefly. It is here that the basis of distinction between the two main types of industrial society comes to focus. I argued that the distinction has mainly, though of course not exclusively, to do with the timing of the process of industrialization. The development of industrial economies for the first time *had* to be independent of predominant governmental initiative. On the other hand, "catching up" occurs in a situation which puts a strong premium on governmental initiative, especially where a strong sense of urgency is involved. I also pointed out that not only is there this primary distinction between the types, but a good deal of variation within each, which can be described in terms of a balance between the various components which have been reviewed.

Within the limits of a single paper, the above analysis has had to select out a very limited sector of comparative considerations. It should, however, be regarded as an essay in comparative sociological analysis. Its validity therefore rests not only on its empirical correctness with reference to the facts of known industrial societies, but also on the way in which it fits into a broader scheme of comparative structural analysis which would include many nonindustrial cases. To be adequate, such a scheme must include, in my opinion, an explicit and well-analyzed evolutionary dimension. It is quite clear that no "primitive" society (defined for example as non-literate) could develop a full-fledged industrial economy. In the long run our ability to handle this type of problem will depend on the level of comparative evolutionary theory of social structures we are able to work out.

TECHNICAL NOTE

The classifications and the treatments of structural differentiation and integration employed in the above analysis all use concepts as well as illustrative references which have been widely current in the literature. My own most important single source, however, has been the system of ideal types presented by Max Weber, in *The Theory of Social and Economic Organization*. Many of the specific forms taken by the definitions and hence the ways in which distinctions are drawn, and the framework of systematization in which the concepts are fitted, are part of a more general attempt at categorizing the analysis of social systems on which I have been working. For the benefit of the reader who is interested in this more technical level of theoretical work, I shall, in this technical note, attempt very briefly to indicate the main ways in which I conceive the elements used here to fit into that more general scheme.

I conceive the structure of all social systems, however complex, to be capable of analysis in terms of the relation of structural forms to a scheme of four functional "system-problems" or dimensions, namely "pattern-maintenance," "integration," "goal-attainment" and "adaptation." Macroscopic and complex systems are characterized by these system-problems and "governed" by the structures and mechanisms organized around them, and subsystems are ordered in cognate terms at various different levels of organization and cultural generality.

Seen in these terms the economy is a subsystem of the society organized about adaptive function (Parsons and Smelser, *op. cit.*). I have therefore organized my own discussion about the problem of the interdependence of the economy with the other three primary functional subsystems of the society, the pattern-maintenance subsystem centering on values, the integrative system centering on institutional norms, and the goal-attainment system, centering on political organization and functioning. Since the emphasis of this paper is structural, I have not entered into any technical analysis of process, an analysis which I tend to attempt to categorize in terms of input-output interchanges between subsystems (Parsons and Smelser, *op. cit.,* especially Chap. II).

Furthermore, it did not seem possible, within the space

limits of the paper, to attempt to present formal classifications within the field either of the pattern-maintenance subsystem or the goal-attainment system at the operative level which is comparable to an economist's treatment of the economy. Indeed I have attempted to be formal in this sense only within the integrative system and even there only for essentially half of it. This is to say that I have not attempted to deal with the highest-level structure of institutional norms, as embodied in particular in legal systems, nor with the details of the structure of systems of social control, in the technical sense used above.

What I have done is to confine this more formal treatment to the areas of economic and political institutionalization which are most directly relevant to the functioning of the economy, what I have called the "economic" and the "political" complexes respectively. These two, in turn, I have dealt with on two different levels of classificatory breakdown. The first concerns the primary modes of integrative control with respect to the functional area in question, economic or political as the case may be, while the second concerns a cognate functional breakdown of each of the subfunctions distinguished in that way. It is these functional differentiations which provide the lines of distinction between the major structural types, and between the components of the "packages" I have discussed.

The paradigm of classification is the same in all cases. Each functional category is "governed" at the highest level by a value-system, which is a *specification* at the relevant level of generalization and of situational reference, of the general societal value system. In its relevance to a differentiated system of units, then, there is a set of norms less generalized than the values, which specify patterns of behavior expected of these units in differentiated functional contexts. These norms then in turn are differentiated by reference, along with their own integrative imperatives and their reference to the values, to each of the two primary aspects of the external situation in which they must be implemented by a unit, the definition of goals it is expected to try to attain, and the definition of expected (permitted, prescribed, prohibited) means to these goals, namely adaptive orientations. The following is a schematic representation of the classifications at the two levels:

HIGHER LEVEL OF GENERALITY

Economic complex   Political complex

A	G	A	G
Means: Property	Goal-specification: Occupation	Means: Regulation	Goal-specification: Authority
Values: Economic Rationality*	Primary Norms: Contract	Values: Organizational effectiveness*	Primary Norms: Leadership
L	I	L	I

* I did not deal with economic rationality or organizational effectiveness as values in the body of the paper. Cf. Parsons and Smelser, *op. cit.*, Chap. III.

LOWER LEVEL OF GENERALITY*

a) Economic Complex

Property

Use	Control
Valuation of Physical Facilities**	Disposal

Occupation

Task Specification	Role Specification
Valuation of Human Services**	Control of Membership Status in Organization

Economic rationality**
(valuation of the factors of production)

Valuation of control of organization**	Valuation of control of capital**
Valuation of productivity**	Valuation of control of human productive capacities**

Contract

Definition of consequences of risk & uncertainty	Definition of legitimate content of agreement
Definition of societal interest in contract**	Definition of legitimate means to assent

* For simplicity I have omitted the titular reference in each box for the classifications at this level—they remain the same as at the more general level.

** These categories were not made explicit in the body of the paper.

LOWER LEVEL OF GENERALITY

b) Political Complex

Regulation

Range or limits of discretion in definition of tasks and access to facilities	Definition of range and limits of technical role-function
Valuation of "technical contributions"	Commitment to the higher level collective interest e.g., "public interest"

Authority

Allocation budgetary resources	Allocation of organization-al responsibility
Valuation of control of membership contributions*	General powers of making binding decisions

Value of Effectiveness*
(Valuation of the factors of powers)

Valuation of collective responsibility*	Valuation of control of facilities*
Valuation of effectiveness*	Valuation of decision-making authority*

Leadership

Definition of consequences of external risk and uncertainty	Definition of collective goals leadership can strive for
Definition of societal interest in leadership*	Definition of legitimate organizational means which leadership can use

* These categories were not made explicit in the body of the paper.

Part III

STRUCTURE AND PROCESS IN POLITICAL SYSTEMS

CHAPTER V

AUTHORITY, LEGITIMATION,
AND POLITICAL ACTION

The general field usually referred to by the term, "authority" is an important meeting-ground between several of the sciences of human behavior, notably political science, sociology, and psychology. Like so many other terms in general usage it has been employed in a variety of different senses, not only by proponents of different disciplines, but within the same one. In such a situation it is often useful to attempt to analyze the different parts of the complex of social relationships with reference to which the term is used by different writers. I shall concentrate my attention on the aspects which lie on the borderline between sociology and political science.

The main problems with which this paper will be concerned involve the inter-relations between three primarily important functional aspects or imperatives of social systems, in the case of primary interest here, societies. The first of these is the way in which values and other aspects of a common culture are shared by the members, and internalized in their personalities and institutionalized in the social structure. The second concerns the ways in which these values are involved with the more differentiated social structure through particular institutions which regulate the main different relationship complexes of the society. The third concerns the way in which the system is organized for the formulation and implementation of effective collective action toward collective or "public" goals, what is usually thought of as the political aspects of the organization of the society. These three, the value aspect, the institutional aspect and the political aspect stand in complex, but, I think, relatively definite, relations to each other.

This classification of problems derives from a general classification of the structural components of social systems. The first, least differentiated level, which can be taken as an analytical point of reference for structural analysis as a whole, is the system of values which, relative to the other elements, must be formulated on a high level of generality. Values are modes of normative orientation of action in a social system which define the main directions of action without reference to specific goals or more detailed situations or structures. The second level is that of institutions. Institutions are still normative patterns, but on a less general level; they are differentiated relative to the situational exigencies and structural subdivisions of the system. Property and authority, as I shall propose to use the term, are institutional patterns or complexes. Institutions are still generalized and "regulate" action at more differentiated and particularized levels. The third level then is what I call that of collectivities. A collectivity is a concrete system of interacting human individuals, of persons in roles. The term group is applicable to at least some collectivities, but not to institutions. In common usage, even in the social sciences, the word institution is often used to designate what I shall here call a collectivity. Whatever words are employed it seems to me essential to make the distinction and keep it clear. One is a member of a collectivity, but not of an institution in my sense—thus to be a "member of property" is clearly nonsensical, but not to be a member of a university faculty. Roles, finally, are the complexes of organized participation of individuals or categories of individuals in the functioning of collectivities.

VALUES AND THE
LEGITIMATION OF ACTION

That a system of value-orientations held in common by the members of a social system can serve as the main point of reference for analyzing structure and process in the social system itself may be regarded as a major tenet of modern sociological theory. Values in this sense are the commitments of individual persons to pursue and support certain *directions* or types of action for the collectivity as a system and hence derivatively for their own roles in the collectivity. Values are, for sociological purposes, deliberately defined at a level of generality higher than that of goals—they are *directions* of action rather than specific objectives, the latter depending on the particular character of the situation in which the system is placed as well as on its values and its structure as a system. Still values (and goals) may be formulated at many different levels of generality. What level is appropriate will depend on what social system is taken as the point of reference for the analysis in question. For purposes of this paper it will be the total society, so the level of generality will be very high.

To illustrate, for contemporary American society, I assume a value system which may be called "instrumental activism." It involves an attitude of active mastery toward the empirical situation external to the society—both physical and psychological nature, and other societies—an attitude which favors increasing the level of adaptive flexibility primarily through increase of knowledge and economic production. This statement does not imply that the American social structure *as a whole* tends to be pre-eminently flexible—for example the constitution has been relatively unchanging. Economic production and knowledge do, however, serve as special instruments of flexible adaptation to changing exigencies. It avoids commitment to a specific societal goal, but is characterized by pluralism on the goal level and a commitment to indefinite generalized "progress." It is also committed to universalization of the prerequisites of valued achievement, hence to relative equality of opportunity and its realization above all through civil rights, education and health. Finally it involves a broadly pragmatic attitude toward organization and authority, accepting them when needed for specific approved goals but repudiating any suggestion of generalized hierarchical superiority.

No value system is ever perfectly internalized and institutionalized, but its status is uneven in different personalities and subcollectivities of the society. The value system does not "actualize" itself automatically but maintenance of relative control in its terms is dependent on whole series of mechanisms of institutionalization, socialization, and social control. It should be clear that using values as the initial point of reference for the structural analysis of social systems does not imply that they are the sole or even the most important *determinants* of particular structures and processes in such systems. I do not think it is useful to postulate a deep dichotomy between theories which give importance to beliefs and values on the one hand, to allegedly "realistic" interests, e.g. economic, on the other. Beliefs and values are actualized, partially and imperfectly, in realistic situations of social interaction and the outcomes are *always* codetermined by the values and the realistic exigencies; conversely what on concrete levels are called "interests" are by no means independent of the values which have been institutionalized in the relevant groups. Thus churches have "interests" just as definitely as do business firms or trade unions though of course the content is different. Marxian theory does not escape this difficulty of circularity since Marx explicitly includes what I have called institutions, e.g., in the form of the law of property, in the "relations of production."

Another problem of interpretation which may be raised relative to this type of theory concerns the stability of values relative to change. In recent discussion value has come to be an overpopular term and there has been a tendency to use it simply as a label for any fairly general type of behavior— thus if people tend to seek security more than in the recent past, the values are said to have changed in the direction of greater security-seeking. This is similar to the uses of the term instinct a generation ago. I do not wish to quarrel over definitions but here I use the term "value" in a technical sense for the *most general directional commitment of persons to action in a social system.* Its content and level of generality are technically defined *relative* to the system of reference. In these terms "change of the value of a social system" has a special technical meaning. Adaptive or equilibrating proc- esses in general do *not* involve change of values, nor does the process of structural differentiation, e.g. most social change in the United States broadly in the last century. If the value system in our technical sense changes it means a profound change in *type* of system. Analysis of such changes involves special problems of technical theory and is not to be equated with "social change" in the most generalized sense.

THE GROUNDING OF
SOCIAL VALUES

I have suggested above that values are in the first instance commitments of the individual personality—they are in some sense ways for him to live with his fellows in society. As such they must be "grounded" in three main directions, first in his *existential beliefs* about the world, second in his own *motivational needs* as a personality and third in his relations to others in the society. On the level of belief the "justifi- cation" of values leads beyond empirical knowledge and roots in the realms of religion and philosophy. The existen- tial propositions which men invoke to answer what Max Weber called the "problems of meaning," the more or less ultimate answers to questions on *why* they should live the way they do and influence others to do so, may thus be called the field of the *justification* of values.

There is, however, also the dimension of "meaning" of values which concerns their integration in the individual personality, their relation to the balance of gratification and deprivation, of personal fulfillment or frustration involved in living up to professed values or failing to do so. This relation may, somewhat tritely, be called the *motivation* of values or value-commitments.

Finally, the third "grounding" of a personal value system is in the social context, the network of rights and obligations in which an individual's value-commitment involves him in his social situation, and which the sharing or nonsharing of his values with others implies. This context, so far as it involves values which can be said to be *common* to the members of a social system, I would like to call that of the *legitimation* of social action.

Legitimation in this sense is the *appraisal of action in terms of shared or common values in the context of the involvement of the action in the social system*. It is a value-reference at what is clearly a very high level of generality, and is as such applicable to any mode or type of action in the social system. It also operates through many different kinds of mechanisms and modes of symbolization.

As I see it legitimation is the primary link between values as an internalized component of the personality of the individual, and the institutionalized patterns which define the structure of social relationships. As an operative process in social systems, legitimation in this sense is not a simple entity the content and strength of which depends only on the nature of the values themselves; it is rather a function of several variables. These variables are, first, the value-content itself, second, the nature and solidity of the cognitive justification involved, third, the mode and order of internalization of the values in personalities, i.e., of their motivation, and fourth, the nature of the situation in which the actor who accepts some kind of commitment to the values is placed in the social system in which he undertakes to implement them.

It may be well to illustrate these points. It may, thus, sometimes be that the justification factor of legitimation is most prominent in some cases where commitment to the relevant values is directly linked with highly explicit transcendental religious beliefs, for example, on the part of the early Puritans. To a psychologically sophisticated observer, however, often in such cases the very emotional vehemence of the adherents of such beliefs (and often currently those of such beliefs as Communism) suggests an insecurity of motivational grounding—the adherents "protest too much." Again it is one thing to be committed to implementation of a value when the situation presents a fairly favorable opportunity of success and when, on the other hand, it is realistically hopeless that anything but martyrdom could ensue from a serious attempt. From the present point of view, "counting the cost" is definitely an aspect of legitimation, though how heavily the cost will be weighed will depend on the particular value-content. Legitimation thus is the set of criteria by reference to which "adherence" to a pattern of values is translated *by the individual* into implementing action—it is, that is to say, the *action* rather than the values themselves, which is legitimated. It is important to understand that action can, however, be legitimated on a variety of different levels of generality—all the way from highly specific acts to the most general directions of action over a lifetime, and involvement in a total society.

The *functions* of legitimation are here defined with reference to the pattern of values itself. The process of legitimation is the bridge by which values are joined to the differentiated subsystems of action and to the situations in which action takes place, looked at from the point of view of the degree to which, and the mechanisms by which, the values can be understood to play a part in the empirical regulation of action. The determination of this degree is, in a concrete case, *always* an empirical question and must never be assumed on a priori grounds.

LEGITIMATION AND
INSTITUTIONALIZATION

The primary reference point for the linkage of values through legitimation with the structure of the social system is *institutionalization*. This I conceive to be a category for the analysis of social systems as such, whereas both values and legitimation are more general than that and apply to *any* systems of action, including cultures, personalities and, in certain ways, organisms.

Institutions are generalized patterns of norms which define *categories* of prescribed, permitted and prohibited behavior in social relationships, for people in interaction with each other as members of their society and its various subsystems and groups. They are always *conditional* patterns in some sense. *If* you occupy a certain status in a social group or relationship, and *if* certain types of situations arise, you are expected to behave in certain ways with respect to these three "P's." Institutions as such incorporate what I have called "value-content." That is to say, they incorporate *legitimated directionality* of behavior. But they also do more than this. They *relativize* rights and obligations to status in the social system, and to the structure of the situation in which persons of a given status are placed, and they define and legitimate *sanctions*, i.e., types of consequences of the action of an individual, "intentionally" (which need not mean consciously or deliberately) imposed by the actions of others in reaction to the person's own. Sanctions, of course, being conditional, may be anticipated and hence within limits may control behavior through motivating the avoidance of negative and the securing of positive sanctions.

Values define, as I have suggested, a broad direction of

action. They do not, however, tell the individual what to do in a given situation; they are too general. When values are institutionalized, statuses and situations are differentiated, and differentiated and graduated sanctions, positive and negative, are attached to them. Conformity with *different* institutional expectations, and different *degrees* of conformity and infraction of the same ones, are ascribed to different categories of statuses and roles in the social system.

Values, as such, are undifferentiated with respect to the internal structure of the social system. A person's values are the same, i.e., are definable and describable, independent of who he is in social status terms, of what situations he faces, and what are the probable consequences of different alternatives of his action for him.

Institutions, on the other hand, are differentiated in the first instance with reference to function in the social system. They define the situation for, and regulate, collective life and, relative to the same shared value system, permit, prohibit, and prescribe different types of action for different parts of a functionally differentiated system. Thus we may speak of complexes of institutional patterns as regulating all the major functional contexts and group structures of a social system, economic, political, integrative, educational, cultural, etc.

Authority, for my particular purposes, I shall define as a category of institutionalization, not one of legitimation as defined above, nor of what below, on a somewhat more concrete level, I shall call "authorization." As such it is cognate with such categories as contract and property. Perhaps a brief delineation of these concepts will be helpful in approaching that of the institution of authority. In a society with a widely ramified division of labor there is an immense network of continually shifting contractual arrangements. The terms of these arrangements are settled *ad hoc* in each particular case by agreement of the parties. But in the concrete structure of the social relationship involved in a contractual relation there is more than the *ad hoc* agreement of the parties; there is a set of socially defined expectations and norms as to what *kinds* of agreements may or may not be made, what means may be employed in securing the other party's consent, how the interests of third parties may affect the agreement, what will happen if, for various reasons, one of the parties fails to fulfill his obligations, and the like. It is norms and expectations on this more general level, which underlie any particular contract, which Durkheim called the *institution* of contract.

Contract, like other institutions is, in a differentiated society, in general, partly defined and enforced by legal process. Thus some types of agreements are clearly approved by law and interpretable and enforceable at law; others, while not prohibited are declared *ultra vires* so that legal sanctions may not be invoked; still others, like those involving slavery, are explicitly prohibited. The essential point, for present purposes, is the existence of a system of relatively general norms which regulate the entering into, and the consequences of, contractual agreements, but which do not prescribe either that any given persons should enter into any given agreements under given circumstances, or, within the institutional limits, what the content of such agreements should be.

The institution of property is a cognate set of norms regulating the relations of persons, individual and corporate, to objects of possession which have economic value. They involve the definition of types of rights of use, control, and acquisition or disposal, with reference to such nonsocial objects. Though in the first instance a set of rights and obligations with reference to nonsocial objects, property always involves and helps to define social relationships in that the right of any actor in relation to an object entails at the very least the obligations of others to respect that right and, conversely, the basis of the obligations of property is the impingement of the owner's rights on the rights of others. It is the social relationship aspect which is at the focus of the *institution* of property.

Authority, similarly, I think of as an institutionalized complex of norms which do not involve the prescription, permission, or prohibition of *particular* acts, but which on a general level define the conditions under which, in the given social structure, and in given statuses and situations within it, acts of others within the same collectivity *may* be prescribed, permitted, or prohibited. In order to say more it is necessary to discuss what I refered to above as the political aspect of a social system.

POLITICAL STRUCTURE
AND PROCESS

It seems to me that what are very generally called the political processes of social systems need to be dealt with in relation to the two different levels of the structure of social systems referred to above, which unfortunately often are not discriminated in the literature either of political science, or of sociology. One is the level of institutions in the sense I have just been discussing, the other is that of *government* as involving a specific complex of *collectivities,* of organizations in which specific decisions are made and specific administrative tasks carried out. The distinction is one which runs throughout the analysis of the structure and functioning of social systems. Thus, property and contract concern the institutional level of the structure of economic function in societies, while the structure of business firms, and of markets which articulate them with each other and the like, concern the collectivity level. Property and contract are not types of firm, and similarly, authority, in my usage, is not a branch or agency of government.

If I may continue with the parallel between economic and political categories, what economists call the *economy* is a functional subsystem of the society—not, as such, a "structure," which primarily *articulates* the institutional and collectivity levels of the organization of social action in this field. An economy is the set of processes by which, *within* a framework of institutional norms, the mobilization of the factors of production, e.g., through employment and investment, and their commitment to the production of goods and services, are carried out. Collectivities are the active instrumentalities of these processes—and, of course, individuals *in their roles* in collectivities. The purely "individual" producer, e.g., the independent artisan, may, from this point of view be treated as the limiting case of a one-man firm. For relatively refined purposes, it is also important to distinguish the *plant* as the collective organization engaged in *physical production* from the *firm* as the superordinate organization concerned with the mobilization and commitment of the factors of production and the disposal of the product through the market mechanism.

Parallel to the economy, in this sense, I believe that we can speak of a functional subsystem of the society in the political area, conveniently referred to as the "polity." The goal or function of the economy is *production;* in the economic, not the physical sense, the product is income or wealth. The goal or function of the polity I conceive to be the mobilization of societal resources and their commitment for the attainment of *collective* goals, for the formation and implementation of "public policy." The "product" of the polity as a system is *power,* which I would like to define as the *generalized capacity of a social system to get things done in the interest of collective goals.* Again collectivities are the active instrumentalities of these processes, operating within an institutional framework. Primarily, but by no means exclusively, in the political case, it is the network of collectivities we call government which constitute such instrumentalities. It is through such collectivities that resources are mobilized and, through the decision-making process, committed to goals, and then the "product" is distributed to the ultimate beneficiaries.

A brief word should be said about the concept of power used here. It seems to me that it is one of the two principal alternatives which are current in the literature of political theory, the other being what may be called the "zero-sum" concept as used, for example, by Max Weber and by H. D. Lasswell. This is the conception that power is the capacity of one unit in a system to gain its ends *over the opposition* of other units—hence if the power of two units is equal there is a stalemate between them. The concept I am using here does not make opposition a criterion as such, though since I am talking about capacity to attain goals, it *includes* the overcoming of opposition. I thus consider the zero-sum concept to be a special case of the more general concept employed here.

Power and wealth have in comon that they are both generalized categories of "means," i.e., of "capacities" to get desired things done. They differ in that though production as such is a collective value, the product, wealth (or income), has no specific reference to *collective goals,* it is a means to *any* goals valued in the society. Power, on the other hand, has specific reference to the goals of the collectivity, and hence implies, for its generation, *integration* of the collectivity with reference to such goals, in a sense which production of wealth does not.

Our immediate concern, then, is with the institutional framework within which power is produced and allocated in a social system, which sets the main norms which must be observed in the process. In coming a little closer to the problem it may be noted that, though in one connection institutions constitute the "spelling out" of values for the more differentiated contexts of social action, in another, institutions constitute the primary focus of the *integration* of a social system. It is only by virtue of institutionalized norms that internal conflict can be held within tolerable limits and that different units of the social structure can be channeled into mutually supportive relations with each other.

Ever since Hobbes, if not much longer, it has been acutely realized that power was a central focus of the integration problem in societies. If a social system is to be stable, the circumstances under which power can be generated, thus "acquired" and allocated, cannot be left unregulated by institutional mechanisms, as well as, on occasion, by overt goal-directed collective action.

POLITICAL INSTITUTIONS:
THE PLACE OF AUTHORITY

Authority I conceive to be part of a wider complex of institutionalization in social systems with reference to power and to political function. The broadest category of political institutions, from which more specific ones may be derived, may be called "differential responsibility" or "leadership." By this I mean that it is a general feature of the institutionalized structure of a social system that responsibility for the effective performance of all functions in the system is not diffusely spread among all statuses in it. In one sense, the division of labor results in differential responsibility in that, *de facto,* different groups assume different specialized functions. But what I have in mind now goes beyond this in one respect in that there comes to be differential responsibility for effective performance of functions which are held to be, for the system in question, "affected with a public interest," i.e., for *collective* goals.

Differential responsibility, in this sense, is an aspect of what sociologists call, "social stratification." The reference, however, is not to stratification in general but is political, namely, to the achievement of collective goals where positive action binding the collectivity and its members is necessary. It is theoretically possible, and in limiting cases in small groups approximated, for all members effectively to bear equal responsibility in such matters, but, in general, and the more so the larger the system, there are fundamental factors making for inequality. Though these are in general familiar, the importance of clarity of decision, range of planning in temporal and subject-matter terms, and symbolization of consensus may be mentioned among the reasons why differential responsibility has a great advantage over too great equalization. On the negative side, it is crucial that any social system, the more so the more complex and larger it is, involves many interests and functions which, in the nature of the case, are distributive rather than central in relevance and are hence decentralized in operation. This means that persons and organizations which specialize in such functions, e.g., much of economic production or simply family living, *cannot* to the same degree specialize in taking the responsibility of leadership in public affairs.

As a very broad historical generalization it can be said that while in earlier civilizations (as distinguished from primitive societies) political responsibility has tended to be institutionalized in the hands of general upper classes or aristocracies, in modern Western society, at least the trend has been in the direction of its coming into the hands of groups with more or less of an occupational character, e.g., "politicians" and civil and military "servants." There is no longer the presumption either that, by virtue of aristocratic status, disproportionate political influence and responsibility will follow as a matter of course, or vice versa, that the politically responsible, influential, or powerful will automatically control all important functions in the society. Of course, imperatives of integration necessitate important relations between the responsible elements in different sectors of a society, but these are not of a simple character.

Differential leadership responsibility in relation to collective goals seems to me to be for the political reference, the parallel, of contract for the economic. Contract is, in proportion to the elaboration of the division of labor, the general institutional framework within which access to the factors of production, and to markets for the disposal of products, is regulated in a society; it is above all the framework which defines the relations of an organizational unit in the productive process to the structured social environment in which it operates. Similarly, differential responsibility is the general framework within which the rights and obligations of leadership, with reference to collective goals, is regulated in a society. Above all it defines the relations of the organizations and roles specializing in performing this type of function in the society to their social environment, the kinds of terms on which they may secure access to the necessary resources, and the kinds of relations they may establish with the recipients of their services.

In the economic case, contract, as the most general institutional category, divides into two main branches or subtypes according to the two most fundamental types of resources employed in production, namely, social and nonsocial. The one branch, through the contract of employment, leads to the complex we speak of as institutions of occupational status and role, and regulates through this the utilization of human services in the productive process. The other, through the contract of investment, leads over into the complex we call the institution of property and regulates the utilization of nonhuman or nonsocial factors in production —of course, at various levels of economic generalization from concrete materials and equipment to purely monetary resources.

I would like to suggest a conception of authority which defines it as one of the two parallel subtypes of institutionalized leadership responsibility, namely, that parallel with employment and the occupational complex. From this point of view, authority would be the complex of institutionalized rights to control the actions of members of the society with reference to their bearing on the attainment of collective goals. That the bearers of differential responsibility should have such rights—differing of course in kind and degree in different cases—is a necessary condition of fulfillment of the expectations defining that responsibility. It goes back to the central point that integration of the collectivity through support of leadership is one of the most central of these conditions. Authority, from this point of view, is the institutionalization of given modes and levels of integration of the collectivity so far as these are essential conditions of effective and legitimized collective action. It is the institutionalization of the rights of "leaders" to expect *support* from the members of the collectivity.

The second main branch or subtype of differential responsibility, I would like to call responsibility for *regulation* of the activities of persons and collectivities with reference to their bearing on the public interest. This is parallel with the contract of investment and the institutional complex of property. I say parallel and not identical because the line of discrimination here is not that between the utilization of social (or human) and nonsocial resources, but is that of the bearing of action on the attainment of collective goals as distinguished from activities which, though in accord and societal values, do not bear directly on political interests in this sense. Leadership, or politically responsible elements, must be in a position to influence such activities with respect to their bearing on the public interest and implement institutional rules which define the requisite borderlines.

There is a common ambiguity in the phrase "public interest" to which attention should be called. On the one hand it may refer to the interest of the social system in the sense of being in accord with the values of the system in relation to its situation—in this sense, for example, sound family life is "in the public interest." But this is, in a society like ours, a peculiarly "private" sphere and severe limits are imposed on the rights of public authority to intervene in family affairs. The other meaning of public interest is the specifically political one, in the sense of the present discussion, namely, having to do with the attainment of collective goals as such. It is in this latter sense that the concept is used here.

Because of the very great prominence of economic production in the activities of American society, it is with reference to this context that the concept, "regulation" has come to be most familiar, indeed that from which its prototype has been taken for purposes of the present discussion. The distinction between authority and regulation is, at the societal level, essentially that between "public" and "private" spheres of interest.

As in the case of any other institution, a pattern of authority will be defined by reference to the four criteria which were outlined above, namely: (1) legitimation in terms of the general values of the society, (2) status in the system of roles or collectivities to which it is applied, (3) the type of situation with which authority-bearers are expected to be faced, and (4) the sanctions which, on the one hand, are at their disposal, on the other hand, can be brought to bear by others in relation to their action.

The values of the society will define the main framework of attitudes toward the attainment of collective goals, the broad types of goals to which commitment is likely to be made, and the degree of legitimized "activism" with reference to such goals. Responsibility for leadership will then be the focus of the claim to authority as a condition of implementing that responsibility. But a third variable will be the type of situation with reference to which authority is expected to be exercised and, finally, authority will differ according to the types of sanctions which are at the disposal of its holders, and the types of counteraction with which they may be expected to have to cope, which are sanctions looked at from the obverse point of view. (This is the point at which questions concerning the use of coercive sanctions, particularly physical force, become relevant.)

MAX WEBER'S
TYPES OF AUTHORITY

It seems to me that all four of these variables need to be taken into account in working out a general classification of types of authority. It is important to note that Max Weber's famous classification dealt with only *one* of them, namely, the bearing of the general values of the society through the processes I have called those of legitimation. It may be worth while to try to state where Weber's three categories fit in terms of the present analytical scheme.

There is an important sense in which the concept of *traditional* authority constitutes the base line of Weber's analysis. This seems to me to be very nearly identical with what I have called "diffuse differential responsibility," in a social system where differential responsibility in the political context has not been differentiated from generally superior status. Such authority may exist, as Weber says, by virtue of a "traditional status," but not necessarily so. The limits to this authority are not confined to a clearly defined context of political functions; there are certain spheres within which there are clearly expected rights to act, and beyond these, a diffuse sphere within which loyalty on a particularistic basis of generally superior status is expected. Though there is no formally defined administrative structure segregated from nonpolitical functions, one may say that the limits of this loyalty are essentially those of acceptability or belongingness in the requisite collectivity of reference. Barnard's well known criterion applies here; defiance of authority is essentially a bid to take over the responsibility of the agent of authority. The outcome of successful resistance to such a bid is, if the defiance is persisted in, extrusion of the bidder from the collectivity—perhaps by the route of execution.

Weber's other two types deviate from the more diffuse character of traditional authority in two directions. The rational-legal type is the consequence of a process of *differ-*

entiation of political from nonpolitical functions in the social system. Authority then no longer rests in a diffusely superior status bearing differential responsibility but in a positively delineated set of powers or rights to exercise *political* responsibility in the social system. The focus of this functional differentiation or delineation is the concept of *office* whch is marked off from general social superiority in nonpolitical respects. The institution of office has this significance even though there is a realistic correlation between incumbency of office and the enjoyment of high status in other respects such as lineage or wealth. Weber, it will be noted, does not distinguish what have here been called authority and regulation, but throws them together as both legally regulated.

Charismatic authority deviates from traditional not by a further process of structural differentiation in the system, but by throwing the legitimacy of the traditional (i.e., institutionalized) status-order into question. The charismatic leader stands in some relevant respects in explicit opposition to the traditional order; he sets his "personal" legitimation over against the institutionalized basis. But the claim is still one in terms of legitimacy; as Weber says, acceptance of charismatic authority is treated by the leader as a matter of moral obligation.

If this analysis is acceptable, it can be concluded that Weber's classification is not one of types of legitimation in terms of different types of values, but, on the one hand, of level of differentiation of the social system with reference to political function and, on the other, of stability of institutionalization of the value system in this respect. Variations which are a function of type of values then, would be expected to be analytically independent of Weber's classification and could be applied to *any* of his three types. It would lead too far afield to attempt to work out here a classification of authority types in terms of values, and of the other three of the four variables outlined above, but this seems to be both an urgent task for the further development of political sociology and one which it is feasible to approach.

LAW AND INSTITUTIONS

The above discussion, and, in particular, the reference to Weber's category of rational-legal authority, raises the question of the relations of law in general to institutions in the sociological sense, and to the institutionalization of authority in particular. My view is that law, or legal process, is a set of mechanisms which operate with respect to *all* categories of institutions in a society in which law itself is institutionalized. It is not, in terms of content, specific to any particular category of institutions. It does, however, have a special relation to the political function in the society since two essential functions of a legal system, the definition of the scope of jurisdiction, and the authorization and implementation of sanctions, inevitably involve political references.

Institutions, I have suggested, have primarily integrative functions in social systems. But as normative patterns they do not operate automatically—to suggest that they did would impute a kind of animistic magic to them. To be legitimized they must be authoritatively interpreted with reference to more general canons of legitimacy. The mutual consistency of norms in a system requires continual adjustment by action directly oriented to such problems since in terms of content the normative system is continually changing. Further, institutional norms must be applied in detailed and particular situations, and the range of sanctions of enforcement must be defined. In advanced societies, legal processes are specially concerned with these functions.

Law is that aspect of the machinery for the definition and implementation of institutional norms which links legitimation through authoritative interpretation with application and enforcement by political agency. Enforcing agencies are not in a strict sense part of the legal system (considered as a subsystem of social action, not of formulated rules) itself at all, but are part of the political organization. Law-enforcement, that is, is a political function. The focus of the legal system is to be found in the courts which are interstitial between political and nonpolitical systems in a sense parallel to that in which political parties are interstitial between government and the "public." The private legal profession is still another interstitial structure which is even less "political" than are the courts, mediating between the judicial processes and the interests of clients.

Seen in these terms, the legal definition of the content and limits of authority becomes an imperative necessity in a society in which functional differentiation has reached high levels. The effect of such differentiation is, as noted, the creation of a whole complex of interests and structures, which cannot be mainly concerned with the implementation of the collective goals of the social system as a whole, but, in this frame of reference, have various bases of legitimation as "private" spheres. The basis for this legitimation is, of course, the values held in common in the society, but the effect of this *must* be to limit the rights of public authority to "interfere" with these interests. The relative specification of the authority of persons and collectivities, defined as carrying differential responsibility, is a direct consequence of the institutionalization of obligatons for the performance of nonpolitical functions in the society. The development of a legal system is thus a major requirement if the society is to reach levels of social differentiation where nonpolitical functions acquire, and can count on, institutionalized rights as well as obligations, in the performance of their jobs. Similar considerations, of course, apply to the importance of legal definition of many other institutional pattern-complexes such as contract, property, employment, and many others.

For perspective, it is important to be aware that law is only one of several mechanisms involved in the operation of

institutional complexes in a complex society. Political processes also operate in this field since, in general, securing
observance of institutional norms is taken to be a goal of
the society. It is in this category that the law-enforcement
functions of political bodies should be placed. But there are
also very important processes which operate, within institutional and legal frameworks, to be sure, but not directly as
legal or as political process. Some of these involve relatively
specialized and directly institutionalized processes as in the
therapeutic treatment of illness, some aspects of religion, of
education, and of family functioning. These, in turn, shade
over into "informal" mechanisms and processes. The sociologist tends to sum up both types of extra-legal process as
"mechanisms of social control."

THE GENERALIZATION OF
INSTITUTIONAL PATTERNS

For purposes of the present analysis, attention has been
focused on the total society. Authority has been treated as a
political institution, on this level, and its relation to law,
stated in broad terms. The generalized analytical scheme
employed, however, is not confined in its relevance to this
level but is meant to be applicable to *any* social system. All
social systems, that is, have integrative problems which are
the focus of processes of institutionalization of values, and all
social systems are differentiated to some extent with reference to the pursuit of collective goals. Hence, it should
follow that authority, or an institutional phenomenon cognate with it, should be a feature not only of the societies in
their political aspect, but of all social systems. By definition,
however, any social system other than a society is a subsystem
of a society. Hence the question arises of the relation between the authority patterns on the highest societal level, i.e.,
those defining its political structure, in the sense we have
discussed it, and on other levels.

The same general principles may be employed in approaching this question as have been used above. The values of a society operate not only at the most general level, but permeate its structure as a whole. Every subsystem has a value system of its own which is a differentiated and specialized version of the general value system, limited by the level and functions of the subsystem in the whole. It is an imperative of cultural integration that there should be a relative pattern-congruence at these different levels. But there must also be differentiation and specification appropriate to the particular subsystem.

When subvalues are institutionalized as such, they, in turn, legitimate subinstitutions which, in turn, are differentiated in relation to the structure and situation of the subsystem in question, and of the requisite categories of roles within it. Thus, we would have variations in mode of legitimation, in the statuses of role-performers within the system, in their situations, and in the institutionalization of sanctions.

In these terms every subsystem within the society has its patterns of authority because on its own level every subsystem has political functions and differential political responsibility. But these will differ for different types of subsystems within the society, by the various criteria by which authority-patterns can and do vary. One of these is the type of function of the subsystem in the larger society. Thus, authority in a military organization under direct political control is naturally different from that in a business firm or in a university. A second basis of variation is the size and scope of the subsystem or collectivity. Thus, a family not only has special functions but it is a small group with a necessarily limited level of structural differentiation. Hence, authority in it must be linked with the diffuse responsibility of the two adult members vis-à-vis their children, in a way in which this need not be the case in a more highly differentiated system. Degree of formalization of authority is linked to, but not identical with, degree of differentiation. In very large and highly differentiated private organizations there is not only conrol through the societal legal system, but there develops something very like a legal system for the organization as such.

When, therefore, the whole ramified structure of institutions in a society and its subsystems is looked at, it is a differentiated hierarchy of permissions, prescriptions, and prohibitions such that the higher level prescribes the limits within which the lower and more differentiated ones may operate. For any given subsystem the relation may be conveniently stated in terms of what is often referred to as the distinction between the "external" and the "internal" systems. In its external relations, i.e., its relations with other subsystems of the larger system, a subsystem of a collectivity is subject to the institutionalized order of the system superordinate to it in the structural hierarchy. For example, a business firm is subject to laws of incorporation, of contract, property, and employment, in its operations in relation to other units through markets and the like. In its internal relations, within institutionalized limits, it can create its own order, its own pattern of authority, rules of property, and the like.

Internal relations are not, however, institutionalized only through the setting of limits to the range of private variability. There is also direct "authorization" of certain types of functions and hence requirements imposed on those who participate in them. A striking example is the generalization of the institution of incorporation in modern societies. The general point is that in many spheres where private agencies undertake socially significant functions in the context of large scale organization which involves complex property relations and organization of personnel with many different types of competence, there is a strong tendency to adopt the corporate form. But this, essentially, is a delegation of *public* authority to a private group, which, in exchange for the privileges of incorporation, places it in a position of fiduciary responsibility for which it is publicly accountable. It is, of course, notable that extension of the corporate form beyond the governmental and ecclesiastical spheres on a considerable scale is a relatively recent thing.

AUTHORITY AND AUTHORIZATION

I have discussed authority in this paper as a phenomenon on the *institutional* level of the structure of social systems and carefully discriminated that from the level of collectivity functioning. In order to round out the picture I would like very briefly to indicate what seems to me to be the cognate concept for the operation of the collectivity as such. This is what I shall mean by *authorization*.

Authority, like other categories of institutionalization, has been defined here independently of any particular goals of the system though very definitely in relation to the goal-attainment *function*. Put a little differently, it is an essential *prerequisite* of the decision-making process in a social system, but not, as such, part of it. An institution is oriented to a general type or *category* of situation, decision-making to a *specific* situation. By authorization, then, I mean that aspect of the process of collective decision-making by which organs or agencies of the collectivity in question, whose status is defined by a given type and extent of authority, are given permission to use this authority in particular situations with reference to particular goals. For purposes of defining the concept, it is indifferent whether the process of authorization involves specification of goals or of measures to be taken to implement a goal. Further, systems may differ according to the degree to which, and occasions on which, authorization is necessary for various types of action.

A classic instance of what I mean here by authorization is one aspect of the function of the legislature relative to the executive in modern governments. Within limits, the executive has authority to act in the light of the exigencies of the situation and to use its authority over implementing agencies and the public to carry out its policy, independently of any decision-making process outside its own branch. But there are other areas in a system like ours, such as the assessment of new taxes, where specific legislative authorization is necessary before the executive action of revenue-collection and expenditure can take place. A military example may also be cited. A commander in the field in general has authority over the units under his command to order them into combat without their consent in the specific case. But he may still require authorization from a higher echelon, e.g., the General Staff, before issuing a particular order of this sort.

The word "authority" has, in general usage, been ambiguous on this point. Sometimes it has meant what is here called institutionalized authority to do certain *kinds* of things with or without specific authorization and, on the other hand, sometimes it has meant permission or prescription to take specific action with reference to the exigencies of a specific situation. Whatever the terms chosen, it seems to me to be important to distinguish these two levels of reference in analyzing the functioning of social systems in pursuit of collective goals.

CONCLUSION

This paper has attempted, in an exceedingly brief compass, to canvass a range of related analytical problems in the theory of social systems which bear particularly on the definition and use of terms in the borderline area between political science and sociology. The most important general aims of the paper have been, first, to discriminate three important levels on which the analysis of social systems can be developed and, second, to locate more precisely than is sometimes done the *political* aspect of social system function relative to others, notably the economic.

The three levels of reference for the analysis of social

systems are values, institutions, and collectivities, respectively. Values, it was suggested, define broad *directions* of orientation of the members of a system, independent of the specific content of system structure, situation or goals. Institutions are normative patterns defining categories of expected (prescribed, permitted, or prohibited) action on the part of persons situated in different statuses in the system, in different situations, and commanding, and subject to, different sanctions. Collectivities, on the other hand, are concrete groups or organizations of persons in roles engaged in activities which have some sort of functional significance in the system of which they are parts.

It was also suggested that the political aspect of any social system concerned its organization and functioning with reference to the processes of facilitating and implementing the attainment of goals imputed to the system as a whole, i.e., collective goals. In a differentiated society, political action is concentrated in a complex of collectivities which we usually refer to as government, but is subject to control through a complex of institutionalized patterns. The generation of power and the formulation and implementation of collective goals and policies are the principal political functions. The formulation of societal values, however, is not as such a political function.

In this connection we suggest usages for three terms which are frequently employed in this general connection. 1) The term, "legitimation," we suggest, may refer to the main link between values and their "spelling out" in the context of the institutional level of the regulation of action. An institutional pattern, that is, is legitimized in terms of the underlying values of the social system. 2) The term, "authority," we suggest, may be appropriately used to designate a particular *class of institutional pattern* of primary relevance to the normative control of political functions in a social system, namely, that where persons or offices bearing differential political responsibility (in a society as a whole or some subsystem of it) are held to be entitled to receive support, or to promote certain types of integration of the system in relation to collective goals, i.e., including the prescription and enforcement by sanctions of certain types of co-operation in promoting the goals and/or the prohibition of certain types of interference with such activity. Finally 3), the term "authorization" seems appropriate to designate the process by which, through decision-making within a collectivity, certain types of measures relative to particular situations and goals are permitted, prescribed, or enjoined which, without that decision process, would not be within the "authority" of the relevant agencies.

It is furthest from the intention of this paper to be dogmatic about definitions of terms. Terminology in this area is not standardized and no one is entitled to legislate a particular usage. What is important is to take cognizance of substantive analytical problems of the order of those which have been reviewed, and, in practice, to avoid confusion between the different problems and levels of analysis.

CHAPTER VI

THE DISTRIBUTION OF POWER
IN AMERICAN SOCIETY

I

It has been remarked that it is relatively rare, in the United States at least, for social scientists to attempt interpretive analyses of major aspects of the total society in which they live. This is particularly true of sociologists, unlike economists, who have made notable attempts in recent years to interpret their societies—for example, Schumpeter's *Capitalism, Socialism and Democracy* and Galbraith's *American Capitalism.* The main exception is Robin M. Williams whose *American Society* is excellent. If for this reason alone, Professor Mills's book, *The Power Elite,* which must be understood as one of a series as yet far from complete, would be worthy of serious attention.

In the nature of the case, to produce such a study is a very difficult enterprise. However operationally useful precise data may be—and Mr. Mills makes copious and, with some exceptions, relatively good use of them—they cannot suffice for a full empirical grounding of interpretive conclusions, not only because on their own level they are fragmentary and incomplete, but because many of the crucial empirical questions arise on a level at which available operational procedures are not of much or any use. This is not in the least to say that observation is not feasible, but rather that it cannot be precise observation in the usual operational sense.

I am referring to questions of the type which are central to Mr. Mills' argument, as to whether and in what sense a relatively small group of the occupants of "command posts" in the society has acquired a paramount position of power, as to whether the relative power of such a group has greatly increased in the last twenty years, as to how unified such a group is, and the like.

There are technical ways of reducing the element of arbitrariness in such judgments and protecting them against at least the grosser sorts of ideological distortion. Checking against all the available precise data is one such method; viewing the problem from the perspective given by wide and deep knowledge, not only of our own society but of others, is another. But I think the most important is exercising control through the use of a relatively well-integrated and technical theoretical scheme. Undertaking as a professional sociologist to review Mr. Mills' book, I am motivated largely by the opportunity to test some of his main conclusions against expectations derived from a type of technical theory that is at best only partially shared by the author of the book. In these terms I wish to take serious issue with Mr. Mills' position on a number of very important points and to outline an alternative interpretation of what I take to be the salient facts of the situation. There are some points at which I differ from Mills on simple questions of fact, but for the most part my criticisms will deal with empirical generalizations and their theoretical background.* These generalizations concern not only the facts he chooses to state and emphasize but others he omits or treats as unimportant.

What is the gist of Mills' argument? I am able here to give only a very brief summary. The reader should not depend on this review alone for his information about the contents of the book itself, but should go directly to Mills' own statement of his case.

* Mr. Mills is clearly writing only partly for an audience of technical social scientists. Though my own argument will be largely based on considerations of technical theory, I shall not introduce explicit justification of my theoretical judgments into this review, but will try to state my case in relatively non-technical terms.

Mills' central theme is the contention—in contrast to what he refers to as the traditional view of the political pluralism of American society—that there has developed to an unprecedented degree, in the last generation or so, a concentration of power in the hands of a small, relatively tightly integrated group of people. These are defined as the people occupying the institutional "command posts" of the society, the places where the decisions are made that have the greatest immediate and direct influence on the course of events in the society and on the shaping of its future and that of the rest of the world, so far as that future is dependent on what happens in the United States. Mills argues that the power of this group has grown disproportionately to the growth in size and power of the society as a whole.

The "command posts" in question are centered in large-scale organizations, which are certainly a prominent feature of American society. The power elite are in general those who occupy the decision-making positions in these large organizations. Mills identifies these in only two basic areas, business and government—although for his purposes the field of government is subdivided into the military and the political sectors; indeed, he almost tends to treat the military as independent of the rest of government. He clearly is thinking of the centralized type of organization where a few "top executives" exercise the main immediate decision-making power, in contrast to the democratic association with a somewhat more decentralized structure of authority and influence. It seems to be largely on this ground that he contends that the executive branch of the federal government has gained a pronounced ascendancy over the legislative. He relegates Congress—even the most influential group of Senators—to what he calls the "middle level" of the power structure; such people do not belong to the "power elite."

Mills broadly identifies the power elite with the "upper class." But he does not agree with Lloyd Warner and his group that the primary element of this upper class is a hered-

itary group of families or lineages; its position clearly
depends on occupational status, though there is also emphasis
on the importance within it of the "very rich," the majority
of whom have inherited their wealth. Contrary to most
sociological usage, Mills restricts the term "class" to an
economic meaning, so that by "upper class" he means, essentially, the rich. But this still leaves open the question of the
substantive relations between inherited and newly acquired
wealth, family status relatively independent of at least very
large wealth, occupational status within various income
ranges, and similar problems.

Generally, Mills is rather vague on the relations between
the power elite and other elements which in some sense
enjoy rather high prestige. He emphasizes the prominence of
lawyers among the "political directorate," but there is no
clear analysis of the role of professional groups in the
occupational structure generally; one presumes that except
for a few lawyers who are successful in politics or business,
and perhaps some engineers, professional people do not
belong to the power elite. Similarly he emphasizes that
members of the power elite have more than the average
amount of education, and in particular he stresses the proportion who have been to select private schools and to "Ivy
League" colleges. In general, he is greatly concerned about
the fact that the power elite are not "representative" of the
population as a whole in the sense of constituting a random
sample by socio-economic origin, by education, by ethnic
group, etc. This is a point to which I shall return.

Neither the "higher circles" generally nor the component
of the "very rich" (Mills' term) are a leisure class in Veblen's
sense; many, if not most of them, "work" in various fields
of business and financial management. Furthermore, the
processes of recruitment are about what social scientists
have come to expect. Mills does not give any exact criteria
for what he considers to be "upper class" as a category of
social origin, but I have the impression that he puts the line

somewhat lower than most sociologists would. But, however that may be, it is clear that there is a considerable element of stability from generation to generation in the higher-status groups in American society. Thus if, to employ a pattern used by Mills, we take a group of prominent persons, the family origin of from two-thirds to three-fourths of them will be the upper third of the American status structure. It is not these essential facts but the interpretation placed upon them which raises questions for us. The only point of fact I would question is whether the recruitment of the very rich has shown a sharper increase through the process of inheritance than through self-earning. It is possible that this is so, but I am inclined to doubt it, and in any case their position does not depend only on the process which Mills calls "cumulative advantage."

Mills radically denies that the group he calls the "very rich" and the "corporate rich" are distinct "classes," in his sense. He explicitly lumps them together and on the whole gives the very rich a greater position of influence than they are usually accorded or than, I think, they actually enjoy. This is in line with his thesis that there is a single, unified power elite. Clearly, it is his contention that the base of the (business) group as a whole lies in command of the very large business enterprises—somewhat erroneously, or at least ambiguously, he puts the primary emphasis on control of property in accounting for this power.

Of the three main subgroups, Mills treats the "political directorate" as by far the weakest. It has, according to him, been greatly infiltrated by the business element, so that it can scarcely be treated as independent. Hence virtually the only element independent of what might be called the business oligarchy is the military—and this, he holds, is coming increasingly to fuse with the business group, or at least to form a close community of interest with it.

The pluralistic components of our older political traditions, Mills feels, are rooted primarily in local groupings—

partly, of course, through the constitutional provisions which establish federalism and make Congressional representation dependent on local constituencies. But the operations of the big organizations have become national in scope, and often international. Hence structures rooted in localism have simply been pushed into a secondary position.

But at the same time Mills contends that the structural base of authentic localism has been progressively atrophied through the development of what he calls the "mass society." The most conspicuous phenomena of the mass society are the prevalence and characteristics of the media of mass communication, which tend to serve as instruments of the power elite out of the reach of locally based "publics" and influential elements in them. The theory of the mass society is only very sketchily presented in one chapter near the end of the book, but is clearly meant to provide one of the main components of the total picture of American society which Mills is presenting.

In terms of recent history, one of Mills' main contentions is that the New Deal period did not represent a turning point in social development, but rather a superficial flurry which only momentarily disturbed the process of emergence of the power elite and the dominance of the business contingent within it. Thus Mills speaks of the economic elite as in due course coming "to control and to use for their own purposes the New Deal institutions whose creation they had so bitterly denounced" (pp. 272-73).

Mills repeatedly disavows any intention of presenting a "conspiratorial" interpretation of American social and political development. He stresses the institutional positions occupied by his elite rather than their personalities and conspiratorial activities. Nevertheless he often comes very close to this implication because of his special theory that a peculiar irresponsibility attaches to the elite and their actions. By this he seems to mean the absence or relative ineffectiveness of formal legal restraints or of a system of "checks and balances" of the sort which has traditionally been associated with our political system. His contention, thus, is that the power elite has been freed from the historic restraints of our society and uses its power in terms of what he calls a "higher immorality"—a conception which is not very clearly explained.

Finally, it should be mentioned that in this, as in some of his previous writings, Mills' general tone toward both men and institutions is sharply caustic. *The Power Elite* certainly purports to be an exposition and an explanation of what has been happening in American society, but it is equally an indictment. There is no pretense of even trying to maintain a scientific neutrality; the book is a fiery and sarcastic attack on the pretensions of the "higher circles" in America, either to competence in exercise of their responsibilities, or to moral legitimation of their position. In such a case, the critic must ascertain the moral position from which the indictment is formulated; I shall have something to say about this later. In his combination of often insightful exposition and analysis, empirical one-sidedness and distortion, and moral indictment and sarcasm, Mills reminds one more of Veblen than of any other figure; that he has attained the stature of Veblen I question, but the role he is cutting out for himself is similar.

II

As I have said, the Mills analysis presents what, to me, is a subtle and complex combination of acceptable and unacceptable elements. Let me now attempt, at some of the most important points, to unravel these elements from each other. I want to try this first on the level of empirical generalization and then to raise one or two more strictly theoretical problems. I shall do so more in my own terms than in those employed by Mills.

In my opinion, two salient sets of processes have been going on in American society during the past half-century, the combination of which encompasses the main facts which are essential to our problem. The first of these is the dynamic of a maturing industrial society, including not only the highly industrialized economy itself but its setting in the society as a whole—notably, its political system and class structure (in a wider sense of the term "class" than Mills')—and the repercussions of the industrial development on the rest of the society. The second concerns the altered position of the United States in world society, which is a consequence in part of our own economic growth, in part of a variety of exogenous changes, including the relative decline of the Western European powers, the rise of Soviet Russia, and the break-up of the "colonial" organization of much of the non-white world. The enormous enhancement of American power and responsibility in the world has taken place in a relatively short time and was bound to have profound repercussions on the characteristics of our own society. Our old political isolation has disappeared and given way to the deepest of involvements.

My first thesis is that these two processes *both* work in the direction of increasing the relative importance of government in our society and, with it, of political power. But their impact has been all the greater because of the extent to which the United States has been an almost specifically nonpolitical society. This has been evidenced above all in the institutions and tradition of political decentralization already mentioned, one aspect of which is the localism which Mills discusses. A second, however, has been a cultural tradition which has emphasized economic values—an emphasis on enterprise and production in an activist sense, not a merely passive hedonistic valuation of the enjoyment of material well-being. Moreover, the virtually unimpeded process of settlement of a continent in political isolation from the main system of world powers has favored maintenance of this emphasis to a greater extent than would otherwise have readily been possible.

At some points in his discussion, Mills seems to look back to the Jeffersonian picture of a system of economic production consisting mainly of small farmers and artisans, with presumably a small mercantile class mediating between them and consumers. Clearly this is not a situation compatible with high industrial development, in either of two respects. First, the order of decentralization of production, where the standard unit is a family-size one, is incompatible with either the organization or the technology necessary for high industrialism. Second, the "Jeffersonian" economy is not one in which economic production is differentiated from other social functions in specialized organizations; instead, the typcal productive unit is at the same time a kinship unit and a unit of citizenship in the community.

In all salient respects, the modern economy has moved very far from the Jeffersonian ideal. The pace-setting units have become both large and specialized. Their development has been part of a general process of structural differentiation in the society which has led to greater specialization in many fields. An essential aspect of the process of development of the economy as a system in *both* these senses is greater specialization on at least three levels: first, the specialization of organizations in the functions of economic production as distinguished from other functions; second, the specialization of functions within the economy; and third, the specialization of the roles of classes of individuals within the organization.

Leadership is an essential function in all social systems which, with their increase of scale and their functional differentiation, tend to become more specialized. I think we can, within considerable limits, regard the emergence of the large firm with operations on a nation-wide basis as a "normal" outcome of the process of growth and differentiation of the economy. Similarly, the rise to prominence within the firm of specialized executive functions is also a normal outcome of a process of growth in size and in structural differentiation. The question then arises whether the process of concentration of firms, and of executive power within firms, has "gone too far" because it has been greatly influenced by factors extraneous to the process of economic development itself.

Mills makes the assertion that the size of the large firm has exceeded the limits of economic efficiency. He presents no evidence, and I think most competent persons would regard this as an exceedingly difficult question. There is, however, one line of evidence not cited by Mills which has a bearing on it. It is true that the absolute size of firms has steadily increased—General Motors today is larger than any firm of the 1920's. But the *relative* share of the largest firms in the production of the economy has remained essentially stable for more than a generation, a fact which points to some kind of equilibrium condition with respect to the degree of concentration in the system as a whole.

A cognate question is whether the power of the executive or managerial class within industry, and particularly within the large firms, has increased inordinately, which, if true, would indicate that factors other than the functional needs of the productive process were operating to skew the internal power structure of firms in favor of the executive groups.

Generally speaking, Mills' argument is that the power of the very rich and the corporate rich *within* the economy, is inordinately great and, by virtue of the factor of cumulative advantage, is becoming continually greater. At the very least, I think, it can be said that his case is not proved and that there is equally good, if not better, evidence for an alternative view, particularly with reference to the trend.

First, I am not able to accept Mills' close identification of the very rich (i.e., the holders of "great fortunes") with the "corporate rich" (the primary holders of executive power in business organizations) as a single class in any very useful sense. Certainly, in the "heroic age" of American capitalism, from the Civil War to just after the turn of the century, the dominant figures were the entrepreneurs who, mainly as the founders of great enterprises and as the bankers and promoters concerned with mergers and reorganizations and the like, came to control these great organizations. But the dominant sociological fact of the outcome of that era was that these owning groups did not, as a group, succeed in consolidating their position precisely *within* their own enterprises and in the economy. It is a notorious fact that the *very* large enterprise, still largely under family control through property holdings, is much more the exception than the rule. Instead, the control has passed—by no means fully, but for the most part—to professional career executives, who have not reached their positions through the exercise of *property* rights but through some sort of process of appointment and promotion.

Mills concedes the main facts of this situation but fails, in my opinion, to evaluate them properly. It seems to be clear that the original "captains of industry," the makers of the great fortunes, *failed* to achieve or to exercise sufficient cumulative advantages to consolidate control of the enterprises in their families and their class ("class" in a sociological, not an economic, sense). This came about essentially because there were factors operating contrary to that of cumulative advantage, which Mills stresses so heavily. The main factor was the pressure to link executive responsibility with competence in such a way that the ascriptive rights of property ownership have tended to give way to the occupational functions of "professionals."

There are, above all, two ways in which Mills' treatment obscures the importance and nature of this shift. First, he continues to speak of power *within* the economy as based on property. To a considerable degree, of course, this is legally true, since the legal control of enterprise rests with stockholders. But, as Berle and Means first made abundantly clear, very generally it is not substantively true. In the old-style family enterprise, still predominant in the small-business sector of the economy, the functions of management and ownership are fused in the same people. In the larger enterprise they have by and large become differentiated. The fact that executives receive large salaries and bonuses is not to be twisted into an assumption that they control, so far as they do, through their property rights. Paradoxical as it may seem, a relatively backward industrial economy like that of France is far more *property*-based than is the case with the United States. In general, property holdings have not, of course, been expropriated, except for their diminution through inheritance and income taxes, which are not as negligible as Mills maintains. What has happened is that their relation to the *power* structure of the economy has been greatly altered. Mills almost entirely passes over this change.

The second problem concerns the process of recruitment in the higher occupational reaches of the economy. It is entirely clear that the process operates in the higher reaches overwhelmingly by appointment, i.e., the decisions of superiors as individuals or in small groups as to who should occupy certain positions. It is also true that the process is relatively unformalized—e.g., there are no competitive examinations and few, if any, formal qualifications of training. But from these facts Mills concludes, and again and again reiterates, that executive competence has very little, if anything, to do with the selection, that it is an overwhelmingly arbitrary process of choosing those who are congenial to the selectors, presumably because they can be counted upon to be "yes men." At the very least this contention is unproved, and I seriously doubt its correctness. There are certainly many difficulties and imperfections in the selection process. But I think it almost certain that higher levels of competence are selected than would on the average be the case through kinship ascription, and that, as such processes go, the levels selected are relatively high.

One final point in this field. It does seem probable that

the factor of cumulatve advantage has a good deal to do with the high levels of financial remuneration of the higher executive groups and with the discrepancies between their incomes and those of governmental and professional people on comparable levels of competence and responsibility. But this is very far from the great fortune level of the founding entrepreneur type, and the evidence seems to be that the discrepancy has not been cumulatively increasing to an appreciable degree, particularly relative to wages at the labor levels; cases like that of the academic profession are somewhat special.

So far I have been speaking about the nature and power position of the elite *within* the economy. The general tenor of my argument has been that, given the nature of an industrial society, a relatively well-defined elite or leadership group *should be expected to develop* in the business world; it is out of the question that power should be diffused equally among an indefinite number of very small units, as the ideal of pure competition and a good deal of the ideology of business itself would have it. But first I question whether the position of power of the business leadership groups is such that a heavy operation of the factor of cumulative advantage must be invoked to account for it. Secondly, I must stress that the business elite is no longer primarily an elite of *property*-owners, but that its center of gravity has shifted to occupationally professional executives or managers. Differential advantages of family origin, etc., are about the same for admission to this group as to other groups requiring educational and other qualifications. Again the evidence is that the proportion of its members recruited from the upper economic and social groups is and remains relatively high, but it has not, in recent times, been increasing, as the theory of cumulative advantage would lead us to expect.

The problem of an elite within the economy must, however, be clearly distinguished from that of an elite in the society as a whole and the power position occupied by such an elite. There are two main orders of questions bearing on the transition from one to the other. Though a thorough consideration of this transition would lead into very far-reaching questions, for present purposes one can be treated rather briefly. Mills gives us the impression that "eliteness" in any society, including our own, is overwhelmingly a question of the power that an individual or a group can command. By this, he means (I shall further discuss his concept of power presently) influence on the "big" decisions directly affecting what happens in the society in the short run. But there are many elements in the society which are relatively powerless in this sense, but nevertheless of the greatest functional importance. Our society has almost divested kinship units as such of important power in this sense. But this does not mean at all that the family has ceased to be important. Closely linked with this is the question of the feminine role. Women qua women by and large do not have a position of power comparable to that of men; but this is not to say that they are unimportant—otherwise how can we account for the extent of our national preoccupations with questions of sexuality? Finally, there is a *distinct* difference between the rank-order of occupations —which, relative to other role-types, are closely involved with decision-making in a society like ours—by power and by prestige. The most striking case is the relatively high position of the professions relative to executive roles in business, as revealed by the famous North-Hatt data. Physicians as a group do not exercise great power, but there is no reason to question their very high prestige, which has been demonstrated in study after study.

The second main context, however, directly concerns the question of power. In a complex society the primary locus of power lies in the political system. There are many subtle analytical problems involved in the delineation of this system and its functions in the society which cannot be gone into here; this formula will have to suffice. Two questions

are, however, primary for our purposes: the degree of differentiation of the political system from other systems; and
its own internal structure. These two problems, it will be
noted, parallel those raised with reference to the economy.

For historical reasons, it seems clear that the development
of the American political system, since the breakdown of the
first synthesis associated with the "founders of the Republic,"
has lagged behind that of the economy. This is a function
primarily of the two factors already noted—the economic
emphasis inherent in our system of values, and the relative
lack of urgency of certain political problems because of our
especially protected and favored national position. Relative
to the economic structure, which had by that time grown
enormously, the political was at its weakest in the period
from the Civil War to the end of the century; this situation
is sketched by Mills in broadly correct terms. Since then,
both internal exigencies and the exigencies of our international position have been stimuli for major changes.

Internally, beyond the more elementary provisions for
law and order and essential minimum services—much of this,
of course, on a local basis—the main focus of the development
of our political system has been *control* of economic organization and processes, and coping with some of the social consequences of economic growth and industrialization. The
process started well before the turn of the century with the
Interstate Commerce legislation and the Anti-Trust Act and
continued through the New Deal era, not steadily but with
waves of new measures and levels of political control.

A major problem in relation to Mills' analysis is whether
this is "genuine" control. His view seems to be that at times
it has been, but that on balance it is the business power-
holders who control government, not vice versa; the above
quotation about the outcome of the New Deal puts it suc-
cinctly. In my opinion this is a misinterpretation. If genuine
and, in some sense, effective controls had not been imposed,
I find it impossible to understand the bitter and continuing

opposition on the part of business to the measures which have been taken. Even some of those most completely taken for granted now, like the Federal Reserve system, were bitterly fought at the time. It therefore seems to me to be the sounder interpretation that there has been a genuine growth of autonomous governmental power—apart from the military aspect, which will be discussed presently—and that one major aspect of this has been relatively effective control of the business system. This control and the growth of "big government" have been generally accepted in the society as a whole. The participation of big-business men in governmental processes is by no means to be interpreted as a simple index of their power to dominate government in their own interests, as Mills often seems to maintain.

To me, another indication of Mills' biased view of the governmental situation is his almost complete failure even to mention the political parties, or to analyze their differences. It seems to me broadly true that the Republican party, though a coalition, is more than any other single thing the party of the bigger sector of business. Four years of a Republican administration—two of them without control of Congress—is certainly not enough to indicate that big business, through its favorite party organ, controls the government on a long-run basis. So Mills is practically forced to the view that the alleged control operates above and beyond the party system. This seems to be connected with his relegation of the legislative branch to the "middle level" of power. I have strong reservations about this, but also it must not be forgotten that the presidency is the biggest prize of all in party politics, and it is its importance which forms the primary integrating focus of our particular type of party system. Surely the presidency is not simply the football of an inner clique which manipulates the executive branch independently of the party.

Mills, of course, recognizes that the aftermath of two world wars, the rise of Communist power, and the relative decline of the older Western Great Powers provide the occasion for the increasing prominence of the military group in our governmental system. Before these changes—and, indeed, to a remarkable extent, as late as the 1930's—the military played a far smaller role in this country than in any other society of comparable scale and organizational and technological development. Part of the change may be interpreted as simply the redressing of a balance. But it seems to me correct to say that for the last ten years there has been a special situation attributable to the extremely unsettled condition of the world at large and to the difficulties entailed for the American system, given its background, in meeting the problem on its own terms. There is thus a sense in which it is true that the higher military officers have tended to fill a vacuum in the field of national decision-making. There are two main points to be made about Mills' treatment of the matter. First, more in this field than perhaps any other, Mills' discussion is marred by a hasty tendency to generalize from very recent short-run developments to the long-run prospects of the structure of the society. Even here he fails to mention that in certain crucial questions the recommendations of the military have been overruled by civilian authority, although the President is a former military man. Secondly, the tone of indictment, particularly evidenced by the quite unnecessary and, I think, inappropriate parading of the term "warlord," is stronger in his discussion of this area than in any other, except perhaps the "mass society."

Related to the position of the higher military officers is what Mills calls the "military metaphysic," meaning the definition of international problems in terms of the primacy of military force. That there has been such a tendency, and that it has gone beyond the objective requirements of the situation, seem to be unquestionable. But I very much doubt whether it is as absolute as many of Mills' statements make it appear, and a swing in another direction is discernible.

This seems to be another case of Mills' tendency to make large generalizations about major trends from short-run experience.

Finally, let us say a word about what Mills calls the "political directorate"—that is, the non-military component in the groups most influential in the affairs of government and politics. Again I think there is a certain correctness in his contention that a definite weakness exists here, and that the high participation both of business and of military elements in the exercise of power is related to this. But a difficulty arises in terms of the perspective on American society which I have been emphasizing throughout. Both the non-political stress in American social structure and values generally, and the recency and intensity of the pressures to build up this aspect of our structure, would lead one to predict that it would be a major focus of strain. American society has not developed a well-integrated political-government elite, in the sense that it has developed a relatively well-integrated business-executive group. For this reason responsibility has been carried—imperfectly, of course—by a very miscellaneous group which includes members of the business and military groups, as would be expected, but also "politicians," in the usual sense of people making an at least partial career out of elective office and the influencing of elections; professional people, particularly lawyers but also economists, political scientists, and even natural scientists (e.g., John von Neumann as Atomic Energy Commissioner); journalists; and, a very important element, upper-class people in more than the purely economic sense that Mills employs, of whom Franklin Roosevelt was one and Adlai Stevenson, though also a lawyer, is another. In my opinion, the structure of the American political leadership group is far from a settled thing. It certainly is not settled in terms of the long-run dominance of a business-military coalition.

Mills holds that the United States has no higher civil service at all, in the European sense, and seems to imply that we should have. There is relative truth in his empirical contention, though I think he tends to underestimate the real influence of "non-political" government officials on longer-run policy. Good examples are the Department of Agriculture and the Reclamation Service of the Department of the Interior—and now, increasingly, the Public Health Service. I think that this is even true of the Foreign Service, and that Mills here, as in so many other connections, seriously exaggerates the probable long-run consequences of the McCarthyites' intervention in the affairs of the State Department.

At least it seems highly probable that, in the nature of the case, the tendency will be toward a strengthening of the element of professional governmental officials who are essentially independent both of short-run "politics" and of elements extraneous to the structure of government and its responsibilities. In fact, the military officer is a special case of this type, and though his role is not stabilized, it presumably must come to be more important than it traditionally has been. However, it is questionable how far the specific models of civil service organization either of Britain or of Continental Europe—particularly, certain of their special connections with the class structure and the educational system—are appropriate to American conditions. Such connections in the American case would accentuate rather than mitigate the prominence of the Ivy League element to which Mills so seriously objects. I think it correct to say that five years of Labour government in Britain, far from lessening the prominence of Oxford and Cambridge educations as qualifications for the civil service, in fact increased their relative importance, by increasing the national importance of the civil service itself.

Above all, I do not think that Mills has made a convincing case for his contention that the power structure impinging directly on American government is in process of crystallizing into a top business-military coalition with a much weaker political "junior partner" whose main function presumably is, by manipulation of the mass media and the political process in the narrower sense, to keep the great majority of Americans from protesting too loudly or even from awakening to what allegedly is "really" going on. On a number of counts which have been reviewed, there is a case on a short-run basis for part of his interpretation. But I think that the kinds of factors brought out in the previous discussion make it extremely dubious that even the partial correctness of his interpretation of a current situation will prove to be a sound indicator of what is to be expected over such longer periods as a generation or more.

My conviction on this point is strengthened by a variety of other considerations which, for reasons of space, cannot be discussed here, but may be mentioned. First, I am extremely skeptical of Mills' interpretation of what he calls the "mass society," which includes the structural position of the great majority of the American population. In this he ignores both kinship and friendship, and the whole mass of associational activities and relatonships. One example is the spread of church membership—which I suppose Mills would dismiss as simply an escape from the boredom of white-collar life, but in my opinion is of considerable positive significance.

Another very important complex which Mills either treats cavalierly or ignores completely involves education at the various levels, and with it the enormous development, over a century, of science and learning and the professions resting upon them. It is true that the people rooted in these areas of the social structure are not prominent in the power elite, and are even subject to some conflicts with it; but they would not be expected to be prominent in this way—their functions in the society are different. Nonetheless, they must be taken very seriously into account in a diagnosis of what has been happening to the society as a whole. One of the most important sets of facts concerns the ways in which the services of technical professional groups have come to penetrate the structures both of business and of government, a circumstance which over a period of time has greatly enhanced the role of the universities as custodians of learning and sources of trained personnel.

Finally, there is one special case of a professional group whose role Mills treats with serious inadequacy—namely, lawyers. First, he dismisses the judicial branch of government as just "trailing along," with the implication that with a slight lag it simply does the bidding of the "real" holders of power. This seems to be a most biased appraisal of the role of the courts. Not to speak of the longer-run record, the initiative taken by the courts in the matter of racial segregation and in the reassertion of civil liberties after the miasma of McCarthyism does not appear to me to be compatible with Mills' views. Similar considerations seem to apply to various aspects of the role of the private legal profession, notably with respect to the *control* of processes in the business world. Mills tends to assume that the relation between law and business is an overwhelmingly one-way relation; lawyers are there to serve the interests of businessmen and essentially have no independent influence. This, I think, is an illusion stemming largely from Mills' preoccupation with a certain kind of power. His implicit reasoning seems to be that since lawyers have less power than businessmen, they do not really "count."

III

The last problem I wish to raise, therefore, concerns Mills' conception of power and its use as a category of social analysis. Unfortunately, the concept of power is not a settled one in the social sciences, either in political science or in sociology. Mills, however, adopts one main version of the concept without attempting to justify it. This is what may be called the "zero-sum" concept; power, that is to say, is power *over* others. The power A has in a system is, necessarily and by definition, at the expense of B. This conception of power then is generalized to the whole conception of the political process when Mills says that "Politics is a struggle for power."

Within limits, every student of social affairs is free to define important concepts the way he prefers; there is no canonically "correct" definition. But choosing one alternative will have consequences which differ from those implied in another, and this is the case with Mills' conception of power. The essential point at present is that, to Mills, power is not a facility for the performance of function in, and on behalf of, the society as a system, but is interpreted exclusively as a facility for getting what one group, the holders of power, wants by preventing another group, the "outs," from getting what it wants.

What this conception does is to elevate a secondary and derived aspect of a total phenomenon into the central place. A comparison may help to make this clear. There is obviously a distributive aspect of wealth and it is in a sense true that the wealth of one person or group by definition cannot also be possessed by another group. Thus the *distribution* of wealth is, in the nature of the case, a focus of conflicts of interest in a society. But what of the positive functions of wealth and of the conditions of its production? It has become fully established that the wealth available for distribution can only come about through the processes of production, and that these processes require the "co-operation" or integration of a variety of different agencies—what economists call the "factors of production." Wealth, in turn, is a generalized class of facilities available to units of the society—individuals and various types and levels of collectivities—for whatever uses may be important to them. But even apart from the question of what share each gets, the fact that there should be wealth to divide, and how much, cannot be taken for granted as given except within a very limited context.

Very similar things can be said about power in a political sense. Power is a generalized facility or resource in the society.

It has to be divided or allocated, but it also has to be produced and it has collective as well as distributive functions. It is the capacity to mobilize the resources of the society for the attainment of goals for which a general "public" commitment has been made, or may be made. It is mobilization, above all, of the action of persons and groups, which is *binding* on them by virtue of their position in the society. Thus within a much larger complex Mills concentrates almost exclusively on the distributive aspect of power. He is interested only in *who* has power and what *sectoral* interests he is serving with his power, not in how power comes to be generated or in what communal rather than sectoral interests are served.

The result is a highly selective treatment of the whole complex of the power problem. There is, in the first place, a tendency to exaggerate the empirical importance of power by alleging that it is only power which "really" determines what happens in a society. Against this, I would place the view that power is only one of several cognate factors in the determination of social events. This bias of Mills is particularly evident in his tendency to foreshorten social processes and emphasize overwhelmingly short-run factors. There is, secondly, the tendency to think of power as presumptively illegitimate; if people exercise considerable power, it must be because they have somehow usurped it where they had no right and they intend to use it to the detriment of others. This comes out most conspicuously in Mills' imputation of irresponsibility to his "power elite" and the allegation, vaguely conceived and presented with very little evidence, that they are characterized by a "higher immorality." It is notable that as he approaches the climax indicated by the title of his final chapter the tone of indictment becomes shriller and shriller and the atmosphere of objective analysis recedes.

Back of all this lies, I am sure, an only partly manifest "metaphysical" position which Mills shares with Veblen and a long line of indicters of modern industrial society. I would call it a utopian conception of an ideal society in which power does not play a part at all.

This is a philosophical and ethical background which is common both to utopian liberalism and socialism in our society and to a good deal of "capitalist" ideology. They have in common an underlying "individualism" of a certain type. This is not primarily individualism in the sense that the welfare and rights of the individual constitute fundamental moral values, but rather that *both* individual and collective rights are alleged to be promoted only by *minimizing* the positive organization of social groups. Social organization as such is presumptively bad because, on a limited, short-run basis, it always and necessarily limits the freedom of the individual to do exactly what he may happen to want. The question of the deeper and longer-run dependence of the goals and capacities of individuals themselves on social organization is simply shoved into the background. From this point of view, both power in the individual enterprise and power in the larger society are presumptively evil in themselves, because they represent the primary visible focus of the capacity of somebody to see to it that somebody else acts or does not act in certain ways, whether at the moment he wants to or not.

There are, in contemporary society, three main versions of this individualistic utopianism, which may be called "liberal" and "capitalist" and "socialist"—I place all three terms in quotation marks deliberately. The liberal version is mainly "humanistically" oriented to the *total* welfare of the individual as a person, and in American terms it is very likely to assume a Jeffersonian cast, to hold up the vision of a simpler and hence almost by definition "better" society against the inhumanities and impersonalities of large-scale modern industrialism and all its concomitants.

The capitalist version is, with all the qualifications which such an assertion must occasion, *primarily* production-oriented. Essentially it says that, whatever the cost to individuals—including even businessmen themselves, or especially so—production must be achieved, carried on, and so far as possible increased. This is the focus of what has been called the "business creed." Understandably it has been highly sensitive to "interferences" on both fronts, from liberal sources which would sacrifice productivity to humanistic values, and from governmentalist sources which would "interfere" with the businessman's primary responsibility for production. Social organization beyond the level of the firm is thus presumptively a limitation of its freedom.

The socialist version has been a secondary theme in American ideology largely because of the apolitical character of American society, which, as I have noted, has been prominent historically. The opposition to capitalism has centered on two fronts, the control of the economy in the interests of preventing abuses of power and the steering of the benefits of productivity in the humanistic direction of "welfare." But the socialist questions whether *control* of the abuses of private enterprise is possible at all; to him, for the state to take over production directly is the only way. From this perspective, furthermore, the "Jeffersonian" version of romantic utopianism seems particularly unrealistic and unacceptable.

From one point of view, the socialist romanticizes the state and the political process. Whereas he distrusts private interests almost totally and feels that they cannot be entrusted with any responsibility, he romantically believes that if public authority alone is entrusted with all responsibilities, all will be well—because some mystical "popular will" or "public interest" controls it—forgetting that public authority, like other forms of social organization, is administered by human beings. And that he does not fundamentally trust even public authority is evidenced by his ultimate ideal that the state should "wither away" and the spontaneous co-operation of institutionally unorganized human beings should take over. The socialist has been put in a particularly difficult position in the contemporary world by the development of Communism which, while still paying lip service to the eventual withering-away of the state, carries the enforcement of its predominance over all private interests, including the liberties of its citizens, to the totalitarian extreme.

Mills does not make his own position explicit in this book. As noted, at times he speaks like a nostalgic Jeffersonian liberal. I understand, however, that he professes to be a socialist—non-Communist, of course. But a basic strain of his thinking is consistent with both wings of the liberal-socialist dilemma on the basically *individualistic* premises that I have outlined: either that social organizaton beyond the level of the family and the local community is a bad thing *in toto,* or that it is instrumentally justified only to get society over a particular hump, the threat of the capitalist evil.

Mills seems to be suggesting that the development of the power elite is bringing that capitalist evil to a climax, to a situation which is intolerable to liberals and socialists alike. I suggest an alternative view: that, though of course accompanied by a whole range of "abuses," the main lines of social development in America are essentially acceptable to a humanistic ethic which in my case is closer to the liberal than to either of the other two outlined here. But it differs in not being in the older sense an individualistic liberalism. If the individualistic assumptions are modified in favor of a set which not only admit the necessity but assert the desirability of positive social organization, much of the ideological conflict between the three positions as total "systems" evaporates. Above all, it can be positively asserted that power, while of course subject to abuses and in need of many controls, is an essential and desirable component of a highly organized society. This position, in asserting and justifying the increased importance of government, thus grants that there is a grain of truth in the "socialist" theme. There is, however, also some justification for the existence of "capitalism," if by that is meant the institutionalization of responsibility for the larger part of economic production in the hands of a variety of private, non-governmental agencies. To my mind, there is no more reason why all important economic production should be controlled by government than why all scientific research should be.

Hence, in my opinion, many of the difficulties of Mills' analysis of a crucial problem in American society arise from his failure to transcend the dilemmas inherent in much of the individualistic tradition in American and, more broadly, in Western thought. It seems to me that he is clearly and, in the degree to which he pushes this position, unjustifiably anti-capitalist. He is partly pro-liberal and probably even more pro-socialist. But in the American scene a choice between these old alternatives of ideological orientation is no longer enough. It is necessary not only to criticize existing conditions from the older philosophical or ideological points of view, but to take serious stock of the ideological assumptions underlying the bulk of American political discussion of such problems as power.

CHAPTER VII

SOCIAL STRAINS
IN AMERICA

To the relatively objective observer, whether American or foreign, it seems clear that the complex of phenomena that have come to be known as "McCarthyism" must be symptoms of a process in American society of some deep and general significance. Some interpret it simply as political reaction, even as a kind of neofascism. Some think of it as simply a manifestation of nationalism. The present paper proposes to bring to bear some theoretical perspectives of sociology in an attempt to work out an interpretation which goes beyond catchwords of this order.

McCarthyism can be understood as a relatively acute symptom of the strains which accompany a major change in the situation and structure of American society, a change which in this instance consists in the development of the attitudes and institutional machinery required to implement a greatly enhanced level of national political responsibility. The necessity for this development arises both from our own growth to an enormous potential of power, and from the changed relation to the rest of the world which this growth in itself, and other changes extraneous to American development, have entailed. The strains to which I refer derive primarily from conflicts between the demands imposed by the new situation and the inertia of those elements of our social structure which are most resistant to the necessary changes.

The situation I have in mind centers on the American position in international affairs. The main facts are familiar to all. It is not something that has come about suddenly, but the impact of its pressures has been cumulative.

The starting point is the relative geographical isolation of the United States in the "formative" period of its national history, down to, let us say, about the opening of the present century. The Spanish-American war extended our involvements into the Spanish-Speaking areas of the Caribbean and to the Philippines, and the Boxer episode in China and our mediation of the Russo-Japanese war indicated rapidly growing interests in the Orient. Then the First World War brought us in as one of the major belligerents, with a brief possibility of taking a role of world leadership. From this advanced degree of international involvement, however, we recoiled with a violent reaction, repudiating the Treaty of Versailles and the League of Nations.

In the ensuing period of "normalcy," until the shock of Pearl Harbor settled the question, it could still be held that the "quarrels" of foreign powers beyond the Americas were none of our concern, unless some "arbitrary" disturbance impinged too closely on our national interests. By the end of the Second World War, however, this attitude could not again be revived by any body of opinion which pretended to depend upon a realistic appraisal of our situation. Our own strength, in spite of our massive disarmament and demobilization, had grown too great; the defeat of France and the disorganization of Germany destroyed such continental European balance of power as had existed; Britain, though victorious, was greatly weakened in the face of world-wide commitments; and Soviet Russia emerged as a victorious and expanding power, leading with a revolutionary ideology a movement which could readily destroy such elements of stability favorable to our own national values and interests as still remained in the world. Along with all this have come developments in military technology that have drastically neutralized the protections formerly conferred by geographical distance, so that even the elementary military security of the United States cannot now be taken for granted apart from world-wide political order.

The vicissitudes of American foreign policy and its relations to domestic politics over this period show the disturbing effect of this developing situation on our society. We have twice intervened militarily on a grand scale. With a notable difference of degree, we have both times recoiled from the implications of our intervention. In the second case the recoil did not last long, since the beginnings of the Cold War about 1947 made it clear that only American action was able to prevent Soviet domination of the whole continent of Europe. It can, however, be argued that this early and grand-scale resumption of responsibility imposed serious internal strains because it did not allow time for "digesting" the implications of our role in the war.

The outstanding characteristic of the society on which this greatly changed situation has impinged is that it had come to be the industrial society par excellence—partly because the settlement of the continental area coincided with the later industrial revolution, partly because of the immense area and natural resources of the country, but partly too because of certain important differences between American and European society. Since the United States did not have a class structure tightly integrated with a political organization that had developed its main forms before the industrial revolution, the economy has had a freedom to develop and to set the tone for the whole society in a way markedly different from any European country or Japan.

All highly industrialized societies exhibit many features in common which are independent of the particular historical paths by which their developments have taken place. These include the bureaucratic organization of the productive process itself, in the sense that the roles of individuals are of the occupational type and the organizations in which they are grouped are mainly "specific function" organizations. Under this arrangement the peasant type of agricultural holding, where farming is very closely bound up with a kinship unit, is minimized; so too of small family businesses; people tend to look to their productive function and to profit as a measure of success and hence of emancipation from conflicting ties and claims; the rights of property ownership are centered primarily in the organization which carries functional responsibility, and hence permits a high degree of segregation between private life and occupational roles for production purposes; contract plays a central part in the system of exchange, and para-economic elements tend to be reduced in importance.

Outside the sphere which touches the organization of the economy itself, industrialism means above all that the structures which would interfere with the free functioning of the economy, and of their adaptation to it, are minimized. The first of these is family and kinship. The American family system, chiefly characterized by the isolation of the nuclear or conjugal family, has gone farther than in any European society toward removing all interferences with the occupational roles of the breadwinning members, and with occupational mobility. A second field is religion. The American combination of federalism and the separation of church and state has resulted in a system of "denominational pluralism" which prevents organized religion from constituting a monolithic structure standing in the way of secular social developments. The third field concerns the matter of social stratification. The United States of course has a class structure; but it is one which has its primary roots in the system of occupational roles, and in contrast to the typical European situation it acts as no more than a brake on the processes of social mobility which are most important to an industrial type of occupational system. Under an effective family system there must be some continuity of class status from generation to generation, and there cannot be complete "equality of opportunity." In America, however, it is clearly the occupational system rather than kinship continuity that prevails.

Linked to this situation is our system of formal education. The United States was among the pioneers in developing publicly supported education; but this has taken place in a notably decentralized way. Not only is there no Department of Education in the Federal government, but even the various state departments are to a large extent service organizations for the locally controlled school systems. Higher education further has been considerably more independent of class standards which equate the "scholar" with the "gentleman" (in a class sense) than has been the case in Europe. Also a far larger proportion of each age-group attend institutions of higher education than in European countries.

Politically the most important fact about American industrialism is that it has developed overwhelmingly under the aegis of free enterprise. Historically the center of gravity of the integration of American society has not rested in the political field. There came to be established a kind of "burden of proof" expectation that responsibilities should not be undertaken by government unless, first, the necessity for their being undertaken at all was clearly established, and second, there was no other obviously adequate way to get the job done. It is therefore not surprising that the opening up of vast new fields of governmental responsibility should meet with considerable resistance and conflict.

The impact of this problem on our orientation to foreign relations has been complicated by an important set of internal circumstances. It is a commonplace that industrialism creates on a large scale two sets of problems which uniformly in all industrialized countries have required modifications of any doctrinaire "laissez-faire" policy: the problems of controlling the processes of the economy itself, and of dealing with certain social repercussions of industralization.

As the process of industralization has proceeded in America there has been a steady increase in the amount of public control imposed on the economy, with the initiative mainly in the hands of the Federal government. This trend was accelerated in the latter years of the nineteenth century, and has continued, with interruptions, through the New Deal. The New Deal, however, was more concerned with the social repercussions of industrialization, rather than with more narrowly economic problems. The introduction of a national system of social security and legislation more favorable to labor are perhaps the most typical developments. This internal process of government intervention has not gone far enough to satisfy European socialists, but it certainly constitutes a great modification of the earlier situation. Moreover, in broad lines it can be regarded as firmly established. It is significant that the major political parties now tend to vie with each other in promoting the extension of social security benefits, that there is no likelihood of repeal of the Federal Reserve Act, and that there is no strong movement to place the unions under really severe legal restraints.

On the whole, business groups have accepted the new situation and coöperated to make it work with considerably more good faith than in Continental Europe. Nevertheless, these internal changes have been sufficiently recent and far-reaching to keep the strains attendant on them from being fully resolved. Moreover they have created an important part of the problems with which this examination is chiefly concerned, problems touching the composition of the higher strata of the society, where the primary burden of responsibility must fall.

By contrast with European countries, perhaps in some ways particularly Britain, the United States has been conspicuous for the absence or relative weakness of two types of elite elements. The first of these is a hereditary upper class with a status continuous from pre-industrial times, closely integrated with politics and public service. The second is an occupational elite whose roots are essentially independent of the business world—in the independent professions, the universities, the church, or government, including civil and military services.

In America the businessmen have tended to be the natural leaders of the general community. But, both for the reasons just reviewed and for certain others, this leadership has not remained undisputed. On the whole the business community has, step by step, resisted the processes of internal change necessitated by industrialization rather than taken the leadership in introducing them. The leadership that has emerged has been miscellaneous in social origin, including professional politicians, especially those in touch with the urban political machines, leaders in the labor union movement and elements in close touch with them. An important part has been played by men and women who may be said to exhibit a more or less "aristocratic" tinge, particularly in the Eastern cities, President Roosevelt, of course, having been among them. An important part has been played by lawyers who have made themselves more independent of the business connection than the typical corporation lawyer of a generation ago. Under the pressure of emergency, there has been a tendency for high military officers to play important roles in public life.

Another important group has been composed of "intellectuals"—again a rather miscellaneous assembly including writers, newspapermen, and members of university faculties. In general the importance of the universities has been steadily enhanced by the increasingly technical character of the operations of the economy; businessmen themselves have had to be more highly educated than their predecessors, and have become increasingly dependent on still more highly trained technicians of various kinds.

The important point is that the "natural" tendency for a relatively unequivocal business leadership of the general community has been frustrated, and the business group has had to give way at many points. Nevertheless, a clearly defined non-business component of the elite has not yet crystallized. In my opinion, the striking feature of the American elite is not what Soviet propaganda contends that it is—the clear-cut dominance by "capitalists"—but rather its fluid and relatively unstructured character. In particular, there is no clear determination of where political leadership, in the sense including both "politics" and "administration," is to center.

A further feature of the structure of American society is intimately related to the residual strains left by recent social changes. There is a continuing tendency for earlier economic developments to leave a "precipitate" of upper groups, the position of whose members is founded in the achievements of their ancestors, in this case relatively recent ones. By historical necessity these groups are strongest in the older parts of the country. Hence the cities of the Eastern seaboard have tended to develop groups that are the closest approach we have—though still different from their European equivalent—to an aristocracy. They have generally originated in business interests, but have taken on a form somewhat similar to the mercantile aristocracies of some earlier European societies, such as the Hanseatic cities. In the perspective of popular democratic sentiments, these groups have tended to symbolize at the same time capitalistic interests and social snobbery. In certain circumstances they may be identified with "bohemianism" and related phenomena which are sources of uneasiness to traditional morality.

As the American social and economic center has shifted westward, such groups in the great Middle Western area and beyond have been progressively less prominent. There the elites have consisted of new men. In the nature of the case the proportional contribution to the economy and the society in general from the older and the newer parts of the country has shifted, with the newer progressively increasing their share. But at the same time there is the sense among them of having had to fight for this share against the "dominance" of the East. A similar feeling permeates the lower levels of the class structure. A major theme of the populist type of agrarian and other radicalism had combined class and sectional elements, locating the source of people's troubles in the bankers and railway magnates of the East and in Wall Street. It must not be forgotten that the isolationism of the between-the-wars period was intimately connected with this sectional and class sentiment. The elder La Follette, who was one of the principal destroyers of the League of Nations, was not a "conservative" or in any usual sense a reactionary, but a principal leader of the popular revolt against "the interests."

It must also not be forgotten that a large proportion of the American population are descendants of relatively recent immigrants whose cultural origins are different from the dominant Protestant Anglo-Saxon elements. A generation and more ago the bulk of the new immigration constituted an urban proletariat largely dominated by the political machines of the great cities. By now a great change has taken place. The children of these immigrants have been very much Americanized, but to a considerable degree they are still sensitive about their full acceptance. This sensitivity is, if anything, heightened by the fact that on the whole most of these elements have risen rapidly in the economic and social scale. They are no longer the inhabitants of the scandalous slums; many have climbed to lower middle class status and higher. They have a certain susceptibility to "democratic" appeals which are directed against the alleged snobbery of the older dominant elements.

Finally, the effect of the great depression of the 1930's on the leading business groups must not be forgotten. Such a collapse of the economy could not fail to be felt as a major failure of the expectation that business leaders should bear the major responsibility for the welfare of the economy as a whole and thus of the community. In general it was not the businessmen but the government, under leadership which was broadly antagonistic to business, which came to the rescue. Similarly, the other great class of American proprietors, the farmers, had to accept governmental help of a sort that entailed controls, which in turn inevitably entailed severe conflicts with the individualistic traditions of their history. The fact that the strains of the war and postwar periods have been piled so immediately on those of depression has much to do with the severity of the tensions with which this analysis is concerned.

My thesis, then, is that the strains of the international situation have impinged on a society undergoing important internal changes which have themselves been sources of strain, with the effect of superimposing one kind of strain on another. What responses to this compound strain are to be expected?

It is a generalization well established in social science that neither individuals nor societies can undergo major structural changes without the likelihood of producing a considerable element of "irrational" behavior. There will tend to be conspicuous distortions of the patterns of value and of the normal beliefs about the facts of situations. These distorted beliefs and promptings to irrational action will also tend to be heavily weighted with emotion, to be "over-determined" as the psychologists say.

The psychology of such reactions is complex, but for present purposes it will suffice to distinguish two main components. On the negative side, there will tend to be high levels of anxiety and aggression, focused on what rightly or wrongly are felt to be the sources of strain and difficulty. On the positive side there will tend to be wishful patterns of belief with a strong "regressive" flavor, whose chief function is to wish away the disturbing situation and establish a situation in phantasy where "everything will be all right," preferably as it was before the disturbing situation came about. Very generally then, the psychological formula tends to prescribe a set of beliefs that certain specific, symbolic agencies are responsible for the present state of distress; they have "arbitrarily" upset a satisfactory state of affairs. If only they could be eliminated the trouble would disappear and a satisfactory state restored. The role of this type of mechanism in primitive magic is quite well known.

In a normal process of learning in the individual, or of developmental change in the social system, such irrational phenomena are temporary, and tend to subside as capacity to deal with the new situation grows. This may be more or less easily achieved of course, and resolution of the conflicts and strains may fail to be achieved for a long period or may even be permanently unsuccessful. But under favorable circumstances these reactions are superseded by an increasingly realistic facing of the situation by institutionalized means.

Our present problem therefore centers on the need to mobilize American society to cope with a dangerous and threatening situation which is also intrinsically difficult. It can clearly only be coped with at the governmental level; and hence the problem is in essence a matter of political action, involving both questions of leadership—of who, promoting what policies, shall take the primary responsibility— and of the commitment of the many heterogeneous elements of our population to the national interest.

Consequently there has come to be an enormous increase in pressure to subordinate private interests to the public interest, and this in a society where the presumptions have been more strongly in favor of the private interest than in most. Readiness to make commitments to a collective interest is the focus of what we ordinarily mean by "loyalty." It seems to me that the problem of loyalty at its core is a genuine and realistic one; but attitudes toward it shade all the way from a reasonable concern with getting the necessary degree of loyal coöperation by legitimate appeals, to a grossly irrational set of anxieties about the prevalence of disloyalty, and a readiness to vent the accompanying aggression on innocent scapegoats.

Underlying the concern for loyalty in general, and explaining a good deal of the reaction to it, is the ambivalence of our approach to the situation: The people in the most "exposed" positions are on the one hand pulled by patriotic motives toward fulfillment of the expectations inherent in the new situation; they want to "do their bit." But at the same time their established attitudes and orientations resist fulfillment of the obligation. In the conflict of motives which ensues it is a natural consequence for the resistance to be displaced or projected on to other objects which function as scapegoats. In the present situation it is precisely those parts of our population where individualistic traditions are strongest that are placed under the greatest strain, and that produce the severest resistance to accepting the obligations of our situation. Such resistances, however, conflict with equally strong patriotic motives. In such a situation, when one's own resistance to loyal acceptance of unpalatable obligations, such as paying high taxes, are particularly strong, it is easy to impute disloyal intentions to others.

Our present emotional preoccupation with the problem of loyalty indicates above all that the crisis is not, as some tend to think, primarily concerned with fundamental values, but rather with their implementation. It is true that certain features of the pattern of reaction, such as tendencies to aggressive nationalism and to abdication of responsibilities, would, if carried through, lead to severe conflict with our values. But the main problem is not concerned with doubts about whether the stable political order of a free world is a goal worth sacrificing for, but rather with the question of how our population is rising, or failing to rise, to the challenge.

The primary symbol that connects the objective external problem and its dangers with the internal strain and its structure is "Communism." "World Communism" and its spread constitute the features of the world situation on which the difficulty of our international problem clearly centers. Internally it is felt that Communists and their "sympathizers" constitute the primary focus of actual or potential disloyalty.

With respect to the external situation, the focus of the difficulty in the current role of Soviet Russia is of course reasonable enough. Problems then arise mainly in connection with certain elements of "obsessiveness" in the way in which the situation is approached, manifested, for instance, in a tendency to subordinate all other approaches to the situation exclusively to the military, and in the extreme violence of reaction in some circles to the Chinese situation, in contrast to the relative tolerance with which Jugoslavia is regarded.

Internally, the realistic difficulty resides mainly in the fact that there has indeed been a considerable amount of Communist infiltration in the United States, particularly in the 1930's. It is true that the Communist Party itself has never achieved great electoral success, but for a time Communist influence was paramount in a number of important labor unions, and a considerable number of the associations Americans so like to join were revealed to be Communist-front organizations, with effective Communist control behind the public participation of many non-Communists. Perhaps most important was the fact that considerable numbers of the intellectuals became fellow-travelers. In the days of the rise of Nazism and of the popular front, many of them felt that only Soviet Russia was sincere in its commitment to collective security; that there was a Franco-British "plot" to get Germany and Russia embroiled with each other, etc. The shock of the Nazi-Soviet pact woke up many fellow-travelers, but by no means all; and the cause was considerably retrieved by Hitler's attack on Russia.

Two other features of the Communist movement which make it an ideal negative symbol in the context of the present loyalty problem are the combination of conspiratorial methods and foreign control with the progressive component of its ideological system. On the one hand, the party has drastically repudiated the procedures of constitutional democracy, and on this issue has broken with all the democratic socialist parties of Europe; it claims the protection of democratic procedures and civil liberties, but does not hesitate to abuse them when this seems to be advantageous. There has further never been any question of the American party determining its own policies by democratic procedures. Perhaps in fact the knowledge of the extent to which the "front" organizations have been manipulated from behind the scenes has been the most disillusioning aspect for liberal Americans of their experience with Communism at home.

At the same time the movement had a large content of professed idealism, which may be taken to account for the appeal of Communism before the Cold War era for such large elements of liberal opinion in the United States, as in other Western countries. Marx was, after all, himself a child of the Enlightenment, and the Communist movement has incorporated in its ideology many of the doctrines of human rights that have formed a part of our general inheritance. However grossly the symbols of democracy, of the rights of men, of peace and brotherhood, have been abused by the Communists, they are powerful symbols in our tradition, and their appeal is understandable.

Hence the symbol "Communism" is one to which a special order of ambivalence readily attaches. It has powerful sources of appeal to the liberal tradition, but those who are out of sympathy with the main tradition of American liberalism can find a powerful target for their objections in the totalitarian tactics of Communism and can readily stigmatize it as "un-American." Then, by extending their objections to the liberal component of Communist ideology, they can attack liberalism in general, on the grounds that association with Communist totalitarianism makes anything liberal suspect.

These considerations account for the anti-Communist's

readiness to carry over a stereotype from those who have really been party members or advanced fellow-travelers to large elements of the intellectuals, the labor movement, etc., who have been essentially democratic liberals of various shades of opinion. Since by and large the Democratic Party has more of this liberalism than has the Republican, it is not surprising that a tendency to label it as "sympathizing" with or "soft toward" Communism has appeared. Such a label has also been extended, though not very seriously, to the Protestant clergy.

But there is one further extension of the association that is not accounted for in these terms, nor is the failure to include certain plausible targets so accountable. The extension I have in mind is that which leads to the inclusion as "pro-Communist" of certain men or institutions that have been associated with political responsibility in the international field. Two symbols stand out here. The first is Dean Acheson. Mr. Acheson has for years served the Democratic Party. But he has belonged to the conservative, not the New Deal wing of the party. Furthermore, the coupling of General Marshall with him, though only in connection with China, and only by extremists, clearly precludes political radicalism as the primary objection, since Marshall has never in any way been identified with New Deal views. The other case is that of Harvard University as an alleged "hot-bed" of Communism and fellow-traveling. The relevant point is that Mr. Acheson typifies the "aristocrat" in public service; he came of a wealthy family, he went to a select private school (Groton) and to Yale and Harvard Law School. He represents symbolically those Eastern vested interests, against whom antagonism has existed among the new men of the Middle West and the populist movement, including the descendants of recent immigrants. Similarly, among American universities Harvard has been particularly identified as educating a social elite, the members of which are thought of as "just the type," in their striped trousers and morning coats, to sell out the country to the social snobs of European capitals. It is the combination of aristocratic associations—through the Boston Brahmins—and a kind of urban-bohemian sophistication along with its devotion to intellectual and cultural values, including precisely its high intellectual standards, which makes Harvard a vulnerable symbol in this context.

The symbol "Communism," then, from its area of legitimate application, tends to be generalized to include groups in the population who have been associated with political liberalism of many shades and with intellectual values in general and to include the Eastern upper-class groups who have tended to be relatively internationalist in their outlook.

A second underlying ambivalent attitude-structure is discernible in addition to that concerning the relation between the totalitarian and the progressive aspects of Communism. On the one hand, Communism very obviously symbolizes what is anathema to the individualistic tradition of a business economy—the feared attempt to destroy private enterprise and with it the great tradition of individual freedom. But on the other hand, in order to rise to the challenge of the current political situation, it is necessary for the older balance between a free economy and the power of government to be considerably shifted in favor of the latter. We must have a stronger government than we have traditionally been accustomed to, and we must come to trust it more fully. It has had in recent times to assume very substantial regulatory functions in relation to the economy, and now vastly enhanced responsibilities in relation to international affairs.

But, on the basis of a philosophy which, in a very different way from our individualistic tradition, gives primacy to "economic interests," namely the Marxist philosophy, the Communist movement asserts the unqualified, the totalitarian supremacy of government over the economy. It is precisely an actual change in our own system in what, in one sense is clearly in this direction, that emerges as the primary focus of the frustrations to which the older American system has been subjected. The leaders of the economy, the businessmen, have been forced to accept far more "interference" from government with what they have considered "their affairs" than they have liked. And now they must, like everyone else, pay unprecedentedly high taxes to support an enormous military establishment, and give the government in other respects unprecedentedly great powers over the population. The result of this situation is an ambivalence of attitude that on the one hand demands a stringent display of loyalty going to lengths far beyond our tradition of individual liberty, and on the other hand is ready to blame elements which by ordinary logic have little or nothing to do with Communism, for working in league with the Communist movement to create this horrible situation.

Generally speaking, the indefensible aspect of this tendency, in a realistic assessment, appears in a readiness to question the loyalty of all those who have assumed responsibility for leadership in meeting the exigencies of the new situation. These include many who have helped to solve the internal problems of the control of the economy, those who in the uneasy latter 'thirties and the first phase of the war tried to get American policy and public opinion to face the dangers of the international situation, and those who since the war have tried to take responsibility in relation to the difficult postwar situation. Roughly, these are the presumptively disloyal elements who are also presumptively tainted with Communism. Here again, admittedly, certain features of our historical record and attitudes provide some realistic basis for this tendency. In fact many elements in both parties have failed lamentably to assess correctly the dangers of the situation, both internally and externally. New Dealers have stigmatized even the most responsible elements of the business world as economic royalists and the like, while many elements in business have clung long past a reasonable time to an outmoded belief in the possibility of a society with only a "night watchman" government. In foreign affairs, some members of the Democratic Party have been slow to learn how formidable a danger was presented by totalitarian Communism, but this is matched by the utopianism of many Republicans about the consequences of American withdrawal from international responsibilities, through high tariffs as well as political isolationism. The necessity to learn the hard realities of a complex world and the difficulty of the process is not a task to be imposed on only part of the body politic. No party or group can claim a monopoly either of patriotic motive or of competent understanding of affairs.

In a double sense, then, Communism symbolizes "the intruder." Externally the world Communist movement is the obvious source of the most serious difficulties we have to face. On the other hand, although Communism has constituted to some degree a realistic internal danger, it has above all come to symbolize those factors that have disturbed the beneficent natural state of an American society which allegedly and in phantasy existed before the urgent problems of control of the economy and greatly enhanced responsibility in international affairs had to be tackled.

Against this background it can perhaps be made clear why the description of McCarthyism as simply a political reactionary movement is inadequate. In the first place, it is clearly not simply a cloak for the "vested interests" but rather a movement that profoundly splits the previously dominant groups. This is evident in the split, particularly conspicuous since about 1952, within the Republican Party. An important part of the business elite, especially in the Middle West and in Texas, the "newest" area of all, have tended in varying degrees to be attracted by the McCarthy appeal. But other important groups, notably in the East, have shied away from it and apparently have come to be more and more consolidated against it. Very broadly, these can be identified with the business element among the Eisenhower Republicans.

But at the same time the McCarthy following is by no

means confined to the vested-interest groups. There has been an important popular following of very miscellaneous composition. It has comprised an important part of those who aspire to full status in the American system but have, realistically or not, felt discriminated against in various ways, especially the Mid-Western lower and lower middle classes and much of the population of recent immigrant origin. The elements of continuity between Western agrarian populism and McCarthyism are not by any means purely fortuitous. At the levels of both leadership and popular following, the division of American political opinion over this issue *cuts clean across the traditional lines of distinction between "conservatives" and "progressives,"* especially where that tends to be defined, as it so often is, in terms of the capitalistic or moneyed interests as against those who seek to bring them under more stringent control. McCarthyism is *both* a movement supported by certain vested-interest elements *and* a popular revolt against the upper classes.

Another striking characteristic of McCarthyism is that it is highly selective in the liberal causes it attacks. Apart from the issue of Communism in the labor unions, now largely solved, there has been no concerted attack on the general position of the labor movement. Further, the social program aimed toward the reduction of racial discrimination has continued to be pressed, to which fact the recent decision of the Supreme Court outlawing segregation in public education and its calm reception provide dramatic evidence. Nevertheless, so far as I am aware there has been no outcry from McCarthyite quarters to the effect that this decision is further evidence of Communist influence in high circles—in spite of the fact that eight out of nine members of the present court were appointed by Roosevelt and Truman.

Perhaps even more notable is the fact that, unlike the 1930's when Father Coughlin and others were preaching a vicious anti-Semitism, anti-Semitism as a public issue has since the war been very nearly absent from the American scene. This is of course associated with full employment. But particularly in view of the rather large and conspicuous participation of Jewish intellectuals in the fellow-traveling of the 1930's, it is notable that Jewishness has not been singled out as a symbolic focus for the questioning of loyalty. A critical difference from German Nazism is evident here. To the Nazis the Jew was the *primary* negative symbol, the Communist the most prominent secondary one. But it must also be remembered that capitalism was symbolically involved. One of the functions of the Jew was to *link* Communism and capitalism together. This trio were the "intruders" to the Nazis. They symbolized different aspects of the disturbance created by the rapid development of industrialism to the older pre-industrial *Gemeinschaft* of German political romanticism. It was the obverse of the American case—a new economy destroying an old political system, not new political responsibilities interfering with the accustomed ways of economic life.

Negatively, then, the use of the symbol "Communism" as the focus of anxiety and aggression is associated with a high order of selectivity among possibly vulnerable targets. This selectivity is, I submit, consistent with the hypothesis that the focus of the strain expressed by McCarthyism lies in the area of political responsibility—not, as Marxists would hold, in the structure of the economy as such, not in the class structure in any simple, Marxian-tinged sense.

The same interpretation is confined by the evidence on the positive side. The broadcast formula for what the McCarthyites positively "want"—besides the elimination of all Communist influence, real or alleged—is perhaps "isolationism." The dominant note is, I think, the regressive one. It is the wishful preservation of an old order, which allegedly need never had been disturbed but for the wilful interference of malevolent elements, Communists and their sympathizers. The nationalistic overtones center on a phantasy of a happy "American way" where everything used to be all right. Naturally it is tinged with the ideology of traditional laissez-faire, but not perhaps unduly so. Also it tends to spill over into a kind of irritated activism. On the one hand we want to keep out of trouble; but on the other hand, having identified an enemy, we want to smash him forthwith. The connection between the two can be seen, for example, in relation to China, where the phantasy seems to be that by drastic action it would be possible to "clean up" the Chinese situation quickly and then our troubles would be over.

The main contention of these pages has been that McCarthyism is best understood as a symptom of the strains attendant on a deep-seated process of change in our society, rather than as a "movement" presenting a policy or set of values for the American people to act on. Its content is overwhelmingly negative, not positive. It advocates "getting rid" of undesirable influences, and has amazingly little to say about what should be done.

This negativism is primarily the expression of fear, secondarily of anger, the aggression which is a product of frustration. The solution, which is both realistically feasible and within the great American tradition, is to regain our national self-confidence and to take active steps to cope with the situation with which we are faced.

On the popular level the crisis is primarily a crisis of confidence. We are baffled and anxious, and tend to seek relief in hunting scapegoats. We must improve our understanding and come to realize our strength and trust in it. But this cannot be done simply by wishing it to be done. I have consistently argued that the changed situation in which we are placed demands a far-reaching change in the structure of our society. It demands policies, and confidence, but it demands more than these. It demands above all three things. The first is a revision of our conception of citizenship to encourage the ordinary man to accept greater responsibility. The second is the development of the necessary implementing machinery.

Third is national political leadership, not only in the sense of individual candidates for office or appointment, but in the sense of social strata where a traditional political responsibility is ingrained.

The most important of these requirements is the third. Under American conditions, a politically leading stratum must be made up of a combination of business and nonbusiness elements. The role of the economy in American society and of the business element in it is such that political leadership without prominent business participation is doomed to ineffectiveness and to the perpetuation of dangerous internal conflict. It is not possible to lead the American people *against* the leaders of the business world. But at the same time, so varied now are the national elements which make a legitimate claim to be represented, the business element cannot monopolize or dominate political leadership and responsibility. Broadly, I think, a political elite in the two main aspects of "politicians" whose specialties consist in the management of public opinion, and of "administrators" in both civil and military services, must be greatly strengthened. It is here that the practical consequences of McCarthyism run most directly counter to the realistic needs of the time. But along with such a specifically political elite there must also be close alliance with other, predominantly "cultural" elements, notably perhaps in the universities, but also in the churches.

In the final sense, then, the solution of the problem of McCarthyism lies in the successful accomplishment of the social changes to which we are called by our position in the world and by our own domestic requirements. We have already made notable progress toward this objective; the current flare-up of stress in the form of McCarthyism can be taken simply as evidence that the process is not complete.

Part IV

THE STRUCTURAL SETTING
OF SOME SOCIAL FUNCTIONS

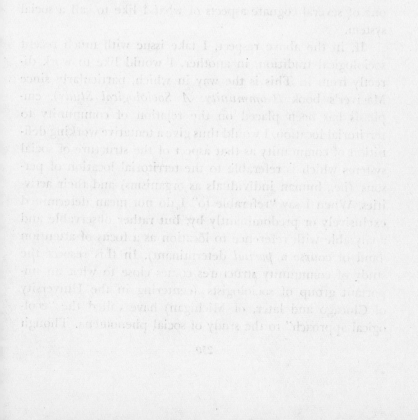

CHAPTER VIII

THE PRINCIPAL STRUCTURES
OF COMMUNITY

Contrary to a good deal of social science tradition, my attempt in this paper will be to treat community not as a type of concrete social unit, but as an *analytical* category. By the term "community" I would thus designate one "aspect" of *every* concrete social collectivity or structure. But by the same token, what I call its community aspect is only one of several cognate aspects of what I like to call a social system.

If, in the above respect, I take issue with much recent sociological tradition, in another, I would like to work directly from it. This is the way in which, particularly since Maciver's book *(Community: A Sociological Study)*, emphasis has been placed on the relation of community to territorial location. I would thus give a tentative working definition of community as that aspect of the structure of social systems which is referable to the territorial location of persons (i.e., human individuals as organisms) and their activities. When I say "referable to" I do not mean determined exclusively or predominantly by, but rather observable and analyzable with reference to location as a focus of attention (and of course a *partial* determinant). In this respect the study of community structures comes close to what an important group of sociologists (centering in the University of Chicago and later, of Michigan) have called the "ecological approach" to the study of social phenomena. Though the territorial reference is central, it should also be pointed out that there is another term to the relation. The full formula, that is, comprises *persons acting in territorial locations,* and since the reference is to *social* relations, persons acting in relation to *other persons* in respect to the territorial locations of both parties. The *population,* then, is just as much a focus of the study of community as is the territorial location.

If the community aspect concerns population in relation to territorial location, then what are the important contexts in which this should be broken down? I would like to take a pluralistic view here and say that we should consider not one such context, but a number of them. The variables according to which these contexts should be discriminated, then, would be found on each side of the relational dyad, namely the territorial and the "personal." And since we are dealing with an aspect of social systems the relevant aspect of the personal category is *role,* which is the organizing and controlling matrix of the many physical *task* performances which make it up.

The main problems for analysis in this paper, then, are the questions of what role-categories of social structure are most directly relevant to the relations of persons to territorial locations; what in turn are the principal categories of *meaning* of territorial location to persons in roles, and how are all these related to each other? From this point of view a territorial location is always significant as a "place where" something socially significant has happened or may be expected to happen. As points of reference always *both* the place where the person of reference is or is to be located, *and* the place where the significant object to which his action is oriented is located, must be considered.

It is further important to note that the human being as a physical organism does not "stay put" in a given location, but moves about a great deal. Therefore you cannot say that a given individual is always in the same unit of community organization. Secondly, the individual person has not one, but a number of roles. Hence, apart from other types of movement, the appropriate unit of community *need* not be the same for any two of the different roles in which he is involved.

More than is usually true in sociological discussion it will be necessary in this paper to refer to many very well-known and hence "obvious" things. I shall therefore have to ask for the reader's patience. I will mention these things, not to tell the reader anything he did not know before, but to *remind* him of things which, though he knows them very well, he might not *think of* as important to the present range of problems.

RESIDENTIAL LOCATION

Let us start with the individual as a primary point of reference. From the point of view of territorial location, the system of actions and participations of a given individual is not randomly scattered. It is clearly organized about a given territorial base which we usually refer to as his "residence," which is a specific physical "dwelling unit" located in a specific physical place. It is perhaps significant that in the English language the place of residence, the "home," is said to be the place where a person "lives," as though, when away from home, he were not alive.

The term "residence," in a community reference, has another set of interesting meanings besides that of dwelling-place, one which will be analyzed further below, namely a reference to the *area* of "jurisdiction" in some respect *within which* his dwelling place falls. Thus, an American citizen is a resident of a local community, e.g., for voting purposes. He is also a resident of a state, and of the United States of America. These are obviously not mutually exclusive meanings of residence, but rather extensions of the dwelling-place meaning to its relevance for different contexts of jurisdiction. Residence, in the dwelling-place sense, is not, however, only a category of the territorial location of the physical organism a large part of the time. It is also a category of *social* structure. In relation to his residence or home, a person plays certain roles which are at least not often so prominent when he is in other places, and these roles are performed in interaction with relatively specified counter-roles. Obviously in our society he typically shares a home with the other members of a nuclear family, though there are of course "households" with different composition where for example relatives other than members of the nuclear family are present, such as particularly the surviving parents of one of the spouses.

Of course there are considerable numbers of persons who "live" outside family households, such as hoboes, or dwellers in rooming houses and hotels, or in monasteries or convents. The "norm" for the great majority of the American population is clearly, however, the nuclear family household.

There is thus a very specific articulation between the territorial distribution of the population with reference to residence and the most important unit of our particular kinship system, and analogous considerations apply in other societies.

But this is *not* to say that, sociologically speaking, all residential kinship units, i.e., households, in all societies are "essentially alike." They are alike in some respects and very different in others. However, the most important uniformity refers to the generality of the association of territorial location in the residential sense (but not in any other senses) with the institutionalization of relationships by "biological position," i.e., by generation, sex and parentage.

Clearly what the typical individual "does" within his dwelling-place and its immediately surrounding "grounds," as compared with what he does outside and within other references of community structure, is variable, both as a function of age and sex role within the household, and as a function of the place of household structures within the larger social system. Therefore one of the important problems for us is to identify which important clusters of territorially located activity for classes of individuals, such as occupational activity, occur *outside* the household. Furthermore, our primary concern is not with individuals for their own sake but with the relational system involving them. Thus many acts within a relational system, such as reading a newspaper or watching television, are performed within the household, for which the *source* of the communication is not only not a member of the same household as the receiver, but is not a household at all.

The nuclear family focuses territorially in the residential premises. But since the composition of the family is the most heavily conditioned by the ascriptive factors of biological position, age, and sex of any major structure of society, it tends to serve as a reference point and partial determinant of several wider structures. Residence is closely linked to what is often called the "style of life." Families with a similar style of life are more likely to feel comfortable living in close contiguity than if styles of life differ greatly. Hence there is a tendency to relative uniformity of residential neighborhoods, and for the "better" neighborhoods to segregate out from the "less desirable" ones. This, in turn, is an important set of reference points for the *class structure* of the society.

Occupation and Work Premises

The next category of territorial reference I shall deal with is that of occupation or work. What is meant by the category of occupation or work is fairly well understood on a common-sense basis and only needs to be brought to attention here in the relevant respects.

Perhaps the best point of reference to start with is the relation to the household. The occupational function from the household point of view is the set of activities of its members on which its "consumption income" is primarily dependent, whether that consumption income be "in kind" or in money terms. Thus while the farmer and the housewife have what may be called occupational components in their roles as members of the household, a full-fledged differentiation of occupational from household roles involves the performance of the functions concerned in a relational context independent of the household. Of course, various modes and degrees of such independence are possible.

The case of the "full-fledged" differentiation of occupational from familial role-components is the case where the work is performed in an *organization* which is structurally independent of any household, which has an organizational goal to the effective attainment of which the role of the individual may be considered to be a "contribution." The performance of such a role is then subject to a "contract of employment." Work is done under relatively specified conditions, generally *on premises* controlled by the organization and not at all by the household of the employee, and he receives money remuneration on agreed terms. There is, that is to say, *both* complete *organizational* separation between household as social organization and employing organization, and complete *physical* separation between residential premises and work premises. This, of course, is an ideal type.

Whatever the incidence of the many borderline cases, clearly the main pattern in our society is the employment of the individual in organizations primarily consisting of occupational roles in this sense. The incumbent works mainly away from home, with people who are not members of his own household, under controls and disciplines organizationally separate from his household. The primary current terms for such premises of occupational work are, of course, the "plant" or factory, the "office," and some others.

Closely assimilated to the occupational role in its community aspects is the role system of formal education. For

teachers and school administrators the roles are occupational; for pupils they may be called proto-occupational.

It is worth noting that, linguistically, descriptive words
used in such contexts often refer to *either* the physical facility or the unit of social organization, or sometimes to both.
Thus "office" or "bureau," "school," etc. Somehow such
double-reference terms are less common in the residential
field; thus "residence," "house" or "apartment" are clearly
physical terms, "household" and "family," social.

One further aspect of the structure of community relations in a wider sense derives from the two fundamentals
of the diurnal and weekly cycles of activity. If *most* of the
time the typical individual spends nights in his home, and
a very large number of individuals spend several hours
several days a week in work premises, naturally there is a
problem of physical transportation back and forth between
them, a problem which does not exist where work and residence are located in the same place. Hence distances
between the two places, means of transportation, and time-
cost factors are all involved in the linkages.

From this point of view, the "local community" is, in one
aspect, in a society like our own, primarily organized about
the complex network of relations between places of residence and of employment of its adult population (and
schooling of its children). There tends to be a process of differentiation of primarily residential *districts* from work districts, which in turn are differentiated by different *kinds* of
work process, e.g., manufacturing, professional work, administrative work, etc., and the residences of different categories
of population.

This clearly implies that a highly differentiated social
structure is commonly associated with technological development so that the typical mode of transportation from home
to work ceases to be unaided walking. Indeed, even so
prosaic a question as whether employed persons habitually
go home for lunch is a relevant one; in many modern coun-

tries such as France this is almost mandatory except in the very largest cities. One may say that a large city, in the sense of a population engaged in a highly differentiated system of social relationships, is also a large city in the sense of the territorial area within which the requisite activities are carried on.

Transportation is the necessary link between residence and work premises. For analytical purposes, however, I shall treat transportation as belonging in what I referred to above as the "communicative" complex. It is necessitated by, and partly conditions, the separation of premises of residence and of work, but the transportation process is subject to different imperatives from either of the other two.

One further obvious qualification of the outline so far presented should also be made explicit. This is that as a physical location the home is not "used" exclusively by persons who "live" there nor is the work-place used exclusively by those who "work" there in the sense of regular employment. One important function of a home is as a place to receive visitors, all the way from the most casual callers to "house guests" over a considerable period. Here again common language distinctions are significant, e.g., between an invitation to "stay with us" and one to "live with us." Entertainment is obviously one of the main modes of relationship of the household to the society outside of it. Similar considerations apply to the work premises, though in this case the most important category of those who are not employed there is those who "have business" there. These may be persons who have supervisory authority over the work organization, but themselves are "located" somewhere else, e.g., in the "central office." Or they may be persons not "belonging to the organization" who have some sort of business with it, as salesmen, customers, or insurance adjusters.

It should also not be overlooked that there are many occupational categories whose jobs require them to "travel," either within the local community, or frequently, outside. In other words only part of their work takes place in one specific location. Here, however, it is usual for such a role to have some kind of a "home base" (one might say an "occupational residence") from which the incumbent goes out and to which he returns. An important distinction, of course, is that between the kind of moving around which still permits returning to the place of residence at the end of a working day, and the kind that requires accommodations which constitute a temporary residence, as someone's guest, or in a hotel. In other words, the question concerns the extent of the relevant area of community within which the individual "operates."

Let me note again that I am dealing with the "work" component of community in an analytical sense. I have already noted some shadings-off between it and the residential focus of community, and cited cases where the two fuse in territorial reference and role-interaction. The same is, of course, often true of shadings-off in other directions, and for both the categories so far discussed. Thus a "church" is both a physical facility and a social organization. Except for the minister it is, as a place, not usually either residential or occupational in function. But it is a place where a determinate group of people engage in organized social interaction and may be said to have a "work" component involved in meeting the "technical" conditions of effective conduct of services and whatever other functions the church as social organization may perform. But another component is communicative in the sense to be discussed and there is even a jurisdictional component, most marked in the case of an "established" church, but present to some degree in all of them.

JURISDICTION

The third element of community structure I shall call *jurisdiction*. By this I mean obligations which are imposed on categories of persons by some process of decision-making where the ultimately relevant agency is held to have "legitimate authority" under a system of normative order. The most important point about obligations, however, is that at some level they imply a conditional procedure of "enforcement." This is to say that in attempting to control the fulfilment of the obligation, it is regarded as legitimate or even mandatory to apply "sanctions." The promise or threat of such sanctions, explicit or implicit, may also, of course, serve as a means of controlling compliance with, or infraction of, obligations.

Sanctions, in the nature of the case, are specific to persons and categories of persons. The effectiveness of sanctions, again positive as well as negative, further depends on their *reaching* the object to whom they are directed. And to reach him, it has to be in a territorial location where he is, or may be expected to be at the relevant time. In its community reference, then, I would like to define an area of jurisdiction as the *area* in which an agency with legitimate authority, which is attempting to control the behavior of persons or categories of persons, has the right to apply sanctions to them.

So far I have referred to sanctions both positive and negative. There is, however, an essential asymmetry between them. This rests on the fact that, in the case of positive sanctions, there is little inducement for the object of the sanctions to question the right of the agent to apply them in the place where he does. In the case of negative sanctions, on the other hand, since there is incentive to avoid them if possible, obvious strategies for such avoidance are to question the right of the agent to apply the sanctions at all, or in the *place* in question, or to escape to a place outside the range of jurisdiction.

For present purposes the difference between right and power is not important. The point is that a social system must be structured not only with respect to the *persons* and categories of them upon which obligations may be imposed, but also with respect to the *places* at which sanctions may be imposed.

The basic reason for the importance of place is, of course, that, if there is no physical organism in a specific place there is no action, and hence no effect of the sanction component of *inter*action. This means that control of the physical movements of people, in the sense of change of location, becomes an aspect of controlling their performance in social relationships. The strategic role of physical force rests on two main considerations: first, that in a "regression scale" of punishment the infliction of pain or injury on the organism is an ultimate recourse when others fail, second, that while there are critical limits on the effectiveness of force or the threat of force in motivation of positive action, in the *prevention* of feared or disapproved action, force is the ultimate sanction. If the magnitude of the force is sufficient *any* person may be prevented from leaving a place or communicating from it, and hence significant action can be blocked. And in the very last analysis, in the human social sense of action, a dead man does not act.

The above statements should not in the least be taken to imply that "in the last analysis human action is controlled by force, or motivated by fear of force." It implies only that certain relatively *specific* conditions which affect systems of action, with special reference to its discouragement or prevention, can be controlled by force. But to imply that because a factor can prevent something or stop it, the whole process is determined by that factor is to argue as if, by equipping a vehicle with sufficiently powerful brakes alone you could make it run and steer it anywhere you wanted it to go.

One further proposition about force is essential, namely that *socially organized* force is inherently superior to what any unaided individual can ever muster. Hence, insofar as force is a *factor* in power, it is the control of organized force which matters, not the strength, or skill of the individual.

It should also be clearly understood that I am not limiting the concept of jurisdiction to contexts where the use of force is institutionalized, or a serious possibility. Thus, it is common for churches to claim jurisdiction over all persons of their faith resident within a territorial area; the parish or the diocese is in one aspect a jurisdictional area. But the church may be forbidden both by its own code and by the law to attempt or threaten to enforce this jurisdiction by force. It is fundamentally for jurisdictional reasons that an organization oriented to the implementation of codes always has a prominent element of territorial structuring. Thus there are usually a "central" office, and perhaps regional and local offices.

If, now, it is clear that jurisdiction in my sense does not as such imply the use of force, it is possible to proceed to develop a few implications of the strategic significance of force which nevertheless remains. The most important of these is that the *combination* of territorial jurisdiction and the attempted monopoly of the legitimate use of organized force is *one* of the primary features of political organization.

There have, in the history of political theory, been many controversies over the delineation of the category "political." I shall not try to review the alternatives but only to state my own view, which derives from the attempt to place political aspects of organization in the context of a general analysis of the social system as a whole. Here I would give primary emphasis to the organization of the social system relative to the attainment of goals accepted as *binding* on the system as a whole.

For collectve action in pursuit of such goals to be effective, there naturally has to be integration of the system with reference to their acceptance and with reference to the distribution of responsibilities and burdens which it entails; this is the "consent" aspect of political organization. But jurisdiction relates to the use of force because if the political authority does not control the use of force, force controlled by other agencies, inside or outside the jurisdictional area, may serve to *prevent* the attainment of *any* goal politically accepted in the system. Hence the special criterion that attainment of a goal should be treated as *binding* would be directly jeopardized if force were not controlled. And because the sanctions of force must be applied to concrete physical persons in concrete physical locations, control of force without territorial jurisdiction is impossible.

Effectiveness in the control of force is, however, obviously a central consideration. This depends on the effectiveness with which a population can be integrated in political terms. Hence, so far political jurisdiction has existed only for limited territorial areas, and many of the wider extensions have proved unstable and broken down rather rapidly.

It seems to be for reasons such as this that the *primary* framework of jurisdiction is found to be in the political reference, and that the boundaries of integrated societal systems have a strong tendency to coincide with the territorial jurisdictions of their political systems.

I have spoken of *tendency* because of the extent to which in fact countervailing tendencies also operate. The mixed "nationalities" problems of central and eastern Europe provide a sufficient example that political jurisdiction and ethnic identity very often do not coincide.

The same general considerations which are relevant to the "state" as the widest area of firm political jurisdiction also apply with qualifications to the subdivisions of it. Here, of course, I mean subdivisions in a sense which does not beg the question of the relations between narrower and wider units of government or political jurisdiction. In the United States, we have both a federal system and a system of considerable local autonomy and "home rule" within the state in the sense of one of the fifty. Other systems are much more centralized and "provinces" are nearer to being branches of the central government, even towns and cities are branches. The central point is not this, but that *whatever* the pattern of centralization or decentralization, the *main* framework of subdivision of political organization is territorial. Government, like all organized subsystems of a society, has to have *functional* subdivisions, but these must in turn be brought together in terms of territorial organization at every level. You cannot *operate* a bureau of internal revenue without access to the taxpayers *where they are,* and they cannot be "got at" wthout the backing of *general* governmental authority in the specific local area.

A general point about social structures is relevant here. This is the distinction between differentiation and segmentation. Two differentiated subsystems of a larger system have different functions in the system so that their "contributions" are complementary; but they do not *do* the same things. The roles of husband and wife in the family are differentiated in this sense. Two subsystems are segments when they are structurally distinct units both performing essentially *the same* functions. Thus two infantry companies in a regiment, or two Ford assembly plants in different parts of the country are segments. Segmentation develops essentially from what economists would call limitations on the economies of scale, if this concept can be generalized so that it is not confined to economically relevant factors. Thus families are very small segments of the social structure. The fact that child rearing is not, in the usual familial respects, carried on in large organizations has something to do with the importance of very great "individualizing" which, in turn, one may suspect has something to do with the extreme "diffuseness" of the relevant communication, as that conception will be noted below.

Any exigency which influences the functioning of a social unit may be a factor in segmentation, but those linked with territoriality and physical processes are certainly prominent among them. The division of governmental units just mentioned is certainly a case in point, and all large organizations which operate in relation to a widely dispersed "public" tend to have segmentary administrative units arranged by territorial jurisdiction.

Another particularly important aspect of this problem is the relation of political jurisdiction to law. In the most general sociological sense, law may be said to be any relatively formalized and integrated body of rules which imposes obligations on persons playing particular roles in particular collectivities. Such a conception implies, I think further, that there is a machinery of authoritive interpretation, i.e., something analogous to a system of courts, and a machinery of the definition and implementation of sanctions, and a relatively clear focus of legitimation. It is quite clear that the concept of obligation from which I embarked on this discussion of jurisdiction, in any at all highly differentiated social system implies law.

Why then does the *highest* level of binding law in a highly differentiated society tend to be, as Dean Pound put it, the law of "*politically* organized society"? The answer, I think, is to be found in the relation of law to jurisdiction. It is because the highest *jurisdictional* authority is political. This, in turn, is true because, first, a system of law must eventually apply to defined categories of territorially located persons in roles. But secondly, to apply sanctions there must, for the reasons discused above, be a jurisdictional reference. Though part of government, the "legal" system in modern societies (legal system in the sense not of the body of rules itself, but of the courts) is a very special part of it, enjoying a special kind of independence from the rest. The main reason why it is in government at all is that the reference to jurisdiction and to sanctions is essential if law is to be *binding*.

I have referred to the political as the "highest" jurisdictional authority. This certainly should not be interpreted to mean, for example, that political obligations are the "highest" human obligations, for instance, in a "moral" sense. I am speaking here of the jurisdictional aspect of the organization of the *society* as a system, and am saying that no society can be effectively integrated which permits other jurisdictional claims to take precedence over those of its governmentally sanctioned legal system. However, human responsibility is not defined only in terms of responsibility in the society. But when the reference *is* to the society, an obligation not "in principle" directly incorporated in the law of the state must fall in one or more of three categories. First, it may fall within the range of freedom allowed and defined by the the law of the state. This is the case with the whole range of *socially* sanctioned "private" interests, be they personal, economic, religious or what not. Second, it may be felt to be an obligation *in conflict* with those imposed by the law. In this case the only recourses are to change the law, or to resort to the various tactics of deviant behavior, e.g., evasion or rebellion. Third, it may fall in an extra-social realm. Thus a person may feel for himself an obligation to "think straight" about a certain personal problem. So long as the consequence is not identifiably expressed in his interactive behavior, the law has nothing to say about it nor any sanctions to impose. In principle, the same is true of "the state of his immortal soul" which, being a nonempirical state of affairs, cannot be reached by empirical sanctions in any earthly jurisdiction.

Some would argue that historically the role of the church did not fit this view of political primacy in the field of jurisdiction. I do not think this is the case if we stick strictly to the treatment of jurisdiction as a structural aspect of a social system. It would certainly be correct to say that the Medieval Church (and churches today as well) claimed to define the highest *moral* obligations of its members, and to impose the ultimate *religious* sanctions in relation to this obligation; but moral obligations are not *ipso facto* social obligations and religious sanctions are not *ipso facto* social sanctions. Only when the moral-religious jurisdiction of the church had been *translated into* political jurisdiction could it be said to be *socially* paramount. This means that, though in the Middle Ages the "state" was organizationally differentiated from the church, it was only in a highly qualified sense *independent* of the church. On the societal level orthodoxy of belief could only become a *sine qua non* of membership in the society in good standing if, as was in fact the case, heresy was a *civil* crime. The church, to be sure, did not "itself" burn heretics at the stake. But if the political authority had not lent *its* jurisdictional backing to the service of the obligations insisted upon by the church, the medieval system of religious unity on the *social* level could not have been maintained.

For the society as a whole, I have argued that political jurisdiction is paramount, and no society can be effectively "politically organized" if a claim of other jurisdictions to supersede that of the law is successfully put through. But this does not mean that the concept of jurisdiction does not apply to *all* subsystems of the society so far as they are governed by a normative order defining obligations, which will be enforced by sanctions. They will of course differ in territorial area, but also in the nature of the obligations and of the sanctions. The cases of "delegation" of the legitimate use of force are on the whole minor, such as parents' rights to spank children. For this reason the ultimate negative sanction of non-governmental collectivities is usually expulsion from membership.

THE COMMUNICATIVE COMPLEX

It is now time to turn to the last of four categories or "foci" of community structure, the one I shall call the "communicative complex." This involves using the term communication in a sense broader than usual.

The three categories so far discussed have, in their territorial references, designated either *places at which* or *areas within which* concerte persons in different roles were located, and to which action-types such as sanctions, are oriented. But since we are dealing with social systems, we cannot omit reference to the processes which go on *between* persons-in-places. The relation of interaction between two persons must, in its physical aspect, relate two discriminable places to each other, and if either is to "influence" the other, there must be a physical process which is transmitted from one organism to the other. This may operate through direct physical contact as through shaking hands or kissing. But most human interaction involves intermediate physical media, such as light waves, sound waves, electrical waves or the transfer of physical objects from the "hands" of one to those of the other.

Communication as an aspect of the structure of community may, for present purposes, be defined as the processes involving, on the one hand, the physical media by which messages and objects are transferred from one person in location to another, and on the other hand, the physical aspects of change of location of persons themselves when this takes place as meaningfully related to communicative performance in a social role. There is thus a continuum from what we would think of as "pure" communication where "only" a message is transmitted, to the cases where physical goods and persons themselves are, as it were, "transmitted," i.e., change their physical location.

Before taking up the modes of involvement of persons-in-locations and the relation of this to the physical media of communication, it is necessary to sketch the components of the process of social interaction through communication on the level of meaning itself, i.e., of *content* of messages. The first category I wish to distinguish is the one already mentioned of *information* as such, which has already been noted. Information is a factor in "defining" the situation for the behavior of its recipient, but giving information does not as such attempt to "influence" that behavior. Informational messages are existentially cognitive in content; as such they merely assert that something is true, has happened, will probably happen, etc.

The interactive process involved in the transmission of information may or may not involve reciprocities of interchange. But so long as we stick to the ideal type of informational communication its receipt changes nothing except the cognitive content available to the recipient.

A second component which I would like to call *opinion* is involved when we assume the existence of an *intentional* orientation to the influencing of the behavior of the recipient. There is, that is to say, an "expectation" on the part of the sender that the recipient will or "ought" to *behave* differently as a consequence of receiving the communication than he would have without it. In a sense in which this is not true of the transmission of information, such a communication implies an element of sanction in the above sense. In some sense, if an "opinion" is expressed that another person or persons "ought" to change their direction of behavior, it is implied that, contingent on what behavior actually ensues, the communicator will, in however mild a degree, feel and somehow express approval or disapproval.

Still a third component of communication involves, however, another order of response, i.e., not just acceptance or non-acceptance in the sense of "agreement" or its reverse, but a *commitment* to specific action on the part of the recipient, or, of course, a refusal to make such a commitment. A message, intended to secure a commitment by the recipient, may be called a *suggestion*. In common usage, this is indicated by a different sense of the word agreement than the above. In response to an opinion one "agrees *that*" such and such is or would be a good thing; in response to a suggestion, however, one "agrees *to*" do something, or declines to agree to.

It may, finally, be made explicit that communication always implies a *common culture*. The minimum of this is a "common language" or, in terms of information theory, a set of rules for relating the processes of encoding and decoding. But beyond this there must be meaningful common "definitions of the situation" in which the communicative process takes place, which provide the "frame of reference" in terms of which symbols can be interpreted. Such a common culture must on some level be a prerequisite of effective communicative interchange. But it is also typically modified and added to, through the process of communication itself. So we may speak of the communicative process starting in a matrix of *given* "understandings" and ending in a modified system.

What, now, are the modes of involvement of physical persons in physical locations in processes of communication? In the first place, all communication requires physical media. Three levels of this physical requirement may be noted. In the first case, no specialized *technology* of communication is required; the ordinary person has both the facilities and the skills which are necessary under ordinary circumstances. The type case here is face-to-face speech. In the second case, a special technological facility has to be provided, but, no physical object needs to be "transported" from the sender to the receiver. Telephone, radio, and television are type cases in this category. The third case is that where a physical object must be transported from the physical presence of the sender to the physical presence of the receiver; the letter is a typical example. Any one of the three above types of media may be involved in any one of the modes of communicating content.

A further question concerns whether the communication channel is one-way or two-way, that is whether it does or does not permit "feed-back." Face-to-face speech is completely symmetrical in this respect as, with their limitation, other media may be also. Media which are technically structured on a one-way basis, like newspapers and broadcasting, involve special constraints on the interactive process. Though, in content, the component of opinion may be heavy, there are substantial limitations on following it up with approval or disapproval, at least of the action of specific persons. It is thus almost impossible to use these media as means of *securing* specific commitments since this requires the specific assent of the recipient. Anonymity of the "audience" is a very important factor here.

Different media of communication have different advantages and limitations which will be of different orders of significance for different functions. Two of the most important ranges of difference concern the importance of direct feed-back in the course of the communication process itself, and the symbolic content of that feed-back. Face-to-face speech has a very wide range of feed-back possibilities, most extensive in the dyadic situation. There is not only the strict semantic content of the utterances of the voice, but tone, cadence, and a variety of cues which are lost when the "same" utterance is put in written form. There is also the visual communication which transmits facial expression, gestures, posture, etc. There is the possibility of actual touch, e.g., patting on the back. Even smell may create "atmosphere," e.g., through a woman's perfume. Hence this type of communication is very "concrete" or "diffuse" in the sense of the range of cues which may have some level of "meaning."

A new set of constraints is already introduced by the presence of a third person, either because there is hesitation about saying and doing things in his presence which might be said and done *à deux,* or because he also has to have opportunity to participate and therefore the time available to any one communicator is, other things equal, cut down. Thus even with physical presence, the communication process in a sizeable "meeting" is very different from what it is between two persons who are alone in a room.

Other limitations are introduced with the distant media.

Writing eliminates all but the semantic content of words, though it may introduce new "contextual" factors through the aesthetic qualities of printing or calligraphy. It also introduces a new degree of freedom in that the message may be preserved and be *repeatedly* consulted. The telephone preserves most of the auditory component of reciprocal speech but removes the visual and other components entirely.

There is no such things as a good or bad medium of communication in an absolute sense, except for the problem of "noise" in the technical sense of information theory. Face-to-face conversation is in a sense the "broadest" but for some purposes it may be better to cut down on cues which can be disturbing. Thus a man may prefer to transmit bad news by letter specifically to *avoid* immediate feed-back.

In its ecological reference, obviously, a highly important range of variation in communications concerns the extent to which physical presence is required, or presents great advantages, and the cases where it is not required, or would even be disadvantageous. Hence transportation is linked with communication with respect to the person, because changes in a person's physical location are often undertaken with a view to facilitating processes of communication, as in the case of a man going to a meeting. But in a very close relation to changing location in order to facilitate communication are the cases where change of location is a consequence of receipt of a communication, e.g., a notification that there will be a meeting at a given time and place. Thus movements of persons in part, like physical media, condition the process of communication. But the processes of communication, in turn, control movements of persons. Indeed the person who himself carries a message from place to place may quite literally be said himself to constitute a medium of communication, whether he carries it in written form, or "in his head."

Furthermore, a linkage exists between the process of communication and the movement of physical objects which is very similar to that which prevails between communication and the movement of persons. In the first place, the medium of communication itself may be a physical object which must be transported, e.g., the letter. Also the presence of the physical objects which serve as the technical means of communication may be a very important condition of successful communication. But the most important case is that where the movement of physical objects is the consequence of processes of communication. Sometimes this does not involve transfer of property rights, but in a highly important class of cases it does, namely the sale of commodities which then become the property of the purchaser. It thus connects up with the problem of jurisdiction because readjustment of obligations in the social system is involved.

I have a special reason for stressing this connection between communication, the change of location of objects, and the transfer of property rights. This is because it is a dramatic illustration of the fact that the mechanisms which control the latter two processes are more closely related to the communication process than is usually realized. Money in particular is both a "language" and a medium of communication, and the relation between language, medium, and physical consequences, is essentially the same here as in other cases of communication.

We are, of course, all aware that communications of decisions to sell or to purchase are "ordinary" communications. But the offer of money is also as much an act of communication, of the type designated above as "suggestion," and its acceptance is a commitment, both to accept the money, *and* to perform the rest of the bargain, e.g., to transfer possession of the goods, and perhaps to "deliver" them in the sense of physical transportation.

Thus a transfer of money from one person to another is an act of communication and what is "tranmitted" is strictly a message. If *physical* money, e.g., bank notes, changes hands, this is a medium. In fact a bank note is quite literally a letter.

Furthermore the same message may be transmitted by different media, as when we recall that in a society like ours the great bulk of monetary transactions do not involve "cash" changing hands at all, but the only *physical* process is giving and following instructions (i.e., communicating in the suggestion mode) the result of which is an alteration of entries in account books.

Money is probably the most striking case of an institutionalized medium which is not ordinarily thought of in the context of communication, but which in fact has all the properties of a medium and language of communication when it is seen in the proper light to bring this out. In my opinion, political power is also such a language and medium which is not comparably quantified and must be regarded as a *component* of acts of communication which take predominantly verbal forms. The essential phenomenon is the *generalization* of commitments and the expectations associated with them. In the case of money, for example, its societal guarantee, partly by public authority (i.e., an exercise of jurisdiction), partly by informal "confidence," makes it possible for it to function as a *circulating* medium. It is not possible to go further into this technical subject here, but it was important to mention it because it provides an essential link between communication processes in the usual senses and the physical movements of persons and goods.

Perhaps I may attempt to generalize this a little. In the context of the analysis of social systems, communication is the main process of *inter*action, by which processes of "action" and behavior of units of the system are "controlled," by which, what one unit does has determinate effects, not only on the state, but on the future behavior of the others. Physical movements of human bodies stand at the "bottom" of this hierarchy of systems of control. The movement of other physical objects under human control, e.g., "transportation," belongs in essentially the same category; at most, it is only one step further removed from "pure communication." As I have noted, furthermore, *all* communication involves physical media, and this includes the transportation of symbolically meaningful objects, e.g., letters. Any classification of the meaning-levels of the content of communication cuts directly across any classification of the media of their transmission.

The content of communications, i.e., "messages" is always "symbolic" and, in some sense, "cultural." The *movement* of persons and physical objects is in some sense "material." The processes in which we are interested are the *co-ordinated* behaviors of physical organisms. This co-ordination, however, is achieved through *inter*personal communication. Mechanisms such as money are those which can "stimulate" the movement of persons and objects very directly. And yet money is not a physical object, nor is a unit of money, e.g. a dollar. Money is a "symbolic mechanism" and its "use," e.g., by "spending," is a process of communication.

The relation between the patterns of movement of physical persons and goods and the control of these movements through money can serve as a kind of general paradigm of the relation between the "communicative" aspect of community structure, that is, the "disposition" of persons and objects in physical locations, and the "symbolic" aspects of the process of social interaction. The essence of the paradigm is a *double* level of interchange. (What I here refer to is the well-known economic paradigm: Goods are exchanged for money (consumers' spending) and wages are paid for labor services.)

At the "bottom" the "issue" is the transfer of rights of possession and the movement of goods. The mechanism which "trips off" this movement is the offer of money. But, at the level of the balance of forces in the system, not of the particular transaction, this "control" cannot be effective unless "what is offered" is "supported in its value" by commitments to production. The commitment which is of salient importance here is that called "labor" by economists. The "input of labor" supports or creates the "purchasing power" which is necessary if consumers are to be *able* to buy the goods produced. This mediating function of money is necessary because the *physical* processes of production and distribution of *goods* cannot be regulated in a social system unless the commitments of the contributors to production are regulated at a *higher* level in the hierarchy of control. The "decisions" by which this regulation operates are very relevant, not only to the outcome of the process of production and allocation of physical goods, but also to the *structure* of the system of social interaction *in which* this physical process takes place. The dual level structure of the economic paradigm derives from the fact that it must articulate *both* with the physical process of production *and* with the structure of the social system. Hence, money is a mechanism on the "lower borderline" of the processes of communication in the usual sense.

The upshot of this discussion of communication is to make it clear that not only must *activities* of members of a social system be spatially located, and hence their distribution patterned, but the physical aspects of the processes of interaction *between* social units must be definitely patterned. Indeed, the conditions, which make it possible to communicate effectively in the relevant respects, constitute one of the most important determinants of the spatial distribution of a population, and of the movements of that population from place to place.

CONCLUSION

There is a sense in which human personality and society must be fitted into the ancient concept-pair of biological theory: organism and environment. As ordinarily understood, both refer to physical categories. In the sense in which this is ordinarily understood, neither personalities nor societies are physical categories. (Of course I mean this statement in a *strictly* analytical sense. I hope it has been evident throughout the above analysis that it is my view that there is no such thing as *concrete* human behavior which is not the behavior of the physical organism in the physical environment. But this does *not* mean that "physical" theory is adequate for the analysis of the aspects of personality and social systems which are involved in such processes as cultural communication and *control* of physical movements. In the sense that a different order of conceptual scheme is required, this scheme must refer to a different category of object. In this sense a personality or a society is not a physical object.) But these action systems are "rooted in" the organism and its physical environment.

The formula with which I began the analysis of community structure is based on this consideration. All individual actors in social systems are, among other things, physical organisms which must be located in physical space and can only change location through physical processes (movements) over time.

The classification of the four categories of community structure which has served as the main logical framework of this discussion is derived from the implications of this starting point. Thus, first, the category of residence is that of the locational reference of persons in the roles in which their status *as persons,* independently of the exigencies of more specified roles, is most salient. This, then, includes the main biologically ascriptive foci of their status, biological relatedness, through birth and parenthood, sex, and age, or generation, as constitutive of their residential status. It is the aspect of social role in which the broader biological references of the categorization of the individual organism are most directly involved.

The category of residence, as an aspect of community structure, may thus be treated as the focus of the anchorage of the individual human person, as person, through the fact that in one major aspect he *is* (not is "attached to") a biological organism, in the physical-organic world. If, however, in residence, the biological and physical reference points of the constitution of social systems are fused, at the same time, residence is the main point of articulation between these and some of the distinctively *social* structures. It is in the family that the earlier stages of socialization of the child take place, which prepare him for roles *outside* the family and which cannot be treated in terms of the properties of the individual organism without reference to considerations of personality, society, and culture. As a point of articulation, the residential focus is thus, though anchored in territory and biology, not just a "case" of these categories.

The work or occupational reference of the structure of community, on the other hand, involves emphasis on the environmental pole of the organism-environment reference system. It is the focus of that aspect of human activities where orientation *to* the environment is paramount, where *adaptive* functions are primarily at issue. And, in one major phase, as we have seen, this is adaptation to the *physical* environment. But this, like residence, is a point of articulation, and just as in the household only some of the activities are primarily concerned with biological needs, so, in work situations, only some of the activities are concerned with meeting the exigencies imposed by the physical environment, notably those which we think of as the processes of physical production of goods. Other "technologies" are concerned with communication and the control of personalities or of social relationships, or with creation of new cultural patterns. But even these must be oriented to certain physical exigencies, notably, they are activities of concrete persons taking place in concrete locations. If they must be co-operative activities, then there must be premises of work in which they take place and the participants can interact through physical media. Thus the reference of an environmental exigency like the biological one is *never* escaped; it is rather that the form it takes changes according to the nature of the activity and the structure of the *social* system in which it takes place. In both the two above cases, personality and social structure have "come between" the two poles of the organism-environment pair so that the structure of human community is not simply a "reflection" of the organic and environmental exigencies, but a point of articulation *between* these exigencies and the specifically psychological and sociological characteristics of systems of human action.

The category of jurisdiction as dealt with here does not primarily concern either of these two poles but rather one of the two primary aspects of the relations between them. It is here that, in territorial terms, the aspect of *area* as distinguished from particular location is primarily significant. This is essentially derived from the fact that *order,* in the normative social sense, implies order in the physical phenomena which are subject to control through the processes of the social system. Insofar as social order operates through normative institutions and rules which are partially dependent on sanctions for their effectiveness, this order must, in the nature of the case, have a territorial reference. Hence the boundaries of a social system as social system must have something to do with the territorial boundaries within which control of physical processes and specification of the categories of persons, to which the order applies, can be made effective.

But again, as in the other two cases, physical boundaries and the jurisdictional authority which orients to them, are not simple reflections of the physical factors or exigencies influencing behavior, but are points of articulation between these physical exigencies and the nonphysical aspects of the social system. The socio-cultural *meaning* of a physical boundary is never statable in geographical terms as such.

The fourth category, the communicative complex, also has the same characteristics. It refers not to the boundaries of interactive systems but to the *processes* of interchange which go on between units of the social system, and to the physical exigencies to which these processes are subject. Just as there are physical techniques of "catching" law-violators there have to be physical techniques of communication. But in this case the *inter-relations* between the physical and nonphysical aspects which are articulated are more patent than perhaps in any other of the four complexes of community structure. For here the clear primacy of communication content over techniques of transmission tends to be taken for granted. But the relation of communication to the movements of persons and goods, and the continuity between "pure" communication and these cases, was stressed above in order to show that this also is a case of *articulation,* with the same basic structure as in the other cases.

CHAPTER IX

SOME TRENDS OF CHANGE
IN AMERICAN SOCIETY:
THEIR BEARING ON
MEDICAL EDUCATION

To the sociologist the medical, like other professions, is an integral part of the society which is the proper object of his studies. I speak therefore as a student of American society and, within that, of the place of medicine and health in its trends of development; within that, in turn, of the place of medical education.

I would like to organize my discussion about one major theme and pursue it through a series of phases of the problem. This is that the United States, as the most fully developed "industrial society" in history, has undergone, and is continuing to undergo, a grand scale process of differentiation in the structure of the society itself and in the culture which expresses and guides its institutions. As medical men with their biological training well know, differentiation must be complemented by processes and mechanisms of integration, which coordinate the functioning of the differentiated parts of a complex whole.

The emergence of medicine itself into a new position of prominence on the national scene about half a century ago was a part and consequence of this differentiation and integration process. Medicine both became more highly differentiated and assumed new and enhanced importance as a mechanism of integration in the society. It is now deeply involved in the process at a later stage. Let me try to follow this theme through in terms of five sub-topics, namely: first, the institutionalization of conceptions of health and illness in society and their importance to it; second, a few highlights of the nature of the development of science that are relevant to medicine; third and fourth, a few aspects of the changing structure of the society itself as it impinges on the individual as a patient and on the organization of medical services; and fifth, the relevance of the changes in science and society, in a few aspects, to medical education. In the nature of the case, I can present only the broadest highlights.

SIGNIFICANCE OF HEALTH AND ILLNESS IN AMERICAN SOCIETY

The problem of illness has been a critical one in Western civilization generally, in its more modern phase, because of the extent to which these societies have been oriented to values of active achievement in instrumental contexts, to the mastery of the physical environment, and to the development of effective social organization itself. Health is vital, because the capacity of the human individual to achieve is ultimately the most crucial social resource. Illness is, to the sociologist, essentially a disturbance of this capacity to perform in socially valued tasks and roles. Education, which is the building up of capacities through learning, and health, which is the maintenance of capacity, are the two great centers for provision and safe-guarding of human resources.

In the American case this generally high valuation of health has been enhanced because of an "individualistic" cast of our society, one that tends to maximize the responsibilities of an expectation for decentralized units of the society rather than the larger collectivity itself. Hence attention, which might in a more collectivistic society be given to the organization of the state, with us, tends ultimately to rest on the capacity of the individual.

Capacity to achieve roots deeply in the state of the organism but comes to flower, on a healthy organic base, in the individual's capacity, at the level of personality, to live with and utilize complex systems of symbols and to conduct highly sophisticated transactions with other persons in human relations. The more developed and mobile the society, the more important the responsibility, self-control, and skills of the individual. It is this context which makes understandable the rapidly increasing importance in our own time attributed to problems of "mental" as distinguished from "somatic" health. Within the general context of our very strong concern with illness and health generally, it is natural that many phenomena of disturbance of behavioral capacities at the higher levels of social participation, which previously were thought of as simple "misconduct," should come to be brought within the health-illness complex. Chronic alcoholism is a prominent example. Another important development is that of a borderline of "psychosomatic" problems where some kind of complex interaction of mental ond somatic factors is postulated. These problems of the nature and boundaries of illness are far from settled in American society. But it seems to be clear that the field of phenomena defined as illness has been steadily broadening and at the same time becoming more highly differentiated. Within this latter category, in turn, the prominence of the mental health problem and the fact that this problem becomes a basis of organizing medical thinking that is not oriented simply to organ-systems of the body stand out. Incidentally, the importance of perspectives such as these makes one somewhat skeptical of the simpler versions of the view that alleged increases in the incidence of mental illness reflect some mysterious degenerative tendency in the population at large.

SOME ASPECTS OF
THE SCIENTIFIC BACKGROUND
OF MEDICINE

Turning now to the second of my main topics, the development of science, let me only mention a very few highlights. As Atchley and Wood made so clear in this Congress a year ago, the whole range of scientific knowledge relevant to medicine has undergone an immense process of broadening and deepening in the last two generations, in a way that has already borne enormously impressive fruit for the control of disease and that will bear much more. The range of detailed knowledge has grown so enormous that it is out of the question for any single human being, to say nothing of an undergraduate medical student, to learn more than a small fraction of it. But fortunately, as Merton has pointed out, this has been accompanied by a marked trend of what James B. Conant has called "reduction in the degree of empiricism." Science has not only grown and differentiated on empirical levels, it has also become more highly organized and integrated through theory. The consequence is that the scientific bases of medicine are becoming more dependent on generalized principle than ever before.

A second development in science is not yet nearly so impressive but, I am sure, is pregnant for the future. This is the emergence within about the last 40 years, in their relevance to medicine, of the so-called behavioral sciences, notably psychology (including psychoanalysis), sociology, and anthropology. These disciplines are, compared with physics, chemistry, and biology, clearly in their infancy and have only begun to have an important impact. That they have genuinely emerged is, in my opinion, one of the major cultural events of our time, and, though an interested party, I think I am justified in saying that there is no serious doubt that they are destined to take their place with their elder sister-sciences both in their ultimate contribution to our understanding of ourselves and of the world we live in and in their practical significance as providing knowledge which can be used to control events in the interest of human values and goals.

The connection of this scientific development with the emergence into prominence for medicine of the problem of mental health is clear. They are, from a sociological point of view, two different aspects of a new stage of development reached by the society. Clearly their emergence poses new problems of intellectual integration. These sciences are themselves now struggling to develop higher-order theory of their own. But at the same time there is a growing necessity to integrate them with the older natural sciences. Medicine occupies a very strategic position for this problem because of its obvious basic interests on both sides. Considerable progress could, were there space, be reported.

There are many implications of these developments for medicine. Looked at sociologically, I may emphasize, with Merton, not only has the corpus of scientific knowledge greatly grown, but scientific investigation and application, as social institutions, have been greatly consolidated and matured in the society. Clearly the modern university is the primary and focal center of this institution. The growth of science means that the connection of medical research and education with the universities, the importance of which Dr. Wood so strongly emphasized, has become more crucial than ever and is likely to remain a cardinal reference point for all medical policy.

SOME DEVELOPMENTS IN
THE STRUCTURE OF SOCIETY

The third of my main concerns is with a few major highlights of the structural development of American society that are not so directly associated with medicine. These may be looked at, first, from the point of view of the individual as patient, and second, from that of the professional groups that must take responsibility for the care of his health.

As recently as a half-century ago, nearly half the American population could be classified as definitely rural; today it is probably below 15%. The change reflects changes not only in residential conditions but in what we sociologists call the role-structure of the society. The biggest change is the progressively sharper and wider-spreading differentiation between the roles an individual plays in his family group, in company with his special intimates, and those he plays in the organizations responsible for economic production, governmental administration, education, and health care, and the like, namely, in his occupation.

The occupational aspect of the social structure has, relatively speaking, been growing rapidly. The overwhelming majority of adult males and of women without major family responsibilities have full-time jobs separated from the familial context, and the proportion of married woman in the labor force has been increasing apace, though it is still a minority. In the occupational world, increasingly I think, status is a function of capacity, of what a person can do, rather than of "who" he is in terms of social class or ethnic, religious, or local background. With all the many qualifications which must be made, this is clearly the main trend.

The consequence has been a major restructuring, both of the family itself and of the local community. The family has become smaller, more mobile, certainly geographically if not class-wise, and more "isolated" from ties both to other kinspeople and to such kinship-like affiliations as the ethnic. It has lost most of its previous functions in economic production and has become focused on the welfare of its members as individual persons, including the all-important bringing up or "socialization" of children. The increasingly general concern with "psychological" problems is undoubtedly associated with this change in the position and structure of the family.

Another aspect of change, which, in a sense, bridges these two, concerns the local community. Clearly, this is overwhelmingly urban, and no longer does it focus to the same extent as before on the big central city, with its Gold Coast and slums, as analyzed by Park and Burgess and their students for Chicago. The manifest change is the rapid growth of the "new suburbia." But I think that the old central lower-class slums are on their way out. For instance, the Negroes in northern cities and the Puerto Ricans in New York are special cases, in all probability the last of an era. More and more work premises will be in outlying areas, and residential areas will be more interspersed with them. Furthermore, residential areas will not be so sharply class-typed. This is in accord with a general tendency to greater complexity of structure rather than sharp hierarchic status-ranking.

There has also been a marked process of general "upgrading" of the population, most conspicuous in education and in occupational status. The lower fringe of the unskilled labor status has been very greatly diminished in numbers and importance, and automation has begun to lessen the proportion of semiskilled jobs, manual and clerical. The numbers in "service" occupations have greatly increased, and, though they are relatively small, the numbers and proportions of the labor force comprising the highly trained managerial and professional groups have been increasing very rapidly.

IMPLICATIONS OF
NEW DEVELOPMENTS

From the point of view of the medical profession this means that the physician is coming to treat different kinds of patients in ways different from before. He has to deal, with increasing frequency and not just in "elite" practices, with educated, skilled and relatively sophisticated people, who nonetheless have their troubles. The old style "charity" wards and clinics, especially in the centers of slum-ridden cities, are likely to diminish rapidly in relative importance. Certainly, special concern will have to be taken for the problem of the "whole patient." But the patient, because his own life is more complex, will have to be looked at in the different "lives" he lives, notably that of his home and that of his job. The trend to specialization in medicine is bound to continue. But new integrations will be needed and bases of differentiation and integration of a higher order worked out. It is my guess that specialization by organ-systems of the body will become less important as the level of generality of medical science itself rises; the "internist" will absorb many previous specialties. Psychiatry, on the other hand, cannot be treated for very long as cognate with urology or dermatology. I also suggest that the organization of medical specialization will have to match the role differentiations of the person, above all in terms of differentiation between "family" medicine and "occupational" medicine.

The implication of the general growth of large-scale organization, and of science, and of the professions, on a wide front, is that medicine will, as a profession, come to be increasingly intimately associated with other professional and administrative groups. The present relation to the lay representatives of the basic sciences on medical faculties is the prototype for a much wider development. I predict that social scientists will soon begin to take their place beside biochemists and bacteriologists. The relations of both these groups and medical personnel in turn to their colleagues in the faculties of arts and sciences of the universities will become increasingly close, particularly as the role of research in the higher-level medical installations continues, as it is certain to do, to increase. But this type of relation is also likely to extend to areas that are not now thought of as directly associated with medical interests, notably the social organization of hospitals, clinics, and medical schools.

There seems to be little doubt that the major trend of the

society is toward an increasingly important role for the professions generally. For the past half-century or so, the business man has indeed been the main "community leader" in the United States. I suspect that his heyday is drawing to a close and that the business groups will decline in relative status as the problems of economic production come to be relatively well "solved" and other functions in the society emerge into greater urgency and salience. Functions of government are certainly among these and I look for both a relative rise in prestige of those associated with it and a marked "professionalization" at least of those aspects associated with its administrative functions. Education and research are certainly also among the rising professions, and the recent relative lag which they have been allowed to suffer cannot continue much longer.

Considerations such as these have, I think, two particularly conspicuous implications for the medical profession. First, medicine was, along with law, essentially the first of the secular, high-level professions. For long, it stood in its field relatively isolated in a comparable status. Now the range of professional development has begun to broaden immensely, most conspicuously through the development of science. Medicine has lost many of its previous prerogatives to science as it bears on health and will lose more. The early stages of the process were dramatized nearly a century ago by the contributions to medicine of the chemist, Pasteur. Just as a large part of "medical" physiology was taken over by natural science, so scientific jurisdiction over much of the earlier "art of medicine" is beginning to be taken over by social science. Medicine hence is becoming in one sense more specialized. As Dr. Sidney Farber has stated, in many contexts like research, the physician is only one of a team of coequal experts in many fields. He is not even necessarily "captain" of the total team even though the problem be mainly "medical." It is essentially where the problem becomes that of responsibility for the welfare of patients that his special prerogative takes precedence. But on a scientific problem he may well have to bow to the superior competence of a layman. Thus, as part of the general process of differentiation in society, not only has medicine been becoming more specialized internally but it has been becoming at the same time a more specialized part of a larger complex of professional specialties.

The second implication of the "professionalization" of the society is that medicine, like law, is less likely in the future to find the higher business classes its most appropriate "reference group," as some social scientists call them. In such matters as the organization of their functions they are less likely than in the past to look to the patterns of economic "free enterprise" for their model. Furthermore, they are less likely to look to the income levels of their neighbors in business occupations for the standards of appropriate medical income.

Points on the Organization of Medical Services

In the light of such considerations as the above, I think that many of the older problems and controversies concerning the social organization of medical services are becoming obsolete. I do not look for what has usually been meant by "socialized medicine" in the future in the United States, nor do I look for preservation or restoration of the pattern where the typical physician practiced on a strict fee-for-service basis. There will not be less but more collective organization.

The technology of medicine, its internal differentiation, and its interlocking with numerous nonmedical specialties and services all require complex and large-scale organization, the importance of which is bound to increase. Medicine, one of the highest of all our technologies, cannot be expected to be exempted from this general trend of the society. But these organizations can be expected to take many forms, including a bewildering combination of governmental and private bases of control. Just as it is today taken for granted that medical schools are needed both in private and in state universities, so it will, according to general social trends, go with the other aspects of medical organization.

With respect to financing, another aspect of the general trend is certainly relevant. This is the taking over of a variety of financial responsibilities, previously carried unaided by families, by different kinds of specialized agencies. We no longer keep our liquid money funds under the mattress; we deposit them in the bank or invest them directly. We save through insurance and contributory, or even noncontributory, pension plans and the like. It is, to my mind, quite unrealistic to expect that the individual family will typically wish to pay for medical care on an *ad hoc* basis, when more effective ways of handling the problem are available. But again I expect there to be a wide variety of such devices with, however, the common features of prearranged provision and pooling of resources. I would also expect it to become increasingly a matter of public policy to assure rather high minima of access to health care to the whole population, independent of the financial resources of the family and indeed independent of the level of "providence" of the individual or his family.

One further point is relevant in this connection. It has already proved true over a wide front that employing organizations are very convenient agencies for the organization of such financial provisions, and I should expect this trend to increase. After all, the employing organization is the principal source of family income, and a relation needs to be established between this source and two primary family financial responsibilities, namely provision for health care and old age.

A related but distinct problem is how far the actual practice of medicine will come to be organized about occupation as a focus. It is my guess that a considerably larger proportion than heretofore will have this character, particularly in those fields where the illness or disability can be considered to be in any direct way connected with the job situation. The family, however, not only remains but in a certain sense has become even more than before the focus of the "personal integrity" of the individual. I should, therefore, expect family-oriented practice, whatever organizational forms it may take, to remain the primary base of operations for concern with the "whole patient." It seems to me reasonable to expect that the family practitioner will lean more and more in the direction of primary attention to psychological rather than somatic medicine. Partly this is because a great many of the problems of the latter are coming to be solved. With their solution the physician is under much less pressure to serve as a kind of glorified nurse, mitigating the anxieties and discomforts attendant on waiting for the spontaneous forces of recovery to operate. Partly, this is at the same time due to the simultaneous emergence of "personality" problems into saliency in the new type of family and the growth of technical knowledge on the basis of which they can be more rationally dealt with.

Such family practice will necessarily have to be closely integrated with the somatic specialties which are traditionally so closely related to family situations, notably: obstetrics, gynecology, and pediatrics, though the latter beyond the early years must be almost equally closely related to the schools. Beyond this there must be a ramified system of agencies by which the patient needing important specialized diagnosis or care can be routed to the proper people. I would look to the more dispersed structure of the modern residential community for the most promising models for the location of the most likely types of hospitals and clinics, rather than to the recently prominent central-city hospital or medical center. With modern transportation within urban areas and the expected concentrations of population, this should not be too difficult to work out.

A Few Implications
for Medical Education

Throughout this brief discussion I have emphasized the fundamental processes of differentiation and integration that have been going on and can be expected to do so in American society. Because of the special role of science and its institutionalization in this process and of the special significance of the health complex for the society, medicine has and should continue to occupy a central strategic position within the society, but it is also exposed to a peculiar degree to the pressures created by the rapidity and fundamental character of change. In this situation medical education faces both formidable difficulties of adaptation and a tremendous opportunity. The difficulties are, I hope, apparent from knowledge common to the profession and from some of the things I have said. The opportunity is to play an even more strategic role in a growing great new society than it has done in the past. I would like to try to specify in three related directions.

The first concerns response to the general situation of the sciences relevant to medicine which, following many others far better informed than I, I have sketched above. One major focus of the problem is the growing length of the process of medical training, which has been such a source of concern to many within the profession. That good medical training should be as long and arduous as that in any profession, I should take for granted. Yet I am inclined to think that it has tended to grow inordinately and that the primary reason for this is a tendency to adhere to too much empiricism, to find it difficult to accept the inevitable codification of knowledge in terms of higher-level theory and the attendant renunciation of great detail except for the range of the field in which the individual is being trained to be a really detailed expert. No individual can pretend any longer to be a detailed expert over more than a fraction of the field of medicine, or, of course, any other of the really big fields of human knowledge and practice. But this need not mean that medical men must be "superficial." They can be trained in the grasp of general theory and much illustrative fact, particularly crucial fact. And, if well trained, they should know when they do not know the detailed answers in particular fields and where and how to proceed to get those answers. In sum, I suggest that the implications of Mr. Conant's aphorism need to be taken very seriously indeed.

The second point is essentially an application to a special case of the first. Unless I am grossly mistaken, both the relative importance of mental illness in the whole field and the scientific knowledge necessary for its competent handling are destined to grow greatly in the coming half-century. I feel strongly that the medical profession as such should be the central agency, in this field as in that of somatic illness, for the responsible treatment of patients. But if the profession is to meet this challenge it must undergo a major reorganization, not least at its growing point of medical education. The present treatment of psychiatry as one specialty among many others, which may not be entered upon without a full "orthodox" training in general medicine, means that it is impossible to increase the number of psychiatrists rapidly. At the same time the demand for their services is enormous and increasing rapidly. If medicine does not meet the demand, then other agencies will step in, which I would greatly deplore.

Clearly, to be competent to handle mental cases the physician must even now not only have more clinical experience with them but learn much more in such fields as psychology and sociology, and, as these sciences develop, this requirement will become more onerous. For a large group to do this in addition to meeting the present requirements is out of the question. The only solution I can see is to train the future "psychological physician" in general medicine in much more general terms than now, except for some fields very close to his own, like neurology. In other words the differentiation between psychological and somatic medicine must reach much farther back than now, into the undergraduate years. And "psychological medicine" must become, not just one specialty among others but probably, one of the two great primary branches of the profession.

My last point concerns the placing of medical practice, through the educational policy of the profession, more fully, with reference not only to the relevant scientific traditions but to the social setting as a whole, including the social organization of science. I think the physician needs to be trained to be not less but rather more responsible, particularly for the welfare of patients, than before. But this high responsibility must, increasingly as the society develops, be discharged in a setting where the patient leads a more complex life and is harder to "get at" as a total person than before and where the profession itself must learn to co-operate with many different lay agencies, starting with the sciences that are not primarily medical. From the "rugged individualism" of a kind of splendid professional isolation of the medical past to integration in this more complex system of co-operating groups and agencies means a major transition.

To accomplish the transition smoothly and successfully, physicians must be trained for it. Indeed in the modern medical school and teaching hospital great steps have already been taken in this direction. If it is fully carried through medicine will have a brilliant future as the key element in a combination of agencies that will ensure a future high level of health on all fronts, which would have been beyond the most optimistic dreams of any earlier generation.

CHAPTER X.

SOME COMMENTS ON THE PATTERN OF RELIGIOUS ORGANIZATION IN THE UNITED STATES

As in a number of other fields, the United States has, in formal constitutions and otherwise, from the beginning of its independent national history presented a rather new and striking pattern of the relation between organized religion and society. On the constitutional level the striking inno-vation was the repudiation of the ancient European institu-tion of the Establishment, through the separation of Church and State on both the federal and the state level, in that the State Constitutions or subsequent enactments, as well as the First Amendment to the Federal Constitution, excluded an established church. On the informal level, the striking inno-vation was acceptance of what may be called "denomina-tional pluralism," namely the presence in the community, with equal formal rights, of an indefinite number of com-peting religious collectivities, or "churches," none of which, however, was allowed to enjoy positive governmental sup-port, though they did have such privileges as tax-exemption, a privilege which has been shared with educational and char-itable organizations generally. Implied also, in the freedom of the individual to belong to, and support, any one of the plurality of denominational groups, was his freedom to dis-sociate himself from all of them. Citizenship did not imply either subscription to any religious creed or subjection to the authority or pressure of any religious body. As far as the organization of political authority was concerned, religion ceased to be a subject of "public" concern and was relegated to the sphere of private affairs, except for political guardianship of religious freedom. In its broad outline this system has proved to be stable over the hundred and seventy years of our national existence, a fairly long period as such things go. There is no sign of a tendency for it to break down now.

This pattern stands in sharp contrast to the main European tradition. There it may be said that the chief background institution has been that of the Established Church where, though political and religious authorities were structurally differentiated from each other, it was understood that the one church should enjoy a legitimate monopoly of religious authority and benefits for the whole politically organized society and that it could legitimately call on political authority to enforce this monopoly by physical coercion, as well as to ensure the financial support of the Church. The prototype of this older pattern was of course the Catholic Church before the Reformation. But the same basic pattern in these essentials was taken over by the main Reformation churches, both Lutheran and Calvinistic, as distinguished from the sects, and in most European countries the further development has been characterized by large elements of this pattern.

The pattern has, of course, been greatly modified in the course of European history since the Reformation. The break in the religious unity of Western Christendom which that movement signalized was, in fact, coincident with the final break in its political unity—the unity of the Holy Roman Empire had already been very seriously compromised by the independence of the English and French monarchies, but after the Reformation the religious schism within its central structure made the "Empire" little more than a fiction. But the formula *cuius regio, eius religio* also proved to be unstable and, more and more, religious unity under an established church within the political unit broke down. The Elizabethan policy of religious tolerance in England was perhaps the first main step in this process. Now, every important European state (except Spain) has at least some important degree of religious toleration and in a few, like France, formal separation of Church and State has been put through.

On the other hand, there are still many residua of the old pattern. Most countries, while tolerating other churches, still permit the privileges of an established church to one, though it is Catholic in some and Lutheran in some, and England has its special Anglican, and Scotland its Presbyterian, Establishment. This is likely to be associated with special privileges in the field of tax-support, education, and other matters.

But apart from the legal privileges of religious bodies, there are other phenomena related to the incomplete resolution of problems stemming from the older pattern. One of the most notable, to Americans, is the persisting tendency to form religiously based political parties. This is least evident in Great Britain, though it may be argued that the ultimate break with Ireland had a good deal to do with this issue, and the religious separatism of Scotland is still a major focus of Scottish nationalism. On the Continent, however, it is prominent in various countries, France with the M.R.P., Holland, Belgium, and Italy.

Very much associated with this tendency has been the tendency for secularism, in the sense of opposition to organized religion in general, also to assume political forms transcending other particular issues. Thus for a century French politics was polarized to a considerable degree about the issue of anticlericalism. In general, political secularism has been a major component of the orientation of the parties of the left in Europe—again apart from Great Britain—and, in the extreme case of Communism, it may be said that the aim has been to set up a counter-Establishment, making militant secularism itself a dogma to be rigidly enforced by a party backed by governmental authority. It may be suggested that the lack of appeal of this European secularist leftism, particularly Communism, in Anglo-Saxon countries, and most especially in the United States, has been associated with the uncongeniality there of any polarization of the body politic over religious issues.

It is understandable that the American institutional structure in this respect should, to many Europeans and to some Americans, appear to be the last stage in the general process of secularization relative to the European heritage, with its roots in Mediæval Catholic unity. How can it be maintained that religion has any vitality if, on the one hand, it has become so splintered that the religious unity of a society cannot be maintained, but an indefinite diversity of denominational groups must be tolerated, and, on the other hand, people's level of commitment to institutionalized religion has sunk so low that they are unwilling to fight for their churches through political means?

As over against this interpretation I would like to suggest that in the United States there has appeared, though probably not yet fully matured, a new mode of institutionalization of the relations between religion and society, which, however, is not secularization in the sense that its tendency is to eliminate organized religion from the social scene, but is rather to give it a redefined place in the social scene. The recent American "religious revival," which has occasioned a good deal of comment, is important evidence for this thesis. There are two primary possible interpretations of this phenomenon. The more popular one, even among American intellectuals, is that, from a religious point of view, it is not really "genuine," but must be explained on extraneous grounds as meeting the needs for neighborliness and security in group memberships of the highly mobile populations of American cities in the industrial age, particularly in the new suburbs. The other is that it is connected with a new equilibrium in the relation between the religious and the secular elements in the social system. I shall comment briefly on this problem later.

A Few Historical
Antecedents of the
American Pattern

It may be argued that at the time of the American Revolution the principle of the separation of church and state was something of a tour de force and was precipitated by two main factors extraneous to the place of religion in the deeper social structure. One of those factors was political expediency deriving from the religious diversity of the thirteen colonies. Clearly the Puritans of New England, the Catholics of Maryland, the Quakers of Pennsylvania, the Anglicans of Virginia, and the Presbyterians of a good part of the South could not have agreed that any one of the denominations could be accorded the privileges of an Established Church, so it was relatively easy to agree that there should be none at all. The other factor was the prominence among the Founding Fathers of a group of intellectuals, typified by Thomas Jefferson, who were deeply influenced by the Deism of the French Enlightenment.

The process of institutionalization of the new pattern has been a long one and has been involved with a general process of social change, the major keynote of which has been structural differentiation. Religious issues have, of course, made their appearance in American politics from time to time, as for example in the various anti-Catholic movements from the "Know-Nothing Party" on. But structurally the separation of church and state has proved stable and there has been no really serious challenge to it.

A good example of the process of structural differentiation involving religion has been the field of education. It must be realized that in the earlier days of the American Republic education at the lower levels was not treated as a public responsibility in any sense but was privately arranged by the privileged upper-class minority for their own children. The focus of formal educational arrangements was in higher education and it, in turn, was oriented religiously to the education of ministers of religion. Even at the time when various groups other than prospective ministers were attending the colleges, the latter were overwhelmingly governed under denominational auspices.

In early, colonial days, a partnership of local church and public authority in the provision for higher education was taken for granted, as in the case of the founding of Harvard College and of King's College in New York, which later became Columbia University. But after the advent of independence, the responsibility fell almost entirely to religious denominations until the beginning of the wave of founding of state universities in the western territories toward the middle of the nineteenth century. This followed closely on the spread of public education at the primary and secondary levels. Though the wider spread of education in the United States occurred under governmental auspices, it should be noted that the local community assumed the responsibility. The pattern still holds in main outline, with state governments carrying a moderate share of responsibility and the Federal Government as yet scarcely any at all. Probably the United States is the only important government in the world which does not have a central department or ministry of education.

It can thus be seen that there is a sense in which in Europe the State took over the educational function from the Church. In the United States it remained in religious hands considerably longer, but then was secularized in the first instance to private bodies, secondarily to public authority, but even there above all to local authority. The colleges, and later universities, have in general evolved from denominational foundations to general private fiduciary agencies with only tenuous denominational affiliations. There has been a similar evolution in the case of hospitals. To an American the difference in the latter connection is striking, for in Europe the nurse, as a "sister," is still hardly distinguishable from the member of a religious order, indeed often is an actual member.

It is perhaps to be expected that in this setting the policies of the Catholic Church should exhibit a certain lag relative to the rest of American society. It has, particularly in the last generation or two, taking advantage of the framework of American religious toleration, set out to create a complete system of religious education whereby, in ideal, the Catholic child will from primary school through the university be educated exclusively in church-controlled organizations. This is only one of the variety of respects in which the Catholic Church occupies a special position in American society, but it may be a question how far it will be able to maintain this special policy in the face of powerful general forces pointing in another direction.

I have suggested that the keynote of the special position of religion in American society lies in structural differentiation. When a previously less differentiated structure becomes differentiated into more specialized subsystems, it is in the nature of the case that, if an earlier and later structural unit bear the same name, the later version will, by comparison with the earlier, be felt to have lost certain functions and hence, perhaps, from a certain point of view to have been weakened. This may be illustrated from a nonreligious case. Thus in peasant societies, where the bulk of the population have been engaged in agriculture, the family household has been at the same time both the main agency of economic production in the society and the main focus of early child-rearing and of the intimate personal life of its members. In modern industrial societies this function of economic production has been largely lost to the family household and transferred to factories, offices, etc. In these terms the family has lost functions and has become a more specialized agency in the society. The modern urban family is clearly different from the peasant family; whether it is better or worse may be a matter of opinion, but the difference of its place in the large social structure surely cannot be ignored in forming that opinion, including the fact that the social and economic advantages of industrialism cannot be secured through a household organization of production.

In order to appraise this type of structural differentiation it is necessary to have in mind a standard for defining the primary functions of a part of the social structure, the nature of which can be conceived to set the limits beyond which the "reduction" of function is unlikely to go. "Secondary" functions on the other hand may, through the process of differentiation, be transferred to other agencies. In the case of the family, just discussed, I think it is clear that the primary functions for the social system as such (physical care of the body being thus excluded) are its contributions to the personality development of the child—what sociologists have come to call "socialization"—and its functions in the stabilization of the personality equilibrium of the adult members. The family, as an agency of society, is above all a set of mechanisms which manipulate the motivational structures of its individual members as these bear on the performance of social roles. Can anything parallel be said about the primary function of religion in society?

This is, in the present state of sociological knowledge, a more uncertain field than that of the family. I should, however, wish to emphasize as the "core" function of religion in the social system the regulation of the balance of the motivational commitment of the individual to the values of his society—and through these values to his roles in it as compared with alternative considerations concerning his ultimate "fate" as a knowing, sentient being, and the bases on which this fate comes to have meaning to him, in the sense in which Max Weber refers to "problems of meaning." Religion, thus conceived, is close in its social functions to the family, though in terms of formal organization it has taken the form of the church.

I think it can be said that the main reference of the "motivational" regulation performed by the family is regressive; it relates to the sources of motivational patterning in the early life experience of the individual, particularly in the family relations in which he is currently growing up or did grow up as a child. Religion, on the other hand, is primarily oriented to the adult phases of life and the problems of meaning involved in its basic limitations, thus including the finiteness of life's duration and the meaning of death. It involves such questions as: What, in the last analysis, am I? Why do I exist? What is the meaning of my relations to others? Why must I die and what happens to me at, and after, death? The cognitive meaning of existence, the meaning of happiness and suffering, of goodness and evil, are the central problems of religion.

An essential cognitive, i.e., philosophical, element is always involved in religion, but, as Durkheim held, the main emphasis is not cognitive, but practical. It is the question of what, in view of my understanding and its limits, are my basic commitments in life. Of course, the influences of others and involvements of various kinds in relations of solidarity or antagonism with others are of very great importance; yet I should contend that in the last analysis religion is an individual matter, a concern of the innermost core of the individual personality for his own identity and commitments. In view of this fact, the nature of the social structuring of religion should be regarded as empirically problematical; it cannot be deduced from the most general characteristics of religion itself.

RELIGION AND THE PROCESS
OF SOCIAL DIFFERENTIATION

My suggestion is thus that a process of differentiation similar to that which has affected the family has been going on in the case of religion and has reached a particularly advanced stage in the United States, producing a state which may or may not provide a model for other societies. It is well known that in primitive societies and in many other civilizations than that of the West, no clear-cut structural distinction could be made between religious and secular aspects of the organization of society; there has been no "church" as a differentiated organizational entity. From this point of view the differentiation (as distinguished from "separation") of Church and State, which has been fundamental to Western Christianity from its beginning, may be regarded as a major step in differentiation for the society as a whole.

Through this process of differentiation religion already had become a more specialized agency than it had been in most other societies. But since the Renaissance and the Reformation a process has been going on which has tended to carry the differentiation further still. The steps by which this process has taken place and the exact patterns which have resulted have been different in different countries. This brief article cannot attempt to trace and compare them all. Besides space, this task would require a level of historical scholarship which I do not command. I must confine myself to pointing out a few features of the American case and of its consequences for the structure of American society.

Perhaps the first major point is that, though a solid structure of Federal Government was established for the new republic, it was, probably more than any European government, built on a system of constitutional restraints on governmental power. The relative insulation of the United States from the politics of the European world—by sheer distance and by the Pax Britannica—then gave our institutions an opportunity to crystallize within the framework of the Constitution without sudden or unbearable pressures to break down these restraints. Then the fact that separation of Church and State was itself written into most of the State Constitutions and into the First Amendment to the Federal Constitution gave a basis for a general tradition that religious issues were not a proper subject for political action. One fundamental consequence of this patterning was that, when the time arrived for governmental initiative in the field of education, predominantly, as I have said, at the local level, there was the strongest presumption that tax-supported schools could not serve the interests of, or be controlled by, any religious denomination.

In the background of all this, of course, lay the characteristics of American religious traditions themselves. Though exceedingly diverse, the main influences were derived from the "left wing" of European, especially English, Protestantism, where the traditions of the Established Church were weakest. To be sure there was a Congregational Establishment in early New England, but by the time of the Revolution it was greatly attenuated and religious toleration fairly firmly established. The fact that, after the first generation, royal governors were present in the colonies reinforced this, because of the fear that if there was to be a firm religious establishment, the Anglican Church would be imposed by British authority. Even as early as the late eighteenth century, the strength of such groups as the Quakers, various Congregational splinter groups, Baptists and, starting at a crucial time, the Methodists, was great. These were all groups which, on religious bases, had opposed the backing of religion by political authority; without their relative strength the American pattern probably could not have survived. Again, it is important that a large Catholic minority did not exist until the pattern was well crystallized.

Another important circumstance lies in the fact that the

great movement of settlement of the newer parts of the country preserved the pattern of religious diversity which had begun in the thirteen colonies. The effect of this was that none of the central political issues which divided the country, above all economic and sectional issues, could be closely identified with a religious division. The main exception has been the concentration, since about the turn of the last century, of the Catholic population in the northern and eastern cities. But, for a variety of reasons, Catholics could not, as such, stably dominate the politics of a solid regional block, and in particular the peculiarities of the South were enough to prevent the emergence of a stable southern-western Protestant coalition against Catholic influence in the East. The upshot is that, though religious issues flared up from time to time, occasionally dominating local issues and alignments, the broad pattern of keeping religion out of politics has come to be stably institutionalized in American society.

Perhaps the second most important context of differentiation involving religion has involved its relation to education, and with it the institutionalization of the intellectual life and its constituent professions. In part, as noted, such differentiation goes back to the separation of Church and State and the fact that when government, even local government, became involved in educational responsibilities, it could not back religious denominationalism in this sphere. The same principle of course had to apply to the state universities as to the locally controlled primary and secondary schools.

How a combination of regional, ethnic, and religious distributions in politically powerful blocks can work out to a different outcome is illustrated by the case of Canada, particularly the Province of Quebec. Here, though there is religious toleration, the educational system is publicly supported but control of the schools is given to Catholic and Protestant religious groups, respectively, with parents given their choice of religious school to which to send their children. That this was tolerated by the English majority (which has been a minority in Quebec) is partly explained by the far greater proportion of Anglicans there than in the United States, with their greater sympathy for the Establishment principle.

As I have noted, private higher education in the United States was originally mainly controlled by religious denominations. Why did its secularization occur? It seems to me probable that among the decisive factors were those involved in the transition from primary emphasis on the college to that on the university. This, in turn, was involved with the rise to immensely increased strategic importance of the secular professions, especially those based on scientific training. It is interesting that the models for this development were drawn largely from the Continental European governmentally controlled universities. But under American conditions, if the private institutions of higher education were to retain their position, some of them had to develop into universities. And again, if, as universities, they were to serve as primary agencies for the training of the whole national professional class of lawyers, physicians, engineers scientists, civil servants, and the academic profession itself, as well as ministers of religion, in a religiously diversified society like the American, they could not do so successfully if they remained denominational organizations in a strict and traditional sense. Above all, particularly the universities aspiring to national rather than local importance could not use denominational loyalty as a main criterion for recruitment either of their faculties or of their student bodies. In any case, whatever the social mechanisms involved, the American system of higher education in both its publicly supported colleges and universities (state and municipal) and its private sector is now firmly secular in its major orientation. The sole major exception is the educational system controlled by the Catholic Church, though there are smaller-scale ones for Lutherans, Jews, etc. The Catholic is a large minority, but there seems to be no basis for believing that its pattern can serve as a model for the reversal of this fundamental trend, if indeed the Catholic educational pattern can itself survive for very long against the trend.

There is one particularly crucial consequence for religion of the secular character of the American educational system. This is that the main standards for the evaluation and inculcation of intellectual culture are not and cannot be controlled by organized religious bodies. Real control of the development of science has long since been lost by religious bodies everywhere—and the attempts of semireligious bodies like the Communist Party to restore that control do not seem likely to be successful in the long run. But the American situation goes farther than this in two vital respects. The first is the extension of scientific methods and theories into the fields of human behavior, a world-wide development which, however, has gone farther in the United States than anywhere else. This development inevitably introduces the relevance of scientific, nonreligious canons into many spheres which have traditionally been considered to be spheres of religious prerogative, such as many aspects of "morals." The second is the secularization of philosophy and the humanities. However seriously the secular philosopher (who may be a practicing member of a religious denomination) may take cognizance of historic and contemporary religious positions on his problems, in the last analysis his professional responsibility cannot be defined as the defense of the official position of any religious body, but is a responsibility to "seek the truth" as he sees it in the light of the general traditions of rational knowledge. No responsible modern American university in the main tradition could appoint him to its faculty on any other assumption.

Finally, reference may again be made to the fact that

rights of predominantly secular orientation are clearly institutionalized in the American system. There is no obligation either of the citizen, in the strictly political sense, or of the member of the community in good standing to accept participation in, or control by, any formally organized religious body. Besides the fields of politics and education, this is perhaps most important in matters affecting the family. In attempting to retain control over various spheres of social life other than a more narrowly defined religious sphere, one of the most tenacious tendencies of religious bodies has been to attempt to prescribe the conditions of marriage and divorce and the responsibilities of parents for children in various respects, particularly education. The American, like the citizen of other countries who violates his church's rules in these matters, may be in trouble with the authorities of that church. But the essential point is that neither his political rights as citizen nor his basic good standing in the American community is conditioned on his conforming with the rules of any particular religious body in these matters. The minimum standards are set by political authority—what constitutes legal marriage and legal divorce, for example. Beyond these, the matter is one of a community opinion which is composed of religiously diverse elements. In religious terms, it seems to be a sort of lowest common denominator which governs—if any one group attempts to impose standards at variance with this common attitude the person in question can, at the cost of trouble with his own group, retain a good general community standing if his conduct is not generally condemned by members of the other groups. This lowest common denominator of institutionalized moral standards must, of course, be carefully distinguished from the deviant behavior which is bound to be fairly prominent in a complex society. It is defined by the consensus of responsible opinion and does not, in general, condone extreme moral laxity.

THE AMERICAN
RELIGIOUS PATTERN

Seen in these terms, it is clear that, by the standard of older ideals of Western Christianity, organized religion has lost much in America. First, it has lost the basic legitimation of the claim to religious unification even within the politically organized society. The right both to religious pluralism and to secular orientation (though not necessarily to combat religion except within limits) is a fundamental institutionalized right in American society. Organized religion has lost the right to claim the support of the state by compulsory enforcement of uniformity or even by taxation either for a single established church or for any religious body. It has lost the right to control the main lines of the educational process, above all perhaps, to prescribe the legitimate framework of secular intellectual culture, with special reference to philosophy. It also has lost the right to prescribe effectively certain vital matters of private morals, with special reference to marriage and family relationships. Has it anything left?

My own view is most definitely that it has a great deal. Ernst Troeltsch, in his classic work, *Social Teachings of the Christian Churches,* maintained that in the history of Western Christianity there had been only three versions of the conception of a Christian Society, one in which the values of Christian religion could be understood to provide the main framework for the value system of the society as a whole. These cases were Mediæval Catholicism, Lutheranism, and Calvinism. All of them involved the conception of a single Established Church as the agent of implementing and symbolizing this fundamental Christian orientation of the society as a whole. Troeltsch considered that the "sects" which did not recognize the religious validity of an Established Church had in effect abandoned the ideal of the Christian Society altogether.

Over against this view of Troeltsch I should like to suggest that in American society there has, in its main outline, evolved the conception of an institutionalized Christianity which is in line with the great tradition of the Christian Society but differs from its earlier version in the fundamental respects outlined above. First, in order of evidence in favor of this view, is the fact that the values of contemporary American society have fundamental religious roots, above all, in the traditions which Max Weber, in *The Protestant Ethic and the Spirit of Capitalism,* called those of "ascetic Protestantism," and that these values have not been fundamentally changed in the course of our national history. The enormous changes which have occurred constitute fundamental changes not of values but of the structure of the society in which those values are maintained and implemented. Essentially by this system of values I mean the continued commitment to values of "instrumental activism," the subordination of the personal needs of the individual to an objective "task" to which he is expected to devote his full energies, and the subjection of the actions of all to universalistic standards of judgment. Associated with this is the importance of universalizing the essential conditions of effective performance through equalization of civil rights and of access to education and health. It should be particularly noted that the shift from a primarily transcendental reference to one with mainly terrestrial focus did not occur as a phase of secularization but, as Weber so strongly emphasizes, within the highly active religious tradition of ascetic Protestantism. It was the conception of the service of the Glory of God, first through helping to build the Kingdom of God on Earth, which was the main focus of Calvinist ethics.

"Secularization" has, essentially, taken the form of differentiation, so that this Kingdom is no longer thought of as exclusively governed by religious considerations, but there is an autonomous secular sphere of the "good society" which need not reflect only man's activities and obligations in his capacity as a member of the church. But this good society may still be interpreted as "God's work" in a sense similar to that in which physical nature has always been so interpreted within that tradition.

The new sectarian or, better, "denominational," form taken by the religious organization itself is broadly in line with the general development which produced Protestantism and then evolved further within it. The keynote of it is the personal intimacy and privacy of the individual's faith and relation to his conception of Divinity. The further this trend of development has gone the more basically repugnant to it have two features of the older traditions tended to become: first, the invoking of secular authority to apply coercive, ultimately, physical sanctions in matters of religious faith and, second, the claim of any human agency to hold a monopoly of all religiously legitimate access to religious goods. This position clearly challenges all claims to authorization by exclusively valid divine revelation, but in the main tradition this consequence has been clearly recognized and accepted. The implication is that the religious body must be a fully voluntary association and that coercion in these matters is contrary to the most essential spirit of religion itself.

A particularly good illustration of the differentiation of religious and non-religious components which have been fused in the past is the increasingly clear discrimination, conspicuous in the United States, between psychiatry and what here tends to be called "pastoral counseling." The most essential point is the emergence of a secular professional tradition for the treatment of disturbances of personality. The elements involved in these disturbances include many elements which in other societies have been handled in a religious or magical context. The line is by no means completely clear as yet, but it is notable that, a few years ago, a strong attack on psychoanalysis by Catholic Bishop Fulton

Sheen was countered by a group of Catholic psychoanalysts and that the Bishop did not then persist in his attacks. Since the Catholic Church is, in this as in various other respects, the largest conservative religious body, the fact that it is not sponsoring a general attack on psychiatry is significant. A careful statement of a limited sphere in which psychiatry was defined as legitimate has recently been made by the Pope.

Denominational pluralism is almost a direct implication of the above two departures from older tradition. If no human agency has a right to claim a monopoly of religious legitimacy and enforce it by coercion, then there is no basis on which to deny the legitimacy of plural competing claims at least to the point that many groups may have enough access to the truth to justify their adherents in each "worshiping God in their own way."

If denominational pluralism of this sort is to be institutionalized as the religious system of a society, then certain conditions must be met. Two of the most fundamental are definition of the limits within which a group of religious associates may claim to be a legitimate "denomination" and, second, the rules of their competition with each other in terms of mutual respect and the like. A third basic problem area concerns the way in which the line is drawn between the legitimate sphere of religious concern and that of the primarily secular institutions which have been discussed.

With respect to the first question, the American pattern is probably not fully crystallized, but its main outline seems to be clear. It draws the definition of a legitimate denomination rather broadly, leaving room for a good deal of free competition. All the main historical branches of Christianity are clearly included. But, so also are now the main branches of Judaism. Also, a good many popular cults of more or less faddist character which do not enjoy the respect of the more highly educated elements are still tolerated so long as they do not become too great sources of disturbance. Similarly, groups which, like Jehovah's Witnesses, are sharply alienated from the normal loyalties of the ordinary society are tolerated though not widely approved. Indeed there is no bar to the toleration of groups altogether outside the main Western traditions, though they do not seem to have gained any serious foothold.

The main core of the tradition is clearly a theistic Judeo-Christian belief complex. The inclusion of Judaism is not strange in view of the fact that similar theological positions have evolved within the Protestant tradition in Unitarianism. Indeed, for reasons like these, it may be said that Judaism presents, at least for the groups which have abandoned Orthodox Jewish separation from the general community, less difficult problems of integration than is the case with the Catholic Church and the real Protestant "Fundamentalists." Clearly there are many degrees of integration and many fringe groups. But there is, as noted, a general Theism, which is even politically recognized—as in the inscription on coins "In God We Trust." Further, sessions of Congress are regularly opened by Protestant, Catholic, or Jewish clergymen offering prayer, and chaplains of all three faiths are provided by the Armed Services.

It is further essential to recognize again that secularism, in the sense of repudiating affiliation with any organized religious body, is clearly institutionalized as legitimate. The central significance of this fact lies, I think, in the relation of religion to the main traditions of the intellectual culture of the society. The institutionalization of rights to secular orientation means that in struggling with the basic problems of meaning which confront the members of any society individually and in their collective capacities, the individual is not rigidly bound within the framework of a particular tradition of beliefs. Individuals and groups are free to define their positions in ways which are explicitly at variance with any of the denominational carriers of the religious tradition.

It seems to me that this protected position of secular orientation is particularly important in determining the circumstances under which, in several areas with which religion has historically been intimately concerned, patterns with secular primacy have come to be institutionalized in positions of high strategic importance in the society. The deeper roots both of religion itself and of some of these secular institutions are so closely interwoven, both historically and in current psychological terms, that any one of the "interests" involved would, if given a monopoly of jurisdiction over them, be likely to bias the balance between the religious sphere and that of the secular "good society" to a deleterious degree. I have in mind here particularly the two spheres of intellectual culture leading up to philosophy and of the attitudes toward a whole range of questions of "morals."

From this point of view, religious and secular orientations may, to an important degree, thus be seen as constituting different aspects of the same system of orientation to "problems of meaning." Indeed the legitimacy of secularism seems to follow almost directly on the abandonment of coercively enforced dogma. But above all secularism is important in defining the boundary between the religious sphere and the secular good society. Just as in a politically democratic society the definition of the boundaries of legitimate governmental authority is not permitted to be a monopoly of the officials of government, so in a "religiously liberal" society the determination of the boundaries of the legitimate sphere of organized religion is not left to the proponents of that position alone; they must compete with proponents of a position which in some respects is hostile to theirs. It is my belief that the secularization of education and of control of certain spheres of morals, which I regard as essential to the structure of the American type of good society, could not have been brought about without the influence of elements willing to oppose the whole weight of organized religion.

But if the religious-secular balance is to work out in a well-integrated social system, the opposition of secularists to religious influence must not be unlimited. And I think it is correct to say that in the United States (and Britain) on the whole, a regulated competition rather than a "state of war" has prevailed. There must be, and are, "rules of the game." From the secularist's point of view his religiously committed fellow citizens are defined not as beyond the pale but as "good people" who differ from him on these points—and, of course, vice versa. Secularism may thus be defined as a kind of "loyal opposition" to the religious point of view. Each side has interests to protect which are vital, not only to the proponents themselves but to the society as a whole. Neither, alone, can legitimately hope to be exclusively influential in the determination of the course of events. The fact that the other "party" is there can serve as an important curb on the extremists on either side. Thus, if a particular denomination tries to put through extreme claims, for example in the direction of denominational control of public education, the more moderate denominations can be relied on to point out that such extremism plays into the hands of the secularists—such claims may come to be identified with "religion" as such. On the other side, extreme secularists who want too aggressively to combat all religion will tend to find themselves restrained by the influence of more moderate secularists who point out that their extreme position —for example, the requiring of civil marriage ceremonies on the presumption that a religious marriage is not "legally" valid—if insisted upon will tend to discredit all secularism and give the "religionists" an undue advantage.

Seen in these terms, the religious-secular balance in American society is analogous to the balance of political parties in a two-party system. The preponderance shifts from time to time—most recently apparently in a religious direction— but the system tends to insure that neither side will gain the kind of ascendancy which would enable it to suppress the other, and basically on the value level most good citizens on the one side do not want to suppress the other. Religion, that is to say, has come to be defined institutionally as quite definitely "a good thing" but equally definitely as not the only good thing, and as confined in its goodness to a fairly clearly defined sphere.

Near the beginning of this paper, the problem of the interpretation of the so-called American "religious revival" was mentioned. A very brief word may be said about it against the background of the above discussion. First, I may point out that a prevailing interpretation stresses the extra-religious phenomena which have appeared in connection with church membership and attendance, above all the ways in which the church has become a center of community social activities and associations. From this observation, it is an easy step to suggest that such interests as those in "sociability," to say nothing of opportunities to "meet the right people," account for the observed facts. A somewhat more sophisticated version of a similar view is the suggestion that the "security needs" of isolated people in a mobile "mass society" constitute the focus of this new tendency.

There seems to be relatively little question about the broad facts. Church membership is currently the highest in American history, not only absolutely but in terms of proportions of the population. The same is true of attendance at church services, money spent in building of new churches, and a variety of other indices. Moreover, relative to general population growth there has been a marked increase in these phenomena in a short generation.

I would suggest that the phenomena of sociability, of desirable associations, and even of the relation to psychological security in interpersonal relations are quite real, but that they are secondary and do not impugn the religious genuineness of the revival. The central phenomenon seems to be the increased concern with values and hence the relation of the individual to his problems of "ultimate concern," to use Tillich's phrase. It is related to a new phase of emphasis on personal "inwardness" in American society, but it is not the first time in our history that this kind of thing has happened. Probably the clearest historical case, which was in some but by no means all respects comparable, was the "Great Revival" in New England in the time of Jonathan Edwards.

A good many writers about the contemporary American scene have noted the prominence of a general "search for values" at a high level of generality. Another phenomenon to which the religious revival seems to be closely related is the prominent increase in concern for the psychological problems of personality, especially with reference to such fields as mental health and child training. Religion generally is very closely associated with the equilibrium of the individual person, and that these two concerns should increase concomitantly makes sense, especially when religion is considered to be so "personal" as in the American case.

It is often suggested that a relative lack of concern with theological problems is an argument against imputing religious "genuineness" to the movement. I question whether this is so. On sociological grounds it is quite reasonable to suppose that such a concern should focus on values rather than beliefs, particularly in the American milieu, where we have a general hesitancy against using too abstract thinking, above all on philosophical levels, and where, in the sense referred to above, the general cultural atmosphere has been highly "secular."

The broader sociological context lies in the fact that American society, in its values and its institutional structure, is organized about a kind of polarization between the external field of instrumental activity, the field of opportunity in economic production, and in other occupational areas, and the capacities and other "internal" states of the acting units, notably the individual person.

We have recently been through a tremendous process of economic growth which has involved not only quantitative expansion but a major structural reorganization of the society, which in turn has very important repercussions on people. They are under pressure to perform such new and different roles that their personal values become involved. I should regard this restructuring of role-values, which is concomitant with the process of structural change in the society, as the main source of the increased concern with religion. It is associated not only with concern with psychological problems but also with the increasing sense of urgency of problems of education and a variety of others. It is most important not to confuse this role-value change with change in the *general* value-orientation of the society as a whole on the highest levels. In my opinion this has, in the American case, remained essentially stable. I am, of course, aware that many others have a different view.

It is reasonable to expect that the salience of religious concern should vary in something of a cyclical pattern, in shape somewhat similar to economic and political shifts, though involving considerably longer periods. It should be interpreted as part of a more general pattern of periodicities which one expects to find in a rapidly developing social system, of what Bales calls a "phase pattern."

I therefore think that the religious revival fits into the interpretation of the place of religion in the structure of the society which has been presented in this paper. If this revival is religiously genuine, as I think it is, the fact that it should occur at all is one more bit of evidence that ours is a religiously oriented society, not a case of "secularization" in the usual sense. Further, the fact that it seems to fit into a cyclical pattern is in line with what we know about the more general significance of such periodicities in this type of society. Finally, the form it takes seems to fit the emphasis on the private and personal character of religion, which is one of the principal features of the American religious pattern and differentiates it from its antecedents in the traditions connected with established churches.

My main thesis in this paper has been that the religious constitution of American society is fundamentally in line with the great Western tradition of a society organized about Christian values, a Christian society in a sense not wholly out of line with that of Troeltsch. Looked at by comparison with earlier forms, religion seems to have lost much. But it seems to me that the losses are mainly the consequence of processes of structural differentiation in the society, which correspond to changes in the character of the religious orientation but do not necessarily constitute loss of strength of the religious values themselves.

The most essential "concession" was made by the Mediæval Catholic Church itself, namely through the view that society should not be a simple "theocracy" but that the secular arm was genuinely independent, responsible directly to God, not simply through the organized Church. From this point on, the basic question has been that of the limits of jurisdiction over the individual of the secular "good society." In the American case these limits have proved to be very different from, and much broader than, those envisaged by the Mediæval theorists; but they did not envisage modern society any more than the modern churches.

The American system is far from being fully integrated. It must contend with important elements which are anchored in earlier patterns of religious organization, notably fundamentalist Protestantism and the Catholic Church, both of which make claims which are anomalous within the main American framework. It must contend with the proliferation of exotic religious movements of dubious longer-run religious soundness, from the "Holy Rollers" to such "inspirationists" as Norman Vincent Peale. It must finally contend with the various aspects of secularism which to many religious people seem to have no place in a religiously committed society. On balance, however, I think that the main trend is toward greater integration of these various elements in a viable system which can be a vital part of a larger society. In this, as in other vital respects, American society is fundamentally an outgrowth of its European heritage, not an exotic "sport."

Chapter I

The most important sources of ideas in the background of this paper are in the work of Max Weber, Chester I. Barnard, and Herbert A. Simon. Cf. especially Weber, *The Theory of Social and Economic Organization,* esp. Chapter III (Free Press, 1957), Barnard, *The Functions of the Executive* (Harvard Univ. Press, 1938), and Simon, *Administrative Behavior* (Macmillan, 1951). Relevant also, as noted in the Introduction, is my own recently renewed concern with problems of the structure of the economy and its relation to the society as a system, documented mainly in Parsons and Smelser, *Economy and Society* (Free Press, 1956). This work directed attention anew to the problems of "organization" as a factor of production with special reference to the contributions of Alfred Marshall, in his *Principles of Economics,* and of Joseph Schumpeter in his *Theory of Economic Development* and in certain respects, in *Capitalism, Socialism, and Democracy.* The problems of "informal organization" have also been important in the background, stemming particularly from the work of Elton Mayo *(Human Problems of an Industrial Civilization* and other writings) of Roethlisberger and Dickson, *Management and the Worker,* of William F. Whyte and a variety of others. William H. Whyte's *The Organization Man* appeared subsequently to this chapter, and did not influence its formulation. Again in the background lie the findings of the research work in small group interaction, particularly of R. F. Bales and his associates. The most comprehensive anthology of this work is A. P. Hare, E. F. Borgatta and R. F. Bales, eds., *Small Groups* (Knopf, 1955).

Chapter II

This paper is so definitely a "follow-up" of Chapter I that essentially the same background influences cited in the latter connection are equally applicable to it. In view of its special relation to education, however, the study of Neal Gross, Ward S. Mason, and Alexander W. McEachern, *Explorations in Role Analysis: Studies of the School Superintendency Role* (Wiley, 1958), should be mentioned as providing especially illuminating case material as well as throwing light on some important theoretical problems.

CHAPTER III

The materials relevant to this study, and to Chapter IV, comprise the wide range of works concerning the factors in economic development in the West and the cognate problems in other parts of the world. At the time of the writing of this paper, in addition to the types of general considerations brought together in *Economy and Society,* I had, of course, been greatly influenced by Max Weber's analysis of the relations of religious values to economic development, not only in the classic instance sketched in his *Protestant Ethic,* but particularly those discussed in his comparative studies in the sociology of religion, as well as those discussed in *The City.* Connected with this, in turn, are problems associated with the studies of Troeltsch, Harnack, and various legal historians like Otto von Giercke and F. W. Maitland. On non-Western societies, besides Weber, I have been particularly stimulated by such work as Granet's studies on China, Ruth Benedict on Japan, and others. More immediately, Robert N. Bellah's *Tokugawa Religion* (Free Press, 1957) and Clifford Geertz's *Religion and Society in Java* (Free Press, 1960). Two other unpublished studies of Dr. Geertz: ("The Social Context of Economic Change: an Indonesian Case Study" (M.I.T. Center for International Studies, 1956), and "The Development of the Javanese Economy: A Socio-Cultural Approach" (M.I.T. Center for International Studies, 1956) and one by Donald R. Fagg, *Authority and Social Stratification, A Study in Javanese Bureaucracy* (unpublished dissertation, Harvard University, 1957), were also very helpful. On certain problems of perspective relative to the American case I am indebted to F. X. Sutton and others, *The American Business Creed* (Harvard Press, 1957), and to Daniel Bell *(Partisan Review,* 1957). Also I am indebted to several publications of, and many personal discussions with, Professor S. N. Eisenstadt.

CHAPTER IV

Since this paper was written after Chapters I-III and is so close to them in subject matter, all of the references quoted in connection with them are relevant. Various of the papers in the symposium, *The Challenge of Development,* in which Chapter III was first published, are relevant, particularly the contributions by Simon Kuznets, S. N. Eisenstadt, and Alfred Bonné. On the psychological side, concerning the internalization of values, a particularly significant set of contributions is the work on the achievement motive by David C. McClelland and his associates. Cf. McClelland et al., *The Achievement Motive* (Appleton-Century, 1953), and several subsequent papers, some unpublished.

Both on the more general perspective of this paper (and of Chap. III) and, in particular, on the family firm as its role has been exemplified in the French economy, I am indebted to David S. Landes, "French Business and the Businessman: A Social and Cultural Analysis" in Edward M. Earle, ed., *Modern France* (Princeton, 1951); *Religion and Enterprise: The Case of the French Textile Industry* (1957, unpublished) and to Jesse R. Pitts, *The Retardation of the French Economy* (unpublished Ph.D. dissertation, Harvard, 1958—to be published by the Free Press).

On some of the comparative points raised I am indebted to many studies of Soviet society, but in particular to Alex Inkeles, *Public Opinion in Soviet Russia,* and to Joseph S. Berliner, *Factory and Manager in the USSR* (Harvard Press, 1957); to the book of Bellah cited above, and to James C. Abegglen, *The Japanese Factory* (Free Press, 1958). A very brief and tentative approach to the comparative problem of the definition of illness is contained in my own paper, "Definition of Health and Illness" mentioned in the Introduction in connection with Part IV of this volume.

CHAPTER V

The concerns of this paper root in the general sociological theory of institutions and their relations to values and to collective action which owe most to Max Weber and Emile Durkheim. Here I am particularly concerned with Weber's "Types of Authority" *(Theory of Social and Economic Organization,* Chap. III), and their relation to Durkheim's analysis of contract as an institution *(Division of Labor,* esp. Book I, Chap. VII). In the recent literature of political theory the most helpful sources to me have been C. J. Friedrich, *Constitutional Government and Politics,* 1st and 2nd Editions; H. D. Lasswell and Abraham Kaplan, *Power and Society,* and David Easton, *The Political System.* It seems to me very important that there is an essential continuity between the treatment of authority for total political systems by Weber and others and by Barnard for the formal organization within the society. On the place of law, I am particularly indebted to two papers by Bryant King in the *Cambridge Law Journal,* 1952-53, and to unpublished papers and personal discussion with Jan van Loon of Leyden, the Netherlands. A particularly clear delineation of the relation between the "external" and the "internal" problems of a social system is given in G. C. Homans, *The Human Group.*

Chapter VI

As a review article this paper does not attempt a discussion of the literature, except for Mills' *The Power Elite* itself. At the beginning it is noted that few sociologists have attempted the kind of general discussion of the society as a whole which is needed for perspective on such a problem. The most important exception is Robin Williams' notable book *American Society,* which is still in a class by itself in this respect. Since this paper was written, Max Lerner's *America as a Civilization* has appeared. It is at least partly sociological and may be used for comparison with Williams in certain respects.

Chapter VII

This paper was written on an immediately contemporary subject without reference to sources other than the press of the period. Perhaps the best single source for related and alternative interpretations will be found in the other papers included in *The*

New American Right, Daniel Bell, Ed., in which this paper also
was included.

CHAPTER VIII

The most immediate reference of this paper is to the literature of social ecology. The widest-known source is Park and
Burgess' text, *Introduction to the Science of Sociology,* and the
whole series of studies done under Park's influence at the University of Chicago. A closely related variant will be found in the
"Michigan school" of which the most important documents are
MacKenzie, *Metropolitan Communities,* and Hawley, *Human
Ecology.* The parts dealing with jurisdiction and communication
have drawn on other sources, notably the literature of political
theory. Here only one source may be specifically mentioned,
namely Laski's *Grammar of Politics,* essentially because, after
long "flirtation" with Guild Socialism, Laski there so clearly
saw how deeply grounded political organization was in the territorial ordering of social relationships. An important part of my
analysis of communication has been drawn from Bales' scheme
of categories as presented in *Interaction Process Analysis.* The
treatment also refers to the analysis presented in *Economy and
Society,* and in Chapter II above.

CHAPTER IX

This paper draws mainly on my long-standing concern with
the structure of American society and its trends of development,
on the one hand, the medical profession and its relations to the
problems of illness and health, on the other. More specifically it
refers to a series of papers presented at the preceding annual
meeting of the Council on Medical Education and Licensure and
published in the *Journal of the American Medical Association,*
June 1, 1957, notably those by D. W. Atchley and W. Barry Wood,
Jr. It is indebted also to another recent contribution to the study
of medical education, *The Student Physician,* R. K. Merton,
G. R. Reader and P. Kendall, Eds. (Harvard Press, 1957). The
reference to the views of Dr. Sidney Farber on the organization
of medical research is to a communication made by him to the
American Academy of Arts and Sciences, May, 1957.

Chapter X

The most important background of this paper in the literature lies in the contributions of Weber and Troeltsch to the understanding of the social aspects of Protestantism, in the *Protestant Ethic* and the *Social Teachings* respectively. It attempts to apply and adapt their broad analysis to the American case, which neither of them dealt with explicitly. Paul Tillich's little book *The Courage to Be* has seemed to me a particularly succinct contemporary statement of the underlying problems of "meaning" involved in religious orientation. The most comprehensive treatment of the problem of American values available is the essay of Clyde Kluckhohn in Elting Morison, Ed., *The American Style*. I do not think Dr. Kluckhohn has made a convincing case for a fundamental change in the last generation, but otherwise it is a most illuminating treatment. I am indebted to Dr. Robert N. Bellah (personal discussion) for much clarification of the role of secularism in American society and its "dialectical" relation to religious commitments.

BIBLIOGRAPHY OF
TALCOTT PARSONS

[Availability in publications other than those in which the works first appeared has been indicated as follows: * — also in *Essays in Sociological Theory* (Rev. ed., 1954), † — also in *Essays in Sociological Theory* (1st ed., 1949), ‡ — included in the present volume.

Papers mentioned in the Introduction to the present volume but not included in it are designated with: §.]—EDS.

1928

"Capitalism" in Recent German Literature: Sombart and Weber. *J. Political Economy* 36:641-661.

1929

"Capitalism" in Recent German Literature: Sombart and Weber. *J. Political Economy* 37:31-51.

1930

Translation of Weber, Max, *The Protestant Ethic and the Spirit of Capitalism;* London and New York, Allen and Unwin, and Scribners; xi + 292 pp.

1931

Wants and Activities in Marshall. *Quarterly J. Economics* 46:101-140.

1932

Economics and Sociology: Marshall in Relation to the Thought of His Time. *Quarterly J. Economics* 46:316-347.

1933

Malthus
Encyclopedia of the Social Sciences 10:68-69.

Pareto
  Encyclopedia of the Social Sciences 11:576-578.

1934

Some Reflections on "The Nature and Significance of Economics."
  Quarterly J. Economics 48:511-545.
Society
  Encyclopedia of the Social Sciences 14:225-231.
Sociological Elements in Economic Thought. I.
  Quarterly J. Economics 49:414-453.

1935

Sociological Elements in Economic Thought. II.
  Quarterly J. Economics 49:645-667.
The Place of Ultimate Values in Sociological Theory.
  Internat. J. Ethics 45:282-316.
H. M. Robertson on Max Weber and His School.
  J. Political Economy 43:688-696.

1936

Pareto's Central Analytical Scheme.
  J. Social Philos. 1:244-262.
On Certain Sociological Elements in Professor Taussig's Thought.
  Viner, Jacob (ed.), *Explorations in Economics: Notes and Essays contributed in honor of F. M. Taussig;* New York, McGraw-Hill, 1936 (xii + 539 pp.)—pp. 359-379.

1937

The Structure of Social Action
  New York, McGraw-Hill; xii + 817 pp.
Education and the Professions.
  Internat. J. Ethics 47:365-369.

1938

The Role of Theory in Social Research.
  Amer. Sociological Rev. 3:13-20. (An address delivered before the Annual Institute of the Society for Social Research, at the University of Chicago, summer 1937.)
*†The Role of Ideas in Social Action
  Amer. Sociological Rev. 3:652-664. (Written for a meeting on the problem of ideologies at the American Sociological

Society's annual meeting, Atlantic City, N. J., December 1937.)

1939

*†The Professions and Social Structure.
> *Social Forces* 17:457-467. (Written to be read at the annual meeting of the American Sociological Society in Detroit, December, 1938.)

Comte.
> *J. Unified Sci.* 9:77-83.

1940

*†An Analytical Approach to the Theory of Social Stratification.
> *Amer. J. Sociology* 45:841-862.

*†Motivation of Economic Activities.
> *Canad. J. Economics and Political Sci.* 6:187-203. (Originally given as a public lecture at the University of Toronto and also published in *Essays in Sociology* ed. by C. W. M. Hart), and in *Human Relations in Administration: The Sociology of Organization,* ed. by Robert Dubin, 1951.

1942

Max Weber and the Contemporary Political Crisis.
> *Rev. Politics* 4:61-76, 155-172.

The Sociology of Modern Anti-Semitism.
> Graeber, J., and Britt, Steuart Henderson (eds.), *Jews in a Gentile World:* New York, Macmillan, 1942 (x + 436 pp.) —pp. 101-122.

*†Age and Sex in the Social Structure of the United States.
> *Amer. Sociological Rev.* 7:604-616. (Read at the annual meeting of the American Sociological Society in New York, December, 1941), and republished in several places, notably Wilson and Kolb, *Sociological Analysis,* and Kluckhohn and Murray, *Personality in Nature, Society and Culture,* 1st and 2nd editions.

*†Propaganda and Social Control.
> *Psychiatry* 5:551-572.

*Democracy and the Social Structure in Pre-Nazi Germany.
> *J. Legal and Political Sociology* 1:96-114.

*Some Sociological Aspects of the Fascist Movements.

Social Forces 21:138-147. (Written as the presidential address to the Eastern Sociological Society at its 1942 meeting.)

1943

*†The Kinship System of the Contemporary United States.
Amer. Anthropologist 45:22-38.

1944

*†The Theoretical Development of the Sociology of Religion.
J. of the Hist. of Ideas 5:176-190. (Originally written to be read at the Conference on Methods in Science and Philosophy in New York, November, 1942.)

1945

*†The Present Position and Prospects of Systematic Theory.
Gurvitch, Georges, and Moore, Wilbert E. (eds.), *Twentieth Century Sociology*, A Symposium; New York, Philosophical Library, 1945.

*†The Problem of Controlled Institutional Change: An Essay on Applied Social Science.
Psychiatry 8:79-101. (Prepared as an appendix to the report of the Conference on Germany after the War.)

Racial and Religious Differences as Factors in Group Tensions.
Finkelstein, Louis, etc. (eds.), *Unity and Difference in the Modern World*, A Symposium; New York, The Conference on Science, Philosophy and Religion in Their Relation to the Democratic Way of Life, Inc., 1945.

1946

The Science Legislation and the Role of the Social Sciences.
Amer. Sociological Rev. 11:653-666.

*Population and Social Structure (of Japan).
Haring, Douglas G. (ed.), *Japan's Prospect;* Cambridge, Harvard University Press, 1946 (xiv + 474 pp.)—pp. 87-114. (This book was published by the staff of the Harvard School for Overseas Administration.)

1947

*†Certain Primary Sources and Patterns of Aggression in the Social Structure of the Western World.
Psychiatry 10:167-181. (Prepared for the Conference on Sci-

ence, Philosophy and Religion at its September 1946 meeting in Chicago, Ill., and also published in the volume issued by the Conference.)

Some Aspects of the Relations Between Social Science and Ethics.
Social Science 22:213-217. (Read at the Annual Convention of the American Association for the Advancement of Science in Boston, December, 1946.)

Science Legislation and the Social Sciences.
Political Science Quarterly, Vol. LXII, No. 2, June 1947.
Bulletin of Atomic Scientists, January, 1947.

Max Weber: The Theory of Social and Economic Organization.
Editor with Henderson, A. M., and translator; Oxford University Press, 1947. †Introduction by Talcott Parsons. Reprinted by the Free Press, 1957.

1948

Sociology, 1941-46. (Co-author: Bernard Barber)
Amer. J. Sociology 53:245-257.

†The Position of Sociological Theory.
Amer. Sociological Rev. 13:156-171. (Paper read before the annual meeting of the American Sociological Society, New York City, December, 1947.)

1949

Essays in Sociological Theory Pure and Applied.
Glencoe, Ill., The Free Press, 1949; xiii + 366 pp.

The Rise and Decline of Economic Man.
J. General Education 4:47-53.

*Social Classes and Class Conflict in the Light of Recent Sociological Theory.
Amer. Economic Rev. 39:16-26. (Read at meeting of the American Economic Association in December, 1948.)

1950

*The Prospects of Sociological Theory.
Amer. Sociological Rev. 15:3-16. (Presidential address read before the meeting of the American Sociological Society in New York City, December, 1949.)

*Psychoanalysis and the Social Structure.
The Psychoanalytic Quarterly 19:371-384. (The substance of

this paper was presented at the meeting of the American Psychoanalytic Association, Washington, D. C., May, 1948.)
The Social Environment of the Educational Process.
 Centennial; Washington, D. C.: American Association for the Advancement of Science; pp. 36-40. (Read at the A.A.A.S. Centennial Celebration, September, 1948.)

1951

The Social System
 Glencoe, Ill., The Free Press, 1951; xii + 575 pp.
Toward a General Theory of Action
 Editor with Edward A. Shils, and contributor; Cambridge, Harvard University Press, 1951; viii + 506 pp.
Graduate Training in Social Relations at Harvard.
 J. General Education 5:149-157.
Illness and the Role of the Physician: A Sociological Perspective.
 Amer. J. Orthopsychiatry 21:452-460. (Presented at the 1951 annual meeting of the American Orthopsychiatric Association in Detroit.) Reprinted in Kluckhohn and Murray, 2nd edition.

1952

The Superego and the Theory of Social Systems.
 Psychiatry 15:15-25. (The substance of this paper was read at the meeting of the Psychoanalytic Section of the American Psychiatric Association, May, 1951, in Cincinnati.) Reprinted in Parsons, Bales and Shils, *Working Papers.*
Religious Perspectives in College Teaching: Sociology and Social Psychology.
 Fairchild, Hoxie N., (ed.), *Religious Perspectives in College Teaching;* New York, The Ronald Press Company, 1952 (vii + 460)—pp. 286-337.
*A Sociologist Looks at the Legal Profession.
 Conference on the Profession of Law and Legal Education, Dec. 4, 1952, Conference Series Number II, The Law School, University of Chicago; pp. 49-63. (This paper was presented at the first symposium on the occasion of the Fiftieth Anniversary Celebration of the University of Chicago Law School, December, 1952.)

1953

Working Papers in the Theory of Action
  (In collaboration with Robert F. Bales and Edward A. Shils.)
  Glencoe, Illinois: The Free Press, 1953; 269 pp.

Psychoanalysis and Social Science with Special Reference to the
  Oedipus Problem. Franz Alexander and Helen Ross (eds.),
  Twenty Years of Psychoanalysis, New York: W. W. Norton
  and Co., Inc., 1953; pp. 186-215. (The substance of this paper
  was read at the Twentieth Anniversary Celebration of the
  Institute for Psychoanalysis, Chicago, in October, 1952.)

*A Revised Analytical Approach to the Theory of Social Stratifi-
  cation.
  Reinhard Bendix and Seymour M. Lipset (eds.), *Class, Status
  and Power: A Reader in Social Stratification,* Glencoe, Illinois: The Free Press, 1953; pp. 92-129.

Illness, Therapy and the Modern Urban American Family.
  (Coauthor with Renée Fox.) *J. of Social Issues,* 8:31-44.

Some Comments on the State of the General Theory of Action.
  Am. Soc. Review, Vol. 18, No. 6 (Dec. 1953), pp. 618-631.

1954

The Father Symbol: An Appraisal in the Light of Psychoanalytic
  and Sociological Theory.
  Bryson, Finkelstein, MacIver and McKeon (eds.), *Symbols
  and Values: An Initial Study,* 13th Symposium of the Conference on Science, Philosophy and Religion, New York:
  Harper & Bros., 1954; pp. 523-544. (The substance of this
  paper was read at the meeting of the American Psychological
  Association in September, 1952, at Washington, D. C.)

Essays in Sociological Theory (revised edition)
  Glencoe, Illinois: The Free Press; 459 pp.

Psychology and Sociology.
  John P. Gillin (ed.), *For a Science of Social Man,* New York:
  Macmillan Company; pp. 67-102.

The Incest Taboo in Relation to Social Structure and the Socialization of the Child.
  British Journal of Sociology, Vol. V, No. 2, June 1954, pp.
  101-117.

1955

Family, Socialization and Interaction Process
 (With Robert F. Bales, James Olds, Morris Zelditch and
 Philip E. Slater.) Glencoe, Illinois: The Free Press; xi +
 422 pp.
‡"McCarthyism" and American Social Tension: A Sociologist's
 View.
 Yale Review, Winter 1955, pp. 226-245.
 (Reprinted under title "Social Strains in America" in Daniel
 Bell (ed.), *The New American Right,* New York: Criterion
 Books, 1955.

1956

Economy and Society.
 (Coauthor with Neil J. Smelser.) London: Routledge and
 Kegan Paul; and Glencoe, Illinois: Free Press.
Eléments pour une théorie de l'action.
 Translated, with introduction by François Bourricaud.
 Paris: Plon.
‡A Sociological Approach to the Theory of Organizations.
 Administrative Science Quarterly, I (June 1956), pp. 63-85;
 II (September 1956), pp. 225-239.
A Sociological Model for Economic Development.
 (Coauthor with Neil J. Smelser.) *Explorations in Entrepre-
 neurial History,* Harvard University.

1957

‡The Distribution of Power in American Society.
 World Politics, X (October 1957), pp. 123-143.
Malinowski and the Theory of Social Systems.
 Raymond Firth (ed.), *Man and Culture,* London: Routledge
 and Kegan Paul.
Man in His Social Environment—As Viewed by Modern Social
 Science.
 Centennial Review of Arts & Science, Michigan State Uni-
 versity, Winter 1957, pp. 50-69.
§The Mental Hospital as a Type of Organization.
 Milton Greenblatt, Daniel J. Levinson, and Richard H.
 Williams (eds.), *The Patient and the Mental Hospital,* Glen-
 coe, Illinois: Free Press.

§Réflexions sur les Organisations Religieuses aux Etats-Unis.

    Archives de Sociologie des Religions, January-June, pp. 21-36.

Società e dittatura.

    Bologna: Il Mulino.

1958

‡Authority, Legitimation, and Political Action.

    Friedrich, C. J. (ed.), *Authority,* Cambridge, Mass.: Harvard University Press.

The Definitions of Health and Illness in the Light of American Values and Social Structure.

    Jaco, E. Gartly (ed.), *Patients, Physicians, and Illness,* Glencoe, Illinois: The Free Press.

Social Structure and the Development of Personality.

    Psychiatry, November, 1958, pp. 321-340.

General Theory in Sociology.

    Merton, Robert K., Broom, Leonard, and Cottrell, Jr., Leonard S. (eds.), *Sociology Today,* New York: Basic Books.

‡Some Ingredients of a General Theory of Formal Organization.

    Halpin, Andrew W. (ed.), *Administrative Theory in Education,* Chicago: Midwest Administration Center, University of Chicago.

‡Some Reflections on the Institutional Framework of Economic Development.

    The Challenge of Development: A Symposium, Jerusalem: The Hebrew University.

‡Some Trends of Change in American Society: Their Bearing on Medical Education.

    Journal of the American Medical Association, May, 1958, pp. 31-36.

‡The Pattern of Religious Organization in the United States.

    Daedalus, Summer, 1958, pp. 65-85.

1959

An Approach to Psychological Theory in Terms of the Theory of Action.

    Koch, Sigmund (ed.), *Psychology: A Science,* Vol. III, New York: McGraw-Hill.

The Principal Structures of Community: A Sociological View.

Friedrich, C. J. (ed.), *Community,* New York: The Liberal Arts Press.

§"Voting" and the Equilibrium of the American Political System.

Burdick, Eugene, and Brodbeck, Arthur, (eds.), *American Voting Behavior,* Glencoe, Ill.: The Free Press.

Durkheim's Contribution to the Theory of Integration of Social Systems.

Wolff, Kurt H. (ed.), *Emile Durkheim, 1858-1917: A Collection of Essays, with Translations and a Bibliography,* Columbus, Ohio: The Ohio State University Press.

Implications of the Study.

(On Marjorie Fiske's study, "Book Selection and Retention in California Public and School Libraries.") *The Climate of Book Selection,* A Symposium of the University of California School of Librarianship. Berkeley: The University of California Press.

Some Problems Confronting Sociology as a Profession.

American Sociological Review, August, 1959.

The School Class as a Social System.

Harvard Educational Review, Fall, 1959.

Mental Illness and "Spiritual Malaise": the Roles of the Psychiatrist and of the Minister of Religion.

Hofmann, Hans (ed.), *Making the Ministry Relevant Today.*

An Approach to the Sociology of Knowledge.

(Read at the Fourth World Congress of Sociology at Milan, Italy, September, 1959.)

Structure and Process in Modern Societies.

(A collection of essays), Glencoe, Ill.: The Free Press.

INDEX